From Joe 12/95

PAVAROTTI
MY WORLD

PAVAROTTI
MY WORLD

by
Luciano Pavarotti
and William Wright

CROWN PUBLISHERS, INC.   NEW YORK

Copyright © 1995 by World Wide Concert Corp. and
William Wright

Published by Crown Publishers, Inc., 201 East 50th Street,
New York, New York 10022. Member of the Crown
Publishing Group.

Random House, Inc. New York, Toronto, London,
Sydney, Auckland

CROWN is a trademark of Crown Publishers, Inc.

Manufactured in U.S.A.

Design by June Bennett-Tantillo

Library of Congress Cataloging-in-Publication Data

Pavarotti, Luciano.
Pavarotti, my world / by Luciano Pavarotti and William
Wright—1st ed.
p.   cm.
1. Pavarotti, Luciano.   2. Tenors (Singers)—Biography.
I. Wright, William, 1930–   .   II. Title.
ML420.P35A3   1995
782.1′092—dc20   95-23264
[B]   CIP
MN

ISBN 0-517-70027-1

10 9 8 7 6 5 4 3 2 1

First Edition

CONTENTS

PREFACE
by William Wright

~

Every so often a personality bursts from the confines of a particular field to win the affection of the public at large. In sports it would be a Joe DiMaggio, a Billie Jean King, or a Michael Jordan. Rudolf Nureyev was known and admired by millions who never saw a ballet. Even bleak corporate boardrooms have produced a Ted Turner, a Lee Iococca, or a Donald Trump. Opera gave the world Enrico Caruso and Maria Callas. Now there is Pavarotti.

In winning such broad acceptance, the serious vocal artist is handicapped by a resistance many feel to the operatic singing style. This is especially true today when the very different style of popular music is reinforced constantly by electronic sound. Still, the supremacy of popular music and a broad aversion to classical singing have proved no obstacle to Pavarotti's enormous popularity.

His appeal seems to pierce boundaries of nationality, culture, race, and age. In part, this is true because no language is needed to appreciate music. It is true also because people of widely different musical cultures—Chinese, Maori, and Pakistani, for example—all seem to recognize in the man himself qualities that lure them into music that might otherwise be alien to them.

Pavarotti's ability to attract people, perhaps to seduce them, to his art is equally successful in breaking down the normal age barriers to operatic singing. Among his fans, Pavarotti can count millions of children too young to appreciate a Beethoven symphony, as well as many people who feel they are too old to delve into unfamiliar music.

I have now written two books with Pavarotti about his life, so I can claim a certain amount of expertise on this phenomenon. Yet it is remarkable how many people, when they learn of my project, immediately set out to explain to me Pavarotti's remarkable appeal. Everyone has a theory, it seems, and all of the theories go beyond the beautiful voice. Perhaps even more remarkable than Pavarotti's popularity is that his millions of fans spend time reflecting on why they like him so much.

The most frequently offered reasons for his all-embracing popularity can be separated out into a few basic elements. Apart from being an artist of the highest rank who possesses a natural instrument of unmatched beauty, Pavarotti has the rare ability to project a nature that appears to be as beautiful as the voice. The expressiveness of his face and of his manner are qualities that can be lost in the opera house but which are ideal for television and film. Thanks to the intimacy of the camera, people in the Australian outback and in Norwegian villages see this aspect of the Pavarotti magic more clearly than boxholders at the Metropolitan Opera. Some opera singers are best experienced from a distance, but from a distance, a significant portion of Pavarotti's impact is lost.

Pavarotti is not only a genius at communicating while singing, he is also remarkably adept at projecting his many likable qualities on television talk shows. His warmth, humor, and feet-on-the-ground humanity are not inhibited by television cameras, nor does he allow himself to be lured into immodesty by trap-setting talk show hosts. Also, I suspect that in this day of the non-celebrity, when an outrageous dress or prime-time rudeness can bring nationwide fame, the public is relieved to have before them for a change a personality who has earned his chair next to Letterman or Leno by being good at something.

All of these elements combine to make him a performer ideally suited to modern technology. And because of his rare appeal coupled with the recent capability for instantaneous global communications, Pavarotti may well have a larger following than any performer in history. When reminded of the vast scale of his success, Pavarotti is at once amazed and perhaps even a little embarrassed by it, yet he is resolved to put it to use for more than just the accumulation of wealth and glory.

First, he realizes his potential for broadening the classical music audience, and to this end, he frequently acts as an emissary into the world of pop culture. He does this by appearing on mainstream television shows and by occasionally doing concerts with pop artists. He is, in effect, striking a deal with the non-opera public: "I'll sing some of your music if you'll listen to some of mine." For many years he refused to perform popular music because he felt he did not do it well. He now realizes that occasional forays into the Top Twenty, even if he sings pop songs with something less than Sinatra's panache, are effective in demolishing the walls that block large numbers of people from the enjoyment of serious music.

This evangelical side of Pavarotti guides many of his decisions. When in 1993 he was approached about doing a second Three Tenors concert, Pavarotti's first reaction was negative. He doubted that he and his two colleagues could ever match the same mood of spontaneous exuberance that so distinguished the 1990 event in the Baths of Caracalla. When it was pointed out to him that staggering numbers of people would be reached, an audience hundreds of times bigger than the first, he saw the boost this would be for classical music and for operatic singing, and he changed his mind. The event that took place in Los Angeles in July of 1994 was broadcast live and reached an estimated two billion viewers, a number that will continue to grow as the show is rerun.

Helping young artists is another way Pavarotti seeks to put his success to good use, and few artists have ever done more to assist unknown singers. Throughout the year, whether bound by a performance schedule or on vacation to rest up for his next engagements, Pavarotti, on most days, takes time to work with aspiring singers sent to him by coaches of other artists.

His Philadelphia vocal competition, started in 1980, is an enormous undertaking that has no aim other than the discovery and fostering of unknown talent. When Pavarotti travels around the world performing, he has the Philadelphia staff set up auditions so he can spend long days listening to young singers in Paris, Buenos Aires, or Portland. It is hard to think of any other artist, in the middle of a major career, who devotes so much time and effort to the aspirations of beginners.

In addition to putting his fame to work for worthy goals, he is constantly seeking new ways to use his own talent. Most artists when they reach the pinnacles that Pavarotti had reached by the 1970s, grow understandably cautious and resist doing anything that might damage their hard-won preeminence. Instead, they settle into familiar and lucrative routines—a season at the Metropolitan, scattered performances at other major houses, and occasional concerts.

This is not Pavarotti; he relishes each new challenge. His fearlessness even led him to star in a Hollywood romantic comedy when his weight was at its heaviest, to sing a concert at Carnegie Hall with rock stars, and to take a full production of *La Bohème* to China. These constant forays away from the traditional world of the opera star have characterized the fifteen years that have passed since the first book he and I did together, which was, for the most part, the story of his rise to fame. This more recent period in his life has been rich and exciting, not so much because of his phenomenal success as because of his appetite for the untried, the unexpected, the risky. All of this says a great deal about his zest for his rare position.

During these years, Pavarotti has also had a number of dramas of a more personal nature. The frightening and perplexing illness of his youngest daughter was an excruciating ordeal for him and his family. A bad knee that required surgery has at times made performing very difficult for him. And of course his ongoing battle with his weight is a problem which causes more distress than he generally shows, and which, as he grows older, becomes an increasing health risk.

Also in his career, despite the catalog of triumphs, he has experienced moments that were not so triumphant: being booed at La Scala, for instance, and the lip-synching flap at the Modena pop concert. He does not shrink from discussing these low points, however, and he does so candidly and philosophically.

As Pavarotti's collaborator, I have made every effort to elicit from him the stories and episodes that reveal the man's true nature. I have sought his comments and reflections on each experience as well as on those matters closest to his heart: family, friends, music, singing, horses, food. I have tried to include anecdotes that reveal his irrepressible sense of fun, his prankishness, his unpredictability, his impulsiveness. I have also managed to sneak by him a few stories that show, usually indirectly, his generosity, his compassion, his empathy, his loyalty, his fundamental modesty—qualities that are combined in a very big heart.

I have used my outsider's prospective in an attempt to evoke for readers the fun and excitement of being around Pavarotti during the high-voltage excitement of performances or when he is relaxing at home in Italy. Because he enjoys his life so much, he and I together have tried to give readers a sense of the fun of *being* Pavarotti.

Having frequently been in his company in the past year, I constantly witnessed actions that struck me as revelatory of Pavarotti's essence, a happy succession of little Rosebuds that dance in biographers' dreams. In his home, it might be the way he grabs a ringing telephone before any of fifteen or twenty family members and employees in the vicinity can answer it (life-hunger), or at lunch stealing rigatoni from his wife's plate (more appetite), or chatting up an airport employee who is a fan while a chartered jet is holding departure for him (unwavering humanity). It might be his refusal to say anything unkind about a colleague, even when everyone around him is doing so (across-the-board compassion). It could be the speed with which he forgets his anger after someone upsets him (absence of rancor).

There is a spontaneity to Pavarotti that produces these small epiphanies with a regularity that makes being around him fruitful for a writer and lively entertainment for everyone else. It has nothing to do with always being "on." It has everything to do with always being Pavarotti. And for him that means seizing the moment, avoiding the routine and the obvious, teasing his friends, making them laugh, or suddenly coming up with a stunt that surprises even those who have known him the longest.

A relatively small occurrence on the China trip was for me typical of the revealing impromptu action that sets Pavarotti apart from most others, especially from other major artists. On the tour, which was arranged with the governmental pomp of a state visit, he was asked to attend a traditional Chinese opera. This is an ancient art form, as stylized as Kabuki, that bears little resemblance to Western opera. Seated in the front row, Pavarotti did what most celebrities would have done, aware that all eyes were on them. As the Chinese singers squealed and grunted before him, he looked

1

SINGING OPERA

ecause I will talk a lot in this book about my life away from opera, I want to talk first about being an operatic singer. More than anything else, that is what I do, that is what I am. Each year I run a big horse show in Modena, I audition young singers around the world for my international vocal competition, I sing concerts in every country, I go on television to talk or to sing, and I appear in the benefit concerts for causes I feel strongly about or for the causes of my friends. I spend time with my family whenever I can, and I try to relax for at least a month each year at my summer house on the Adriatic at Pesaro.

With all the time I spend with these activities, I never forget that I am above all a singer of opera. That has always been the most important thing for me, and will remain so for as long as I am able to sing. I love opera very deeply, I love the music by itself, but I love even more the mixture of music and drama that can produce a powerful effect on an audience, an effect not like any other.

I grew up in opera. My father had an operatic tenor voice—at eighty-two he still does—and I heard him singing throughout my childhood. I have spoken before about when I was a very little

1

boy—about six, I think—and I climbed up on the kitchen table in my family's apartment just outside Modena and sang a little bit, then announced to everyone that I wanted to be a tenor when I grew up. I'm sure many little boys do that in Italian homes—boys who do not become tenors—but I think it is worth mentioning that at least one little boy made good on his bragging.

All of my training was to be not just a singer but an opera singer. From the beginning I had to learn how to use the voice, certainly, but I also had to learn how to interpret a score, to put drama and character into the music. Like all opera students, I also had to learn the most important roles for my kind of voice. Even during those first six months of serious voice training with my teacher, Arrigo Pola, when I sang nothing but scales and vocal exercises, I knew where I wanted to be: on the opera stage.

When Maestro Pola accepted a job to teach in Japan, he sent me to another vocal coach, Ettore Campogalliani in Mantua, who was also teaching my childhood friend Mirella Freni. She and I would ride the train from Modena to Bologna together for our lessons, and during the trip we talked about little except the opera careers we both wanted to have. As it turned out, Mirella established herself as an international artist long before I did.

In those early years of struggle, I often thought of giving up and going into teaching or selling insurance, but I knew that if I continued my effort to be a professional singer, it would be as a singer of opera, never any other kind. Then, when I won the vocal competition in 1961 and began to get jobs as a singer, they were jobs in opera, nothing else. And since then, although I have branched out into concerts, television, and several nonmusical areas, the most important part of my year still is, and has always been, my opera performances. So when I say I am an opera singer, I do not mean I am a man who sings opera or a man who earns his living that way; I mean that is who I am.

In addition, much of what I do outside of the opera house has, among other motives, the motive of drawing more people to opera. When I perform with pop singers or go on a talk show or get frantic putting together my horse show, I am hoping to convince people that I am not a museum piece left over from the nineteenth century, a historical relic, or an artist high in a tower. I want non-opera people to see that I am a human being just like them, a person who likes sports, popular music, good food, and pretty women—but who also has a passion for opera. Maybe what I hope to get across is the idea that it is not necessary to be old-fashioned, eccentric, or weird to love opera.

It makes me very happy that opera is becoming more popular. This is certainly true in Italy. When I started my career, people in Italy had already been saying for twenty years that opera was dying. The opera houses, even La Scala, had empty seats. The audience that did go to the performances seemed to be made up of the same people over and over. That is not true today. Most performances are sold out, the audiences change, and there are many more young people than there used to be.

This makes me very happy not only because I love opera but because there are so many important masterpieces in the repertory and also some of the greatest music ever written. As an art form, opera is a rare and remarkable creation. For me, it expresses aspects of the human drama that cannot be expressed in any other way, or certainly not as beautifully. Also, my native country has made such important contributions to this musical form—we created it, in fact. Opera is the blood of Italians, or at least of this Italian and many others, and I want to see it survive and flourish.

That is why, no matter how busy I get or how much I am tempted by new adventures or by financial offers that cannot be matched in the opera world, I always include operatic engagements in my schedule for each year, even though I know what that means—hard work at rehearsals, the nuisance of makeup and getting my too-big body into costumes, the ridiculousness of a well-fed middle-aged man portraying a twenty-year-old hungry artist in a Paris attic.

I also know that singing opera performances means suffering the terrible nerves that come from worrying not only about your own performance but also about the hundreds of other things that can go wrong in an operatic production and turn something beautiful into a fiasco. Grand opera is big in every sense. In addition to the big spectacle and the big artistry, it is very big in risks. An incredible number of things can go wrong. And of course, if it is done badly, it is not helping the cause of opera; it is hurting it.

Some friends who give me advice ask me why I continue to sing in operas. They point out that I no longer have to go to so much trouble, singing roles I have sung many times, singing a number of performances of the same opera over and over in a short time. They say I have proved myself as an opera singer, I have sung most of the important roles that suit my voice.

They also tell me that the people who like me—the ones who come to my concerts and buy my records and videos—they don't care whether or not I sing opera in an opera house to an audience that is very small compared to the audience for concerts, television, and records. Most of them are hardly aware that I sing opera performances, and maybe it's true that most of my fans don't even care if I perform in operas. But I care very much. Not only do I love opera and enjoy performing in it, I owe my career to it.

The large opera houses make their plans very far in advance, and most of us well-known singers know exactly where we will be singing two or three years ahead. It is a gamble for the managements, because the person who is singing wonderfully when he signs the contract in 1994 may not sound so good in 1996. That is the risk everyone takes. Even if you are singing like a frog, if you have the contract in your hand, they must let you sing anyhow, and pay you too, of course. You get paid the same whether you sing well or badly.

It has happened that singers who no longer have a voice insist on singing what they have contracted to sing, but generally a singer in such a predicament will ask to be excused. If the problems are real rather than imaginary, the opera house is usually extremely happy to let such singers out of their contracts. I like to believe I will know when it is time for me to quit and that I will not insist on singing like a frog just because I have a contract.

When I agree to sing a role at a particular opera house, the entire procedure, from invitation to opening night, follows a regular pattern. The most difficult step is, of course, when I agree to undertake a new role. So many roles that I sang for the first time, I sang in San Francisco. I like the opera audience in San Francisco very much. They are knowledgeable, but they are not unfair. And the opera company there had a coach, musical director Otto Guth, whom I particularly liked to work with when I learned a new role.

I must always work with a coach when I learn a new role. It is not true that I can't read music, as they say about me. But I prefer to study a role with a coach because I learn so much better and faster if I *hear* the part rather than read it in a score. I like an expert musician to sing each phrase for me as the composer intended. For me this is the best way to lock the music in my brain. I also need someone else to listen to what I am doing and tell me immediately when I am doing it wrong. If I make a mistake when I study a score alone, I might lock the mistake in my mind until I am corrected at a rehearsal. With a coach, I get rid of the mistakes as soon as I make them.

I remember when I first sang in *Aïda* for the San Francisco Opera in 1982. As the time approached to begin rehearsals, I knew I did not have the role of Radamès down in my brain absolutely correctly. I pleaded with the general manager, Kurt Adler, to bring Maestro Antonio Tonini from Milan to help me. Tonini was one of the great musicians and coaches of La Scala for many years. I said to Kurt Adler, "Tonini *is* La Scala." I try not to make special requests like that, but this was an important debut for me and for San Francisco. Kurt agreed to bring him, and I think this extra help prevented a disaster. If you are not absolutely certain about the music—the notes, the tempi, the inflections—other bad things can happen on the stage.

Often I agree to sing roles I have sung many times before. I do this because I love certain operas and feel they are particularly well suited to my voice and my personality. Also, there is not always time to learn new roles. Three of my favorite parts that I have sung often in different opera houses around the world are in *La Bohème, Un Ballo in Maschera,* and *L'Elisir d'Amore.* I love these operas for many reasons, but each of these great works means something special to me. *Bohème* is almost my signature opera. It was the opera in which I sang my very first performance on a stage anywhere, and I made my New York debut in it. *Ballo* is a brilliant opera, less frequently done than *Bohème,* and has in its score perhaps the broadest range of musical styles for tenor singing. I have often said that if I were allowed one opera and only one to sing for the rest of my life, it would be *Ballo.*

L'Elisir I love because I see myself in the tenor character, Nemorino. He is a simple country boy like me, but has a lot of naive intelligence. Also, the second act aria, "Una Furtiva Lagrima," is one of the great tenor arias. It is different from the other great arias in the Italian repertory because it does not have a sensational climax. The music is very restrained which, for me, makes it more difficult to sing correctly.

A typical operatic engagement for me took place when I sang *Un Ballo in Maschera* at the Teatro San Carlo in Naples in December of

1994. Rather than take you on a tour from city to city, saying a little about each place in which I have performed in the past few years, I will describe in more detail this one experience.

In the summer of 1992, the directors of San Carlo came to see me at my summer house in Pesaro to invite me to sing an opera at their theater. When I take a vacation on the sea each year, I try to relax totally and free my mind from work problems. Most of the year I always try to set challenges for myself, but these challenges make you always a little anxious. Pesaro is for not being anxious. This makes it the best time to consider and discuss new projects for the future.

I was interested in the San Carlo invitation. I have always loved Naples, and that is not true of all Italians, especially Italians from the north. But I love the city's beauty, its vitality, and its major place in the history of Italian opera. It had been twenty years since I had sung an opera there. I was eager to sing in Italy again after the problems at La Scala during *Don Carlo* when I lost control of my voice for a musical phrase. People booed, and the critics booed in their way, too. (I will discuss that unfortunate perform- ance in greater length in a chapter in which I have grouped to- gether many of the bad things that have happened in these past fifteen years.) Naples seemed to me an ideal place to prove to my countrymen that I could still sing.

I knew I could not win my reputation back by singing a con- cert. It had to be an important opera in a major opera house. By picking Naples, I was not trying to sneak back into my native country through a less dangerous city than Milan. The major Ital- ian newspapers are read throughout Italy, and in Naples I would be facing the same critics who had disliked my *Don Carlo*. In addition, I knew the Neapolitan audience could be every bit as difficult to please as the audience in Milan.

Verdi knew how tough the Neapolitans could be. In fact, their critical attitude made him angry. He wrote in a letter: "because they have had Palestrina, Scarlatti, Pergolesi, they think they know more than anyone else." Unlike Verdi, however, I take the view that, with the incredible operatic history of Naples, the people there are entitled to think of themselves as experts. In addition to the great composers Verdi mentioned, Naples also had Rossini, Donizetti, Bellini, and Verdi himself. It is not a city where you can get by with second-rate opera.

In addition to its high standards, the Teatro San Carlo in Naples is the oldest opera house in Europe that is still operating. It was built in 1737, forty-one years before La Scala and fifty-one years before La Fenice in Venice. Except for two years—1874 and 1875—San Carlo has been in continuous operation since it was built. Not even a terrible fire in 1816 or the Second World War closed it down.

The musical history of the theater is even more incredible. Rossini was artistic director of San Carlo for eight years, and many of his operas were first performed there. He was succeeded by Donizetti, who served as musical director for sixteen years. During his time in Naples, Donizetti composed sixteen operas for San Carlo—one for each year he was there. Among these operas were *Roberto Devereux, Maria Stuarda,* and one of the greatest operas of all, *Lucia di Lammermoor.* Can you imagine a work like *Lucia* being "this year's opera" by the resident music director?

A single event in San Carlo's history, however, interested me the most. Giuseppe Verdi had written *Un Ballo in Maschera* for this theater in 1857. When he completed this masterpiece, it got into trouble with the Neapolitan censor, a representative of the Bourbon monarchy, who was not happy about a libretto in which a king is assassinated at the final curtain. Verdi refused to make the story changes the censor demanded. Neither side would back down, so Verdi withdrew his opera and took it to Rome.

La Scala also wanted to produce *Ballo,* but Verdi wanted his opera done as close to Naples as possible to teach the censor there a lesson. Finally, in 1857, this great opera was produced in Rome with the title it has today. Of course, *Ballo* has since been performed many, many times in Naples, but I very much liked the idea of singing it in the city for which Verdi had written it—and where it would have had its premiere except for one man.

I love *Ballo* for many reasons besides the one I mentioned above: that it gives the tenor an opportunity to show off different singing styles. The music is superb from the beginning to the end. The story is strong, and the tenor character, Riccardo, is a good man who is deeply in love with his friend's wife. I sympathize with him, not because I have ever been in love with a friend's wife, thank God, but because I know how powerful love can be and how it can make a man do things that he knows are wrong. Riccardo knows that what he has done to his friend is very wrong, and he accepts his fate at the end.

I had another idea about going to Naples that was a little sentimental. Like most tenors, I worship Caruso, and this was the city of his birth. When I filmed the television special for PBS in Naples in 1987, *Pavarotti Returns to Naples,* I visited the place where Caruso was born, which is in a crowded, busy section of the city. I was so moved to see his apartment, the streets where he grew up. When word spread through that quarter of Naples that a present-day tenor was inside a building paying his respects to the great earlier-day tenor, I came down to find the street so full of people that I could not cross it to reach the car.

Not only are the Neapolitans extremely proud to have given the world Caruso. They are proud, too, to have given the world so much of the music he sang, especially the traditional Neapolitan songs. Like me, they are very respectful of true greatness, and like me, they are sentimental.

On that last visit to Naples I had stayed at the Hotel Excelsior. When I learned that Caruso liked to stay next door at the Hotel Vesuvio, I told myself that the next time I visited the city, I would

stay at the Vesuvio, in his suite, if possible. It is hard to explain why
I wanted to do this. Maybe it was an homage, maybe sentiment,
maybe superstition. Perhaps I thought that while I lived there he
would teach me something about singing.

When the people from San Carlo came to Pesaro and asked me to
sing an opera for them to open their 1994 season, I suggested *Ballo*.
Because it was to be the first opera of the year, it almost had to be
Verdi. I also wanted it to be an opera in the standard repertory, one
that was well known, and one I had sung before. In this way it
could serve as a test of whether or not I was starting to slide down-
hill. With an opera I know well, I can concentrate on the singing.
When you are always worried about the notes of a new role, you
are in far greater danger of making every kind of mistake.

The directors of San Carlo were happy with the idea of *Ballo,*
but first I wanted to think it over and discuss the idea with others.
I have pretty strong ideas about what I want to do and don't want
to do, even three years from now, but it is always a good idea to
discuss an important plan with others, as there can always be con-
siderations you did not think of. Basically, I make the decision
myself. And of course my agent, Herbert Breslin, discusses the
terms of my employment. I hate talking about money; I have a real
problem with that side of life, which makes me glad I am in a
profession where other people must do it for me.

After a little while I contacted the people at San Carlo and
told them I was happy to accept their invitation. Herbert made the
financial arrangements, and then the contracts were drawn up and
I signed them. Once you consent to a project like this, you put it in
your appointment book. And my appointment book is my bible,
my master. I try to keep it always near me wherever I am. As soon

ising just as gracefully to the south to tell you where you
egendary volcano also stands to remind us how fragile,
ble, and cruel life can be. When my secretary, Nicoletta,
rapist, Larisa, and I arrived at the Hotel Vesuvio on Via
, we could see the lovely and famous Santa Lucia fishing
ctly in front of our hotel. Just behind this harbor is the
Castello dell' Ovo. Centuries ago Santa Lucia was a sepa-
outside of the city's center, but it is now a major section
wn Naples. Most of the city's best hotels are right in

Lucia harbor is the subject of two of my favorite Nea-
gs, "Santa Lucia Lontano" and "Santa Lucia." It was
to have this famous harbor that has inspired such beauti-
sitting right below my hotel window. Santa Lucia also
ber of restaurants that are lit up at night with neon signs
l of people eating. The restaurants are even more popu-
summer when everyone eats outside.

not sure it was such a good idea to have right below my
his reminder of the wonderful Neapolitan food. Santa
staurants, naturally, specialize in seafood, and it was hard
t to look down without thinking of the delicious tiny
ongole, that are better in Naples than anywhere else, espe-
n served on steaming linguini with a little tomato, pars-
arlic—fantastic!

staying in Caruso's suite, which was magnificent—a
ving room with comfortable furniture, large-scale which
ndsome paintings, an upright piano that they tell me
ayed, and a large dining table in the room's center. The
re on the fifth floor, and when I went out onto the balco-
both the living room and my bedroom, I could see
nta Lucia and over the top of the Castello, to the shining
he famous island of Capri off in the distance. From my
n this mythical island, even on days that seemed clear,

as I agree to an engagement, I put into my book the date I must arrive in the city, the approximate rehearsal schedule, and the exact performance schedule. I make sure everyone I work with understands the dates. And most of all, I must remember the dates. I am pretty good about this and don't have to refer to my book too often; I know from memory when I must move from here to there.

From time to time in the next months, the San Carlo people telephoned me to discuss other members of the Ballo cast they were considering, kindly assuring me they would choose no one I might not be happy to work with. I almost never have problems with another singer's personality, though. I have worked with many who have terrible reputations for being difficult and have had totally pleasant experiences. For instance, many people were talking about Kathleen Battle's temperament, but I did L'Elisir d'Amore with her at the Met, and she was always very nice.

I do have problems sometimes with the ability of another singer. If I don't feel a singer is of high vocal quality, I am afraid that singer will make the rest of us less good. I prefer they find someone else. But if I am given a chance to complain at the beginning yet agree to work with a singer, I never say anything later, no matter how bad somebody may be singing. None of us sing our best all the time, and the other singers must take the same chance with me. It's the ones who never sing well I try to avoid.

In the two years after I made my arrangement with San Carlo, I sang operas at the Met, at La Scala, and in Vienna, Frankfurt, and Tokyo. I sang concerts in New York, Miami, Houston, Philadelphia, Chicago, Boston, London, Paris, Berlin, Oslo, Ravenna, Modena, Zurich, Tel Aviv, Honolulu, Seoul, Singapore, and many other cities I can't now remember. I worked like crazy on my horse shows and on the Philadelphia vocal competition. For one year we prepared the second Three Tenors concert scheduled for Los Angeles in July of 1994. But through all of this activity, one part of my mind was quietly preparing me for the *Ballo in Maschera* I knew I would be singing in Naples in December of 1994.

The summer before I was to sing *Ballo* I was working mostly on the music of *I Pagliacci,* which I was to sing at the Metropolitan Opera's opening night. This was a role I had recorded and sung in concert with Riccardo Muti and the Philadelphia Orchestra, but I had never sung it in a full stage production. In fact, when I was singing at the San Francisco opera in 1976, Terry McKuen, the general manager, urged me to sing *Pagliacci,* but I knew my voice was not yet right for it.

Now, eighteen years later, I was finally going to take on this role that had been made unforgettable by so many great tenors. I had to make sure I knew the part down to the last sixteenth note before I went out onto the Metropolitan stage with it. Gildo Di Nunzio of the Met, who is my good friend and often prepares me for roles, could not come to Pesaro that summer, so I imposed on my friend Leone Magiera to come up from his summer home in Ancona to work with me on the *Pagliacci* score.

Apparently we didn't work hard enough. When I arrived in New York that fall for the rehearsals, Gildo told me he had listened to a rehearsal and had marked places in the score where I made mistakes.

I was not happy to hear this. "Were there many places?" I asked him.

"Lots," he said.

I nodded, but thought maybe he said this to convince me I should not work with anyone but him. Later I asked him to come over to my apartment; he lives only a few blocks away. For several hours we worked on the mistakes. They were little things, but he was correct: I had been making some revisions in Leoncavallo.

All my thoughts that autumn had been on *Pagliacci.* As soon as

the opening was behind me, I g
to study it, working either alon
I know this part as well as I k
sometimes mix things up. Sin
memories when trying to bring
cated as an operatic role. Also as
notes in your head, you are alwa
tions, new ways to present th
thoughts to discuss with the cor
in rehearsal to see if you and he

I heard my former secreta
when I was about to perform I n
watching television, making ph
the time my mind was on the p
and over the score in my head
much my work is always on my

It was only natural that, as
proached, the score of *Un Ballo*
my head—how I would sing th
that note—every one of a thousa
performance. When I wasn't v
someone, Verdi's opera would r

The acting was very much
ideas for variations in the traditi
cardo, and I planned to offer my
Directors are usually happy to
hearsals, but will tell you quickly

~

It is always a great pleasure for me
beautiful, sitting on that grac

Vesuvius
are. The
unpredicta
and my th
Partenope
harbor di
medieval
rate villag
of downt
front of it

Santa
politan so
incredible
ful music
has a num
and are fu
lar in the

I wa
window
Lucia's res
for me n
clams, *le v*
cially whe
ley, and g

I wa
very big l
I like, ha
Caruso pl
rooms we
nies from
beyond S
bay with
hotel roo

as I agree to an engagement, I put into my book the date I must arrive in the city, the approximate rehearsal schedule, and the exact performance schedule. I make sure everyone I work with understands the dates. And most of all, *I* must remember the dates. I am pretty good about this and don't have to refer to my book too often; I know from memory when I must move from here to there.

From time to time in the next months, the San Carlo people telephoned me to discuss other members of the *Ballo* cast they were considering, kindly assuring me they would choose no one I might not be happy to work with. I almost never have problems with another singer's personality, though. I have worked with many who have terrible reputations for being difficult and have had totally pleasant experiences. For instance, many people were talking about Kathleen Battle's temperament, but I did *L'Elisir d'Amore* with her at the Met, and she was always very nice.

I do have problems sometimes with the ability of another singer. If I don't feel a singer is of high vocal quality, I am afraid that singer will make the rest of us less good. I prefer they find someone else. But if I am given a chance to complain at the beginning yet agree to work with a singer, I never say anything later, no matter how bad somebody may be singing. None of us sing our best all the time, and the other singers must take the same chance with me. It's the ones who *never* sing well I try to avoid.

In the two years after I made my arrangement with San Carlo, I sang operas at the Met, at La Scala, and in Vienna, Frankfurt, and Tokyo. I sang concerts in New York, Miami, Houston, Philadelphia, Chicago, Boston, London, Paris, Berlin, Oslo, Ravenna, Modena, Zurich, Tel Aviv, Honolulu, Seoul, Singapore, and many other cities I can't now remember. I worked like crazy on my horse shows and on the Philadelphia vocal competition. For one year we prepared the second Three Tenors concert scheduled for Los Angeles in July of 1994. But through all of this activity, one part of my mind was quietly preparing me for the *Ballo in Maschera* I knew I would be singing in Naples in December of 1994.

The summer before I was to sing *Ballo* I was working mostly on the music of *I Pagliacci,* which I was to sing at the Metropolitan Opera's opening night. This was a role I had recorded and sung in concert with Riccardo Muti and the Philadelphia Orchestra, but I had never sung it in a full stage production. In fact, when I was singing at the San Francisco opera in 1976, Terry McKuen, the general manager, urged me to sing *Pagliacci,* but I knew my voice was not yet right for it.

Now, eighteen years later, I was finally going to take on this role that had been made unforgettable by so many great tenors. I had to make sure I knew the part down to the last sixteenth note before I went out onto the Metropolitan stage with it. Gildo Di Nunzio of the Met, who is my good friend and often prepares me for roles, could not come to Pesaro that summer, so I imposed on my friend Leone Magiera to come up from his summer home in Ancona to work with me on the *Pagliacci* score.

Apparently we didn't work hard enough. When I arrived in New York that fall for the rehearsals, Gildo told me he had listened to a rehearsal and had marked places in the score where I made mistakes.

I was not happy to hear this. "Were there many places?" I asked him.

"Lots," he said.

I nodded, but thought maybe he said this to convince me I should not work with anyone but him. Later I asked him to come over to my apartment; he lives only a few blocks away. For several hours we worked on the mistakes. They were little things, but he was correct: I had been making some revisions in Leoncavallo.

All my thoughts that autumn had been on *Pagliacci.* As soon as the opening was behind me, I got out the score of *Ballo* and began to study it, working either alone or with Gildo and other coaches. I know this part as well as I know any, but your memory can sometimes mix things up. Singers must constantly refresh their memories when trying to bring back anything as long and complicated as an operatic role. Also as you review the music, locking the notes in your head, you are always thinking about new interpretations, new ways to present the music. You store away these thoughts to discuss with the conductor, or maybe to try them out in rehearsal to see if you and he like the innovation.

I heard my former secretary, Judy Kovacs, tell people that when I was about to perform I might look like I was goofing off—watching television, making phone calls, cooking risotto—but all the time my mind was on the performance, that I was going over and over the score in my head. Judy was right. She knew how much my work is always on my mind.

It was only natural that, as the date to travel to Naples approached, the score of *Un Ballo in Maschera* was more and more in my head—how I would sing this phrase, how long I would hold that note—every one of a thousand details that go into an operatic performance. When I wasn't watching football or talking with someone, Verdi's opera would rush back into my head.

The acting was very much on my mind as well. I had a few ideas for variations in the traditional way to act the part of Riccardo, and I planned to offer my suggestions to the stage director. Directors are usually happy to let you try something during rehearsals, but will tell you quickly if they think it is not a good idea.

It is always a great pleasure for me to arrive in Naples. The city is so beautiful, sitting on that gracefully sweeping bay and with

Vesuvius rising just as gracefully to the south to tell you where you are. The legendary volcano also stands to remind us how fragile, unpredictable, and cruel life can be. When my secretary, Nicoletta, and my therapist, Larisa, and I arrived at the Hotel Vesuvio on Via Partenope, we could see the lovely and famous Santa Lucia fishing harbor directly in front of our hotel. Just behind this harbor is the medieval Castello dell' Ovo. Centuries ago Santa Lucia was a separate village outside of the city's center, but it is now a major section of downtown Naples. Most of the city's best hotels are right in front of it.

Santa Lucia harbor is the subject of two of my favorite Neapolitan songs, "Santa Lucia Lontano" and "Santa Lucia." It was incredible to have this famous harbor that has inspired such beautiful music sitting right below my hotel window. Santa Lucia also has a number of restaurants that are lit up at night with neon signs and are full of people eating. The restaurants are even more popular in the summer when everyone eats outside.

I was not sure it was such a good idea to have right below my window this reminder of the wonderful Neapolitan food. Santa Lucia's restaurants, naturally, specialize in seafood, and it was hard for me not to look down without thinking of the delicious tiny clams, *le vongole,* that are better in Naples than anywhere else, especially when served on steaming linguini with a little tomato, parsley, and garlic—fantastic!

I was staying in Caruso's suite, which was magnificent—a very big living room with comfortable furniture, large-scale which I like, handsome paintings, an upright piano that they tell me Caruso played, and a large dining table in the room's center. The rooms were on the fifth floor, and when I went out onto the balconies from both the living room and my bedroom, I could see beyond Santa Lucia and over the top of the Castello, to the shining bay with the famous island of Capri off in the distance. From my hotel room this mythical island, even on days that seemed clear,

of those people couldn't remember to bring my costume and a little mineral water each day.

At one of the first costume rehearsals, an important part of my shirt ripped a short time before I had to be onstage. Nicoletta went running outside my dressing room to the lady attendant who sat at a desk there. I think her job was to help with such emergencies. She had a small box of pins—but not the right kind of pin. Two people were sent to find the costume lady, but she was nowhere near the rooms where we were putting on costumes. They returned with a much bigger box of pins. We went through it, but still could not find the right one, though I knew it was not an uncommon type.

More and more people began running around backstage looking for the right pin. It seemed we had half of Naples looking for this pin. Finally they found the tailor, and—miracle of miracles—he had the sort of pin that would not stick into me during the performance, and he was able to put my costume together again.

Maybe they do need two hundred people.

The important thing, the preparation of the opera, went very smoothly. Our conductor, Daniel Oren, comes from Israel, but he has done much work in Italy. He is a superb musician and a total professional who can go quickly to the problem spots and work them out. Daniel works hard for perfection, which I try to do too. I am always happy when I find this quality in a colleague.

His job was made easier by an excellent cast. Our Amelia was the wonderful Bulgarian soprano Nina Rautio, who has been establishing a reputation in European houses. Renato was to be sung by Paolo Coni, a handsome baritone with a rich, powerful voice and a strong stage presence. He has a very good future, which makes me happy because he is a client of my wife's management company. Victoria Loukianetz was physically perfect for the part of Oscar, the clever page—small and spirited but with a brilliant soprano voice they could hear on Capri.

When I am working on an opera with the others in the cast, I am completely serious about getting the work done and making the opera that we do together as excellent as possible. I think everyone who works with me knows that. But I also like to have fun and make the work as pleasant as possible for everyone.

One day when there was no rehearsal, the weather was sunny and beautiful so I told Nicoletta and Larisa we were going on a trip. With our driver, Roberto, we drove the autostrada south from Naples to the Sorrentine peninsula and over the big hills to Positano and Amalfi. Even in December the Amalfi drive is one of the most beautiful in the world. Neither Nicoletta nor Larisa had seen it before, and they were thrilled.

When we got back to the hotel late in the afternoon, who was coming out from the entrance? Bill Wright, who had arrived from New York to work with me on this book. It is a compliment to Bill that when I see him, I know it means more work but I am still glad. Bill was happy, too. He lived in Naples for a year as a young man. He knows the city well and loves it as I do. He had booked a room in the Vesuvio, so each morning he would come with Nicoletta, Larisa, and me to the theater for rehearsals. When I was not needed on stage, he and I would talk in my dressing room.

People don't realize how different the life of an opera singer is from the life of other people. During a break in the rehearsals for *Ballo* in Naples, for example, Bill, Nicoletta, and I wanted to eat more than my usual piece of fruit at lunch. We all felt like eating real food, but

I didn't want to go outside the theater. The December day had turned cool and windy from the mild weather we had been having and was now the perfect weather for catching a cold. Plus I was feeling like I might be about to catch something. With the opening night approaching, I was more worried than usual about my health.

A woman who worked backstage told us a solution: there was a restaurant in the theater—not the coffee bar, but a complete restaurant with hot meals for people who worked in the opera house. She said she would take us there. We start out following her through the backstage corridors, going down a flight of steps past long piles of scenery. Finally we get to a door which leads out into a large courtyard. I stop. It is outdoors. The woman looks puzzled that I refuse to go outside.

"But it is private, Signor Pavarotti," she said. "We only must cross this courtyard. Only people who work for the opera can go to this restaurant."

I explain the air is not private, and the cold air is what gives me a sore throat so I won't be able to sing in two days. Nicoletta says she will go back to the dressing room to get my hat and scarf. Bill and I wait. I am sure the woman thinks I am crazy. She knows I don't want to go outside, but to her walking quickly across a courtyard is not exactly "outside." I believe that abrupt changes in temperature can cause problems with the health. Also, I don't know how long it takes the wind and cold to do their damage.

Of course I go outside when I go home in the evening and when I go from the car into the hotel. But with the opening performance so close, I don't want to do this any more than absolutely necessary. It is sad for me, because I love fresh air. I sometimes feel like I could eat it. When I am in my apartment in New York, I look out at Central Park thinking how much I would like to go down for a walk. But if I have a performance coming up, I do not dare. If I get sick, even a little sore throat, I disappoint thousands of people, I make everyone mad at me, and I don't get paid. If this happens, I ask myself if I needed that walk in the park so much.

The day before the dress rehearsal was a day of rest. I told Bill we could spend as much of the day working on this book as he liked. When I woke up, however, I felt terrible. I had pain everywhere, but especially in my throat. The disaster I feared had arrived. Bill phoned to see if he could come down from his room so we could start working on the book. I told him I was sick and had to remain quiet all day. He understood how important it was for me to throw off whatever was trying to keep me from singing the next day.

In Italy, dress rehearsals are like full performances. The house is always full, usually with people who are connected to the opera house one way or another. More important to the singers, the critics often come. And the critics from our most important national newspapers like *Corriere della Sera* and *Repubblica* would be present as well. I wanted to show them that when I stumbled in *Don Carlo* at La Scala, I was not finished but had only had a bad night, but I could not do that if I went onto the Naples stage feeling sick and sang badly again.

So it was very important that I not be sick, that I feel all right. I was sorry about putting off Bill, however, because I knew he had come from New York so we could talk. I felt it was essential that I stay in my room and be completely quiet, not using my voice at all—or my brain, either—maybe watching television and sleeping whenever I could.

This time I was lucky. The next morning I felt much better and my throat felt all right. After I had taken a hot shower and gotten dressed, I sang a little at Caruso's piano, and the voice was there. Actually it sounded pretty good. Thank you, Signor Caruso, or whatever angel was looking after me that day.

Every day when I arrived at the theater there was always a small crowd standing outside to greet me. On this day of the dress, the crowd was much larger and we had to force our way through. There was a big atmosphere of excitement and suspense. Everyone I had worked with for the past month knew how important this performance was for me, and I could see in their eyes they were anxious for me. All the people I passed backstage wished me *"in bocca al lupo,"* which means "in the mouth of the wolf." This is the Italian way of wishing luck—like "break a leg" in English. I am good at concealing my nerves and appearing as relaxed and cheerful as I usually am, but terrible things were happening inside me as I walked to my dressing room.

The dress rehearsal went wonderfully—an incredible relief. I was very happy as I changed from my costume and took off the makeup. Even though it takes only ten minutes to drive from the theater to the hotel, I had Nicoletta use the cellular phone to order steak dinners for her, Larisa, Bill, and me. I wanted it waiting in my suite when we arrived. I felt far more relaxed. Not only was my voice in good shape, but I had a day and half to rest my throat before the opening two nights later.

The next day Herbert flew in from India, and my wife, Adua, and two of my daughters, Giuliana and Cristina, drove down from Modena. My wife always attends my openings in Europe, but this time she had also come to hear her client, Paolo Coni. Now she is not only giving me moral support, she is able to do business as well with all the opera people who come to important openings.

About six o'clock on the evening of the premiere, my driver, Roberto, drove me, Nicoletta, Larisa, and Bill from the hotel to the opera house. The trip took us past the Palazzo Reale and the Castel Sant' Angelo, which are always lit up at night, but on this evening they appeared more brightly lit and more beautiful. As we turned from the port area up through the Piazza Municipio to the theater, I saw spotlights moving across the sky and I knew that Naples was making a special display for the opera's opening night. The crowds at the stage door were enormous and greeted me so noisily that I felt like a bullfighter as I made my way through them.

I always like to allow a lot of time to get into makeup and costume. With all the concerns that make you nervous, you don't want to add rushing to the list. This time my costume was laid out and ready. Once I struggled into the terrible boots I had to wear, I felt the worst part of my preparation was over. I am usually ready long before it is time to go onstage. I am happy to wait. For these final minutes I don't like to greet people and usually sit and talk with people very close to me like my family or Herbert.

The opening-night performance of *Ballo* went wonderfully for me and for everybody. The audience did not restrain themselves in showing their approval. The Neapolitans can be super-critical, but they can also be super-enthusiastic, as they were that night. The tension that had been building over months was gradually melting away. My family and Bill went to a reception afterward that Daniel Oren and his wife gave in the opera house, but I went back to the hotel to eat something light and go to bed.

When the newspapers came out the next day, the critics were also very favorable. We could now call the Naples *Ballo* a big success. Of course, I was very happy that I had shown my fellow Italians I could still sing, and maybe this victory would erase the bad impression created by my La Scala *Don Carlo*. But the joy I felt came more from what happened in Il Teatro San Carlo that night between me and maybe two thousand Neapolitans than from the good reports that others heard about later.

A life like mine is mainly about performing before an audience, connecting with that audience, pleasing them and making them like you. With many members of the audience, you must

meet their expectations. The expectations may come from having heard you sing before, from hearing your records or just
from hearing *about* you. As a singer's reputation gets bigger and
bigger, it becomes more and more difficult to meet those expectations. It is not enough to sing well. You must somehow give
the audience a thrill that justifies the big reputation. You must
not disappoint them.

I am very glad that I can still do this most of the time. When
the audience tells you they are not disappointed, it is for me a very
great thrill, maybe the greatest. Pleasing audiences is my life, and it
is at the center of who I am. It is difficult, however, to describe in
the pages of a book the feeling this gives me.

Maybe I am not so different from everybody. We all want to
do the best with what we have been given and to get appreciated
for our efforts. With me that may be a stronger desire because I am
so aware I have been given something special. The worst thing for
me would be to think I wasted the gift or have not used it in the
right way. The best thing is when others make me believe I have
used it well.

The day after the opening I had to fly up to Switzerland for a
business meeting. When I returned to the Hotel Vesuvio that evening, Bill had checked out and returned to New York. In a note he
left for me, he praised the opening night's performance and told
me I had sung "like Pavarotti." I am 99 percent certain he meant it
as a compliment.

2
ONSTAGE ADVENTURES

I have had so many fantastic experiences during these thirty-five years of performing on opera-house stages it is hard to remember all of the ones that had a special meaning for me. There was the enormous excitement of singing for the first time with an orchestra in the Reggio Emilia *Bohème* in 1961. As a voice student, you have been hearing this orchestra in your mind for years. When you finally hear it for real, it is an incredible thrill. The *Rigoletto* I sang the following year with Tullio Serafin in Palermo was my first experience with a major conductor who took an interest in my development.

Another unforgettable experience from the early years of my career was working with Herbert von Karajan for the first time when I sang Rodolfo at La Scala in 1965. As if that wasn't enough excitement for a young tenor, later the same year I went on a tour of Australia with Joan Sutherland. This was an extremely important experience for me, as it was while working with Joan that I polished my technique and learned from her how to be consistent in my performances.

A standout of all my operatic experiences in the years that

followed was a *La Bohème* at La Scala in 1979 with the incredible Carlos Kleiber conducting. Mirella Freni was the Mimi. Something happens to all singers when we work with truly great conductors. These geniuses can make you hear things in the music you never heard before, and they make you alert to new possibilities in the drama. Kleiber inspired me to try different approaches to passages I had sung many times in a different way. Difficult places in the score that had caused me problems before, I found myself singing without effort.

As an example, it is traditional to transpose "Che Gelida Manina" down a half tone to spare the tenor the difficult high C at the end. Although few people were aware of it, most of the great tenors of the past had done this. But Kleiber made me sing the aria in the original key. Somehow I soared up to the high C with no strain. It may sound like superstition, but I am sure that was due to the inspiration of working with him and the way he conducted.

Another wonderful recollection of *La Bohème* was when I sang it at a benefit performance with Montserrat Caballé as Mimi. After "Che Gelida Manina" the audience went crazy and Montserrat, standing beside me on stage, went out of character and joined in the applause. That was a wonderful moment for me. If the bad notes in my singing get written about in every newspaper in the world, you must let me talk a little about my good ones.

It is not always a matter of wild ovations and legendary performances. Sometimes you are just happy to get through an opera without trouble. Many things can get in the way of singing your best, and the biggest obstacle is illness. For an opera singer, the possibility of bad health is a problem that hangs over you all the time like an evil spirit waiting to turn a beautiful event that makes everyone happy into a disaster that makes everyone mad. One of the most frightening times was when I sang for the first time in Buenos Aires. It was in 1987, and the opera was *La Bohème*.

The trip started off beautifully. I had never sung at the Teatro Colón before, and I knew it was one of the world's great opera houses. Caruso had sung there, and so had most of the other great singers of history. One of them, the legendary soprano Maria Caniglia, once said to me, "It's easy to have good acoustics in a small theater, but in a large theater, the most beautiful acoustics are in the Teatro Massimo in Palermo and the Teatro Colón in Buenos Aires."

Buenos Aires has an enormous Italian population—someone told me over half the people are of Italian background—and they made a big celebration over my arrival. There were banners up in the principal streets, signs everywhere saying "Welcome, Pavarotti." It was already wonderful for me to see this beautiful city, but all these signs of the city's appreciation and excitement made it even better.

Leone Magiera, our conductor, had arrived with the other principals a few days before me. My first day in the city had been set aside for me to recover from my trip, and I didn't have to rehearse until the second day. I think they wanted me to stay in my room and rest and I know I should have, but I was too excited. I asked if I could be taken on a drive through Buenos Aires to see the sights. That was my big mistake.

The city was fantastic—beautiful old buildings and the widest boulevards I had ever seen. When we passed by the theater on the principal boulevard, I got so overwhelmed at seeing this shrine of opera that I wanted to see the inside of it, too. When we entered the auditorium, an orchestra rehearsal was in progress, but I was bowled over by the beauty of the theater. In spite of the dark—the only light came from the musicians' stands—I could see the boxes and the ceiling with their fantastic colors, all gold and yellow and blue.

The metal fire curtain was down and, in the pit, Leone was holding an orchestra rehearsal of the Act One music. Someone whispered to me that they were having a separate staging rehearsal behind the curtain. I wasn't supposed to come to the theater until the next day, but many people working in the house had seen me arrive. These people looked surprised, and I could see that crowds of backstage workers were forming in the doorways.

I didn't want to interrupt the rehearsal, so I went quickly to a seat in the first row near Leone. I just wanted to drink in the beauty of that wonderful place with Puccini's music playing. At that moment, the orchestra was arriving at my cue for "Che Gelida Manina," and I am afraid I got carried away and began to sing my aria. Leone was startled, but when he turned and saw me sitting there, he smiled and continued conducting.

Hans Boon, who works with Herbert Breslin, told me later that he had been standing in the back of the theater when I began to sing and the rear seats quickly filled with all the people working backstage in the opera house. He said that the acoustics were as magnificent as we had been told and that the sound of me singing from an orchestra seat that famous aria was one of the most wonderful things he ever heard. It was wonderful for me, too. When I finished, the place went wild. All of these people—the orchestra, costume people, stagehands—were not just clapping for the aria, they were also welcoming me to Buenos Aires.

The experience put me in such a terrific mood that I wanted to work right then. I asked them to bring our Mimi, Kallen Esperian, who was a winner of my vocal competition, from the rehearsal behind the curtain. She came out, and we sang the rest of Act One with her aria, "Mi Chiamano Mimi" and our duet, "O Soave Fanciulla." By now it seemed like all of Buenos Aires had found its way into the theater, and there was a huge ovation when we finished.

I have sung *Bohème* many, many times, but few times were as moving for me as that impromptu rehearsal in the Teatro Colón. When I made my movie, *Yes, Giorgio,* they tried to write in a similar scene. They wrote a scene for me to enter the back of the Metropolitan Opera House during a rehearsal and I start to sing. But as always when you try to re-create something that was completely spontaneous and natural, it came out plastic and forced.

Sadly, I paid for this thrill in Buenos Aires. The rehearsal went well, but the day before the dress rehearsal I woke up feeling horrible. I was very, very sick with the flu. I am superstitious about doing more than I am scheduled to do. It seems that every time I do, I get sick. I had not been scheduled to ride around Buenos Aires that first day after a long airplane ride, or to have a full singing rehearsal with orchestra. I was supposed to stay in my hotel and rest. When I break the rules that way, I am asking for trouble.

My family had arrived from Italy, and my wife, Adua, was looking after me. Herbert had not yet arrived in town, so I telephoned Hans Boon and asked him to come to my room so I could tell him the terrible news. He found me with my head wrapped in towels, a hot water bottle on top, and a thermometer in my mouth. Adua was standing next to the bed putting her hand on my forehead every five minutes.

"Look at me, Boonino," I said. "I am sick as a dog. This is the same flu I had in Salzburg. It took me fourteen days to get over it." I recognized all the symptoms. Over the years I have become a connoisseur of flu.

Hans looked stunned. He said, "But, Luciano, that will knock out all of the performances. We leave Buenos Aires in thirteen days."

We were both silent. Then he said, "Well, what can they do if you're sick? Kill us?"

But I knew he was thinking that the city was turned upside down for my first appearance there. For me to cancel would be a major disaster, almost an international incident. I told him to give me my appointment book.

Looking at the dates, I figured out a plan and explained it to Hans. The dress rehearsal was the following night. It would be a full performance with all the wealthy patrons of the opera coming as invited guests. The following day was a day of rest, and the opening was the night after. If we did not do the dress rehearsal as a performance, I told Hans, and instead had my cover sing for me, I could have two full days, almost three, to recover from my illness. There was one performance that I was not scheduled to sing. The cover tenor was to sing in my place. I would sing that one, and all of the patrons who missed the dress rehearsal could come.

Actually, this plan worked. The theater management was able to arrange this by switching tickets around. I had the next two days off and concentrated on getting rid of the flu, but of course it is more difficult to get well when you know you *must* get well.

To make the crisis even worse, our soprano, Kallen Esperian, also caught my flu and was very sick. The day of the opening, I felt a lot better, but I still wasn't sure if I could sing. I went to the piano in my room and tried out my voice. It seemed to be working okay. I called Kallen to ask how she was feeling. She said she was still sick and did not think she could sing. I told her to come to my room; I would vocalize her and then I would tell her whether or not she could sing for the opening.

When Kallen arrived, looking miserable, we went to the piano. I could see that she was sick and that she had some problems in her throat, but I also heard that, underneath, the voice was fine.

"You can sing tonight," I told her. "No problem."

She looked surprised and a little panicked, but said she would do it. Later that day Hans Boon and one of the other singers came to my room very upset. They had been outside Kallen's room, they told me, and had listened to her vocalize. She sounded terrible, they said, nothing like her normal voice. They said I mustn't let her sing that evening.

Getting a production of an opera on a stage is an enormously complicated process. Hundreds of people are involved, and all of them must do their job, but in the end all of these people and the entire audience, also, depend on the condition of two or three sets of vocal cords. The people involved know this, and they are as concerned about these vocal cords as if they were their own and as if they were expected to sing. These few principal voices belong to the entire group, and every member of the group gets as nervous for you as you get for yourself.

These colleagues in Buenos Aires knew how sick Kallen had been the past few days. Perhaps that knowledge made them hear something different when they heard her sing. I could hear something different too, but it was the kind of difference that clears up with vocalization.

Since I had loved Kallen's singing from her first audition in Philadelphia and had watched her develop as a singer, I felt I knew her voice better than these other people. Also, I was maybe a little extra protective of her because she was one of my Philadelphia competition winners.

I was confident that Kallen would be fine by the evening. I was less confident about myself. Throughout the day I sang the aria that tells me the condition of my voice, "Una Furtiva Lagrima" from L'Elisir d'Amore. I know that if I can sing that aria, my voice is working properly. I can hear the resonance and know exactly where the voice is. Adua says she is sure she heard me sing the aria twenty times that day.

On this day, however, I wasn't sure. As the hour approached to go to the theater, I still wasn't certain I would be able to sing. I know how this doubt drives everybody around me crazy, as well as all the people at the theater. You try to keep from them the bad news until you are sure the disaster is unavoidable, but this time my condition was no secret. Because the dress rehearsal had been re-scheduled, everyone in Buenos Aires knew I was sick.

About six in the evening, I was feeling okay, and I left for the theater. I was in that strange state when you are not sick and you are not well. From my attempts to sing "Furtiva" I was pretty sure the voice was okay—for one aria, at least. Whether or not I would be able to sing an entire opera was a different story. As I was getting into my costume and makeup, Hans came into the dressing room.

"You feel fine. Right, Luciano?"

I looked at him and said, "I will go on, but if it doesn't sound right on the first high note, the performance is over."

As it turned out, everything went beautifully. Kallen and I were both in excellent form. Maybe our relief at being able to sing gave our singing an extra luster. In any case, the people of Buenos Aires were more than satisfied and were as enthusiastic about Kallen as they were about me.

After the performance everyone in the company was so happy, they all decided to celebrate at a popular nightspot called the Tango Club. Not me. I knew I had not fully recovered and could not go. I told Kallen that she too must go home to bed, but she had already decided the same thing herself. When I was back in the hotel, I began to feel very sorry for her. I was with my family, but Kallen was alone. She had sung so beautifully and so coura-geously and I had sent her to bed like a naughty child. I had an idea. I called room service and ordered dinner for four people on a cart.

Next I telephoned different hotel rooms hoping to find some of Kallen's friends in the company. I suspected many would stop at the hotel to change their clothes for the Tango Club. Each time I got an answer I asked the person if they would eat dinner with Kallen. They could go to the club later. When I found three who agreed, I met them in the lobby and we went up to her floor to wait for the cart. The cart arrived, and I pushed it to Kallen's door and knocked.

When she saw me, the three others and the cart, she looked very surprised. I said, "Here is your dinner and here are some friends to eat with."

I don't believe in pampering singers, especially young singers who must learn that singing opera is a difficult profession. But Kallen definitely deserved special attention. Earlier that day she had felt sure she could not sing. She did it only because I told her she could. This took a lot of trust and the courage of a lion. When I pushed the dinner cart into her room and removed the covers from the food, Kallen looked very happy. I went back to my room and went right to sleep.

Many of the things that have gone wrong for me onstage seemed to have happened in Paris. I wonder if that city may be a little jinxed for me. One of the worst was in 1984 when I had just hired a new secretary, Giovanna Cavaliere. She and I made our arrangements before I left New York in October. Then in November she flew over to Paris, where I was singing *Tosca*. We were staying at the Claridge Residences on the Champs-Élysées.

For a new secretary of an opera singer the day of the first performance is like the first real day on the job. In Giovanna's case, the day was a total nightmare—for us both. It started when I asked her to go out to buy some food for us to eat in the room. I especially like chicken before I sing and asked her to find some that was already cooked. Every street corner in Paris has wonderful take-out food places, but she came back with chicken that was so dry and tough we could not eat it.

She also brought cooked zucchini, which is one of the few

vegetables I do not much like. I wouldn't have minded so much, but when you start with a new secretary, you are super-critical of everything she does, and I worried about what kind of secretary I had hired. (She turned out to be wonderful.)

But it was at the theater that the real trouble happened, and it was in no way her fault. I always like to arrive in plenty of time, and we got to the Paris Opera House at 6:15, which gave me an hour and forty-five minutes to get into makeup, vocalize a little, then relax in my bathrobe until about fifteen minutes before I was called onto the stage. To avoid wrinkling the costume, I do not put it on until I must.

At about 7:20 the conductor, James Conlon, who is now the artistic director of that company, came by my dressing room to wish me luck. I wondered why he was coming by my room so far ahead of the curtain time, but decided he must have other things to do before the opera began. A few minutes later Giovanna said she could hear the orchestra and later told me she thought Conlon must be doing a last-minute rehearsal. When I decided it was time to put on my costume, I told Giovanna to wait outside and keep anyone from coming into the dressing room.

Suddenly I heard her yelling, "You can't go in! Mr. Pavarotti is in his underwear."

My door burst open and the stage manager pushed in with Giovanna trying to stop him. "Where are you? The curtain is up. You should be onstage right now and you are in your underwear." Then he added in French, *"Nous commençons."* We are starting.

I looked at him and said in my bad French, *"Nous arretons."* We are stopping.

This was not a good moment. At that time I went into a panic, but later it made me a little angry. Every night that we had rehearsals, we had begun at eight o'clock. Opera houses all over the world start performances at eight o'clock. The Paris opera has 1,400 employees. Not one of them had told us that the performance would start at 7:30, not 8:00. I couldn't believe it. There was no way I could get out on the stage in time for the opera to proceed, so they brought down the curtain and told the audience there were "technical difficulties." They waited till I had my clothes on, then they started the opera again.

I think this is a performer's worst nightmare. You are supposed to be onstage, a hundred musicians have arrived at the place in the score where you are supposed to sing your first notes, everyone is looking at the place onstage where you should be standing, but you are in your dressing room in your underwear.

People often ask me about things that go wrong on the stage. I tell them that almost nothing had ever gone wrong on the stage for me. I had been very lucky—until the Paris *Tosca*. That night the singing was fine, but *everything* else went wrong.

In the second act, my character, Cavaradossi, is brought into Scarpia's office after being tortured offstage. They have hurt him so much he cannot stand and he collapses on a stool. During rehearsals I looked at the stool carefully. It was made of carved wood. It looked delicate, too delicate to hold me.

I went to the director and said quietly so no one would hear, "I don't think that stool is strong enough. If I sit on it, I will break it."

He said, "Don't worry, Luciano. We have had it reinforced with steel."

I was still worried, but it worked all right for the dress rehearsal. But on the night of the first performance, when that moment in the opera arrived, I was dragged onto the stage by Scarpia's guards and placed on the stool. The Tosca was the wonderful soprano Hildegard Behrens. She was supposed to come over and throw her arms around me as we had done in rehearsal many times. But Hildegard is a very powerful actress, and she got carried away by her performance. For some reason she ran across the stage and threw herself on top of me.

They are still looking for that stool.

Even with the extra steel, it had collapsed completely. We were both in a pile on the stage. The audience was so stunned that no one laughed. In the first place, they could not see the stool, and I think they thought our collapsing onto the floor together was part of our performance. Also, one of the guards was standing beside us, but he was too stunned to move. It looked like Tosca and her lover were having a wrestling match on the stage of the Paris Opéra. No one came near us until we got to our feet and continued singing.

I pitied poor Giovanna. She had started the day with the wrong chicken. Next she had seen me undressed in my dressing room when I was supposed to be onstage singing. Now she had ended the day seeing her boss on his back on the stage with a soprano on top of him. I tried to explain to her it was not always like this.

Sometimes directors get carried away with what they want from you onstage. They ask you to do things that you know will make you look ridiculous. I am lucky that the directors I work with understand how much I can move because of my size and because of my knee problem. For instance in the Met's beautiful production of *Tosca* my character, Cavaradossi, is an artist. When the opera begins, he is working on a large painting in a church. The set designer had wanted the picture to be enormous and had built a scaffold for me to stand on as I painted the religious mural. It was all right at the beginning of the opera after I make my entrance because, even with my bad knee, I could climb up to the scaffold on the steps he provided.

The problem was that I had to come down during the act to sing my duet with Tosca and after that to hide from Scarpia's police. The only way to get down was this narrow wooden stair-case—very steep, like the stairs on a ship. With my knee problem, there was a good chance I wouldn't be able to come down—or that I would come down faster than anyone wanted. One possible solution would have been to ask Tosca to join me on the scaffold-ing so we could sing together. But she was in a long skirt and there was no point in her climbing the steps, as she was not painting. It was a big problem.

To solve it we arrived at the idea that I would be working on a *small* painting of the big painting, a sketch or cartoon. It made sense to place this on an easel down on the stage. I could say good-bye to that scaffolding. The set designer's original idea was an ex-cellent one from the visual point of view—me working halfway up a huge portrait that everyone in the audience could see clearly. But it turned out to be a very bad idea, given what I could and could not do. Sometimes you must remind set designers and directors they are working with human beings, not acrobats.

When I am working on an operatic production, I may joke around with my colleagues during rehearsals, but I never do this during a performance. I know that in the past some opera singers have done this and there are many stories. Caruso was a champion of jokers. He loved to play pranks—like lovingly taking the soprano's hand and leaving a hot sausage in it.

I think I have a sense of humor, but I am very against doing such things on the stage. I take opera and singing too seriously. I would never do anything that might throw other singers off their concentration, and I would advise my colleagues not to try any tricks with me. Performing an operatic role is too difficult a busi-ness and there are too many ways a production can get into trouble. To me it seems very unprofessional and far too risky to add to the problems with childish pranks.

Even though everyone knows I feel this way, I still haven't always been safe from pranks. Last fall, while I was onstage, one of my colleagues at the Metropolitan Opera played a trick on me that took me completely by surprise. He didn't have to worry too much about my reaction because he was my boss at the Met, the company's artistic director, Jimmy Levine. That night he was conducting *Tosca,* which we had done many times together. (*Tosca* and Paris seem to be my two trouble spots.)

I had just completed my big aria, "E Lucevan le Stelle," in the final act. Cavaradossi is writing a good-bye letter to his beloved Tosca before being shot by the firing squad. The music of the aria is extremely beautiful and moving, I sang the aria well, and there was a huge ovation when I finished. When the audience grew quiet, Jimmy started the orchestra up again.

The first notes sounded right. Puccini wrote a very brief repeat of the aria's theme before going on to Tosca's entrance. Suddenly I realized this was not the next page of music. Jimmy was playing the opening bars of my aria again. For a moment I was confused, totally confused, and thought maybe I hadn't sung the aria yet, only thought I had. When your concentration is thrown off while you're onstage, your first thought is that you have done something wrong. Then I saw a big smile on Jimmy's face and I realized what he was doing. He was making me respond to the applause by singing the aria a second time.

I should explain that the Metropolitan has a very strict policy against encores. Other major opera houses are not so strict about this and sometimes allow them if the audience insists, but at the Met—never. The New York audience can clap for an hour and still not earn an encore. That is why I was so confused. But I pulled myself together and sang "E Lucevan le Stelle" a second time, and the audience went crazy. They could see from my confusion that I was not expecting this, and they knew encores never happened at the Met.

Backstage afterward Jimmy gave me a big hug and said, "It was my little Halloween joke, Luciano." It was October 31.

This surprise encore was so unusual that the next day, the *New York Times* had an article about it. They quoted Jimmy: "Because it was Halloween, I wanted to do trick-or-treat. The trick was on Luciano, the treat was for the audience."

One thing that bothers me very much when I am performing on stage is when a colleague, a singer performing with me, is working in isolation, when that person ignores my presence on the stage. This is particularly terrible when I am supposed to be in love with the soprano. If the soprano sings all the time to the audience, if she doesn't even look at me, how can anyone believe she is in love with me?

It is not only lovers with bored expressions that can hurt the drama. When the Conte di Luna in the first act finale of *Il Trovatore* confronts Manrico before the final trio, he hates him and wants to kill him. If the baritone looks at the tenor like a stranger he is passing on the street, there is no tension. I know I am not Laurence Olivier, but I try to put myself into the part I am playing and react to the other performers. If the others are not reacting to me, it makes it twice as difficult for me to appear believable.

Although I make an effort to act, I must sometimes draw the line at other people's notions of how best to get the drama across. For instance, the character I play in *I Lombardi* dies and returns as a spirit in the last act. To show the audience that I had really died earlier and was now a spirit, the costume designer dressed me all in white, like an angel. He also wanted me to wear white feathered wings like the lady in *Angels in America*. I refused to do this and said absolutely not. The man asked me why not. I looked at him. "If I am an angel," I said, "you are Abraham Lincoln."

3

PERFORMING
WITH MY
HANDKERCHIEF

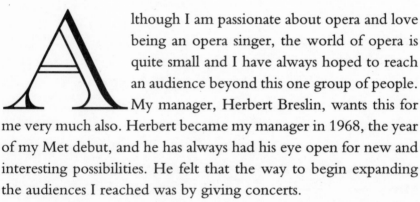

lthough I am passionate about opera and love
being an opera singer, the world of opera is
quite small and I have always hoped to reach
an audience beyond this one group of people.
My manager, Herbert Breslin, wants this for
me very much also. Herbert became my manager in 1968, the year
of my Met debut, and he has always had his eye open for new and
interesting possibilities. He felt that the way to begin expanding
the audiences I reached was by giving concerts.

In 1973, as I was finally becoming very well known in opera,
Herbert heard about a rich man in Liberty, Missouri, who had died
and left money for a foundation to bring international performing
artists to his town. What a wonderful thing to do for your city, and
it is a nice thing for artists, too. Because I had never done a full-
length concert alone, and also because such concerts present many
problems, Herbert thought it would be a good idea for me to try
this idea in Missouri.

There are many things that make concerts difficult. First of all,
you must sell the tickets. There must be enough people in that city
who want to hear you sing to fill a hall. Then, instead of singing

maybe three or four arias, as you do in the course of an opera, you must sing fifteen to twenty arias and songs in one evening—five times as much singing as you do in an opera. And you do it alone. There is no chorus music or soprano arias to give your voice a rest.

Although singers make bigger fees if they can fill concert halls, it is a lot more work. It's also a much bigger risk. You are completely exposed and vulnerable, far more so than when you perform an opera with a hundred other people. In a solo concert many things can go wrong. That is why Herbert thought it would be good to try this idea outside of New York, where you may get only one chance. As it turned out, the concert in Liberty went very well—the audience was happy and so was I. So, later that same year, 1973, I did a concert at Carnegie Hall. That, too, was a success, and I've been doing concerts ever since.

I do not forget that Herbert pushed me to do that first concert, and I am very glad that he did. I think that's one reason Herbert and I get along so well: we're both always eager to try new adventures, new challenges. We've been doing new things together now for twenty-seven years.

Very soon after the success of the concert in New York, I had my first televised concert. That was with Joan Sutherland from the Metropolitan Opera. It's very exciting to think that your singing is reaching so many people at one time—not just three or four thousand, but millions of people. But at the same time you're aware that if you don't sing so well, or if you hit a bad note, millions of people will know it. So it's very frightening. But the televised concert went well, and I was now established in another type of performing besides opera.

Opera is an effort from a group, and I like that very much. Of course, it makes you feel wonderful when you get applause for your aria or take a solo bow, but basically the artistic effect of an opera must come from the group, with all of the musicians performing their best and working well together. When the people I am singing with perform well, it makes me as happy as when I perform well alone. It is like a sports team. Different individual players may score the goals, but all the others are just as important for the final result. I have felt that way about singing opera since my first performance in 1961.

Even though I love the teamwork of the opera stage, there is a different thrill from singing a concert. It is not just ego. On a concert stage with only a piano, or even with an orchestra, you feel much closer to the audience. There is no drama and fantasy to put a screen between you and them. In fact, there is nothing between you and them. With an opera, it is the work itself that is communicating with the audience. We artists are merely the instruments for the artistic vision of Verdi, Donizetti, or Mozart.

But on the concert stage, you as an artist are communicating more directly with the audience. I love very much this feeling of direct contact. While I know some will scoff at this, I feel this contact as much in a stadium with 50,000 people as I do in a recital hall with a hundred. I can even feel it with television, when the numbers become too big to imagine.

Since those first concerts, I've given concerts all over the world—in Russia and South America, Japan, China, Southeast Asia, Mexico. There are very few places where I haven't sung.

Of all the many wonderful concerts, several stand out. One was in Russia in May of 1990. It was a time when Mikhail Gorbachev was in political trouble and was not going out in public. They told me he was afraid he would be booed and that the newspapers would write about it or, worse, that it would be shown on television. But when I sang my concert in Moscow, Gorbachev came to the hall and sat in the back of a box so no one would see him. I was very touched; I was also very impressed to meet him later.

I am not a strongly political person. I feel that you must know much more than I know to have strong political opinions. But I do believe that Gorbachev and Ronald Reagan must be given credit for ending the cold war. For all of us who lived so long under that black cloud of fear, the end of that hostility was a fantastic thing. I do not believe it ended by accident. Many powerful people on both sides wanted the tension to continue. So because I am convinced that Mikhail Gorbachev must take half of the credit for bringing about this enormous improvement in the world we live in, it was a great thrill for me to meet him.

Another concert that will always be for me one of my best memories was in 1991 when I sang in London's Hyde Park. The concert was free for almost everyone, except for a few rows in the front. If people wanted to sit up close, they had to pay money. But everybody else in London who wanted to come could come for free. I was very excited about this, but unfortunately the day of the concert it poured rain and did not want to stop. We could not cancel or postpone the concert because it was being shown live on television. We had to go through with it. The stage and orchestra were in a covered shell, but everyone in the audience was in the open air. When I say everyone, I am not joking. Sitting down in front I could see the Prince and Princess of Wales, Prime Minister John Major and his wife, and many other dignitaries—everyone but the queen herself, to be accurate.

When the concert began, most of the people sitting out in front of me had their umbrellas up. It looked like an enormous field of umbrellas. But after my first aria, an announcement came over the loudspeaker asking all of the people to put their umbrellas down. The voice explained that no one could see anything except the umbrella in front of him.

When they made that announcement, there was a huge burst of applause. Except for the people on the front row, everybody was happy to have the umbrellas go down. Princess Diana immediately put down her umbrella, and so did everyone else. From up on the stage, it was incredible to see all those thousands of people sitting there with the rain pouring down on them. It made me feel very strange and uneasy to be under a roof, dry and comfortable, and to look down and see, a few feet in front of me, the Prince and Princess of Wales and the prime minister of England with water running off them.

The concert was produced by Tibor Rudas, an important person in my life whom I will talk much more about later. He and Herbert and their wives were sitting in the front row getting as wet as the royal people. At one point during the concert I made a gesture toward all of my friends and toward the royalty to indicate my frustration at their situation. I put up my hands and tried to show with my face that I was unhappy for them.

Some people in the audience were lucky; they had raincoats and rain hats, but others just sat there getting wet. It was even more painful for me, I think, because I am always so terrified of catching cold. But no one seemed to mind, and that's what made the whole experience so incredible for me. I've never had a more enthusiastic audience. The spirit was wonderful. I was there to make them happy, and they were there to be happy.

Earlier when I was singing operas at Covent Garden, I had been invited to have dinner at Buckingham Palace and had been asked to some other very formal parties. I had seen Charles and Diana on these occasions, and I liked them both very much. The prince loves opera and will travel a great distance to see a particular performance. He is also good friends with many opera singers. Both Charles and Diana are very nice people, and I am deeply sorry for the problems they have had.

Before the Hyde Park concert, I asked Prince Charles if he would permit me to dedicate a song to his wife. He said yes. Toward the end of the concert, I stopped everything and made an announcement to the audience. I told them that, with Prince

Charles's permission, I was going to dedicate the next aria to Princess Diana. "Donna Non Vidi Mai" ("I never saw a woman such as this") from Puccini's *Manon Lescaut*. When I said that over the loudspeakers, the audience went crazy. In England they love Diana very much.

When the concert was over, the prince and princess came backstage to congratulate me. Princess Diana must not have had a rain hat during the concert, because she was soaked, totally soaked, her blond hair streaming down on both sides of her face. Even so, she still looked beautiful and like a princess. She also looked very happy and excited.

Princess Diana is so lovely, so kind, and so poised, you look at her and you think, this is a person who will go through life with only good things happening to her. It does not seem to be turning out that way. But I think I made her happy that night. In the backstage tent that served as a greenroom, she told me that my dedicating the aria to her was one of the nicest things that had ever happened to her.

After their separation, Diana came to New York, and she and I were both invited to a dinner given by Nelson and Leona Shanks. He is an artist who had painted her portrait as well as mine. The dinner party was at the National Arts Club, and a limo was sent to pick me up first, then was to pick up Princess Diana. But at the last minute, the British embassy decided they should drive her to the party instead, for security reasons. On the way to the dinner, our car got caught in terrible traffic. Something had happened in the streets, and nothing was moving. When we finally arrived, Diana was already there. I felt very bad. I try always to be on time, and I don't like it when others are late for me. I certainly wanted to be on time for the Princess of Wales.

At dinner we all ordered different things, and she ordered broiled shrimp that looked wonderful. I said to her, "Princess, those shrimp must be very good, yes?" She said they were excel-

lent. Later I said they must be really delicious. She smiled and nodded enthusiastically. Finally, I said, "Listen. I tried twice with no
success. Now I ask you directly. May I have one of your shrimp?"

She got very flustered and apologetic. "I am so sorry . . . I
didn't realize . . ." Then she smiled in a shy way and said, "I am not
accustomed to sharing my food." If that is true, she would have a
terrible time at my family table.

I am a friend to both Princess Diana and the Prince of Wales,
so I don't speculate on their problems, even privately. I think,
however, that her life is very sad now. I believe she is lonely. I
don't mean that she has no people around her. I'm sure there are
many people in her life, but not people she can kick off her shoes
with, really relax with.

That is a terrible thing that can happen to famous people. At
one time, years back, as my life began to grow more complicated
with operas in different cities, touring, concerts, and the star treatment everywhere, I saw that this same thing could happen to me
too. You fall into a routine so that you only see people who are
working for you and helping you get where you must be next. I
worked very hard to make sure that didn't happen to me, and I
think I have succeeded. At least the people around me don't mind
if I kick off my shoes.

The pressure of singing concerts is enormous. It's even worse than
an opera. If you are in the cast of an opera and something goes
wrong with your voice or if you get sick, the managers always have
somebody who can sing in your place. Like singers, the men and
women who run opera houses know about the unpredictability of
the human voice. My sickness in Buenos Aires was more of a crisis,
of course, because the city was making such a special event of my
singing there. Usually opera houses can adjust, but with a concert,

they cannot put in a substitute. Everything depends on you, and many things can go wrong.

One time I was singing a concert in Pittsburgh and my secretaries, Nicoletta and Larisa, who were responsible for packing everything I needed, had forgotten to pack my white tie and tails, which I wear when I sing. Each one thought the other had packed them. When they realized their mistake, they knew how upset I would be and were afraid to tell me until they figured out what to do.

They got an idea. They telephoned Andrea Griminelli who was going to perform with me. He was still in New York and would be flying to Pittsburgh in a few hours. They told Andrea to go to my apartment, find my white tie and tails, and bring them with him on the plane. They pleaded with him not to tell me.

He must have forgotten their request, because we spoke on the telephone about a small change in the program, some details we had to work out. I asked him what plane he was taking out. Then he said, "Don't worry, Luciano, I have your white tie and tails."

"You have what!" I couldn't believe it. The concert was to begin in a few hours and I had no clothes. I went a little crazy. Andrea could get on the wrong plane, or my clothes could get on the wrong plane. Of course, Nicoletta was furious with Andrea, I was furious with Nicoletta, everybody was furious with everybody. You get very nervous and upset on the day of a concert.

I have a good quality, however. No matter how angry I get at anyone about anything, I forget about it very quickly. Whatever it was, it is finished the next day, completely gone. Nicoletta tells me I am too much this way. She gets very upset if she sees me being nice to someone she thinks has done something bad to me. She cannot understand how I can forget that this person lied to me, betrayed me, or did some other bad thing to me. I tell Nicoletta to forget it. None of us is perfect, and people do what they must do.

My clothes arrived in Pittsburgh in time, and everything was okay. Maybe Andrea was making me suffer a little bit the way I had made him suffer before a concert we did together before Pittsburgh. Actually the joke I played on him was terrible, but sometimes you must do things to break the tension before these performances. Andrea performs on a beautiful gold flute which is his most important possession. It is very valuable, and he is extremely proud of that flute. Backstage about an hour before our concert was to begin, he brought his flute into my dressing room and asked me to watch it while he ran an errand.

When he came back, the flute wasn't there. He looked everywhere, but could not find it. I told him, "I'm very sorry, Andrea. I left the dressing room for one minute only. Somebody must have stolen it."

Well, of course, he went crazy—out of his mind. I let him suffer a few moments, and then I pulled the flute from the sleeve of my dressing gown. That was not very nice of me. My friend Gildo tells me I have a mean streak. I don't think I do, but I think what I did to Andrea was definitely mean, because for a performer not to have his instrument just before he performs is probably the worst nightmare an artist can have. It is the same as when I lose my voice. Terrible. But at least with Andrea, I could give his voice back to him.

Andrea has performed over seventy concerts with me and we are good friends. He gives me credit for his success, but I remind him that he plays the flute, not me. Andrea is intelligent; he is nice to be with, and people like him. He is very serious about his career and knows how to seize opportunities. He deserves his success.

Like me, Andrea has had problems with clothes. At one of the Central Park concerts we did together, he arrived from his apartment wearing blue jeans. He carried his formal clothes for the concert in a clothing bag over his arm. When he opened the bag, he discovered that his black pants were not inside. There was only about an hour to go before the performance, and he had to have the right pants; he couldn't appear onstage in a formal black jacket, a white tie, and blue jeans. So he told the production people his emergency. They had an idea and said to him, "There are police cars just outside. We'll get the police to drive you from the stage out of the park to your apartment so you can pick up your black pants."

Andrea started out in the police car, but the crowds coming into the park were so huge that the police car could not pass through the people who were walking on the park roads. The police knew that if they succeeded in getting Andrea out of the park, the crowds would be even worse when they returned and they would not be able to get him to the stage in time to perform.

They turned their car around and brought him back. Andrea had no idea what he would do, and I couldn't help. I only had my own pants. The musicians needed theirs. The stagehands were all in work pants or blue jeans. With the concert starting in a few minutes, Andrea was sitting in his dressing room without any pants on in a daze. A friend came to his dressing room to wish him well before the concert. He looked at his friend's pants. They were black, and the friend was about Andrea's size. Before the man knew what was happening, his pants were off of him and onto Andrea. He made it onto the stage in time.

When you see one of us performers up on a stage taking our bows—smiling, happy—you must always think that maybe ten minutes before the performance, we had no pants. We may have a good voice, or we may play the flute well, but we are humans and we do stupid things.

When one of my concerts is being filmed for television, I am sometimes very concerned about the angle of the camera. If it is positioned a certain way, it can make you look bigger, and that is the last thing I need. One time I was singing the Verdi Requiem in white tie and tails, and Kirk Browning, who was directing a film version for Public Broadcasting, had set up his equipment on one side of the stage, but it was the side where I was the first of the four singers. When I saw some shots he had filmed of us in rehearsal, I was horrified. I was particularly heavy at the time, and all you could see was me. I completely covered everybody. You couldn't see the soprano, the mezzo, or the bass—only me.

I told Kirk he had to move his camera to the other side of the stage. He said that was too difficult at this point. I insisted; otherwise it would look like Verdi had written the requiem for a solo tenor. Finally he agreed, and the other singers were visible.

If people think I am happy about my weight, they are wrong. I am happy *in spite* of my weight. That is very different. Often I hate to see how I look to others. I look in the mirror and I say, "Oh, my God!" So I am self-conscious about the way I am photographed. When people are taking my picture with other people, even a casual snapshot, I always put one of the others in front of me. Otherwise the picture has too much of me.

It is worse for television. One time when Kirk was filming me in a concert, we looked at some shots he had done at the dress rehearsal. I had worn studs with my white-tie outfit. In some shots he showed too much of me. You could see three or four studs and much too much stomach. For another shot he moved the camera in closer and showed only two studs. It was ten times better, and I told him that was the one he should use.

Just before the concert began, I saw Kirk backstage and I held up two fingers and yelled at him, "Remember. Two studs only."

When I perform in concerts, I use certain tricks that make me feel more secure. Everybody knows about my white handkerchief, which I used in that first concert in Missouri in 1973, in case I started to perspire. I find that I feel much better if I have it out there with me. It has a function, but it's also for good luck.

Also, when I am singing a concert that has music which is new to me, I feel much more comfortable if I have the score nearby. I remember when I gave my first big concert in Madison Square Garden in 1985, it was going to be televised live on public television. The producer from PBS, a nice man named David Horn, came up to me during one of the last rehearsals and he started to move the music stand with my scores on it. I grabbed it from him. David said, "Surely, Luciano, you're not going to keep the music stand for the actual performance."

I said to him in my best Italian-American, "You take-a my stand, I kick-a your butt."

In 1981 a very interesting man entered my life who changed things a lot for me: Tibor Rudas was in his late fifties, born in Hungary, but had worked for many years as a producer of entertainment in Australia and later America. For some time he had produced revues for the Las Vegas casinos and was then hiring performers for Resorts International in Atlantic City. He had brought to Atlantic City such great entertainers as Frank Sinatra, Dolly Parton, and Bill Cosby. Mr. Rudas came to see Herbert with an invitation for me to sing at his resort hotel in Atlantic City. As I later heard the story, Herbert threw him out of his office.

You must understand several things about Herbert. He cares very much about serious music, about opera. He also cares about me. He is very proud of what I have done in my career, and he is also proud of his part in it, as he should be. Because of all this, he can be very protective.

I know that people come to him all day long in his New York

office with requests for me to sing, not just for every good cause under the sun but also for school events, sporting events, social events—even for the opening of a new pizzeria. (Although I didn't sing there, I did attend the opening of a pizzeria last year, but I did it because the owner was a friend.) I sing many benefits and try to give 10 percent of my appearances to them. But if it weren't for Herbert I would find myself doing nothing but benefits.

Herbert knows that my schedule is made two or three years in advance. When I do have some time, he knows the kind of event that will interest me. I trust him completely to say no to things he is certain are not possible. He is always polite on the first exchange. He listens to the proposition and gives his answer. Most often he says no and explains why it is not possible for me to accept the invitation. If people continue their efforts to persuade him, telling him who else will be there or whatever they think might change his mind, Herbert is suddenly not so polite. That is what happened when he told Rudas to leave his office.

Tibor later told me Herbert's exact words: "Mr. Pavarotti is one of the greatest singers in the history of opera. You want him to sing in a gambling joint? Not in this lifetime!" When Rudas tried to make him change his mind, Herbert told him to get out. Herbert's way of telling people no is not my way, but Herbert has his style of operating.

We learned that Tibor Rudas had his style, too. He came back to Herbert's office several times, each time offering more money for just one concert. And from the beginning the offer was very large. Each time he received the same answer: "Go away." The Breslin office is on West Fifty-seventh Street in the same block as Carnegie Hall. Herbert and all of his staff sit in one large room, no partitions or doors. It is like a small newspaper office. Anyone entering from the hall comes right into the room where Herbert and his employees sit. One day the door opened and

Rudas stuck his head inside. Everyone looked up. He yelled one thing: "A hundred thousand dollars!"

Herbert told him to come in.

In 1981, you must remember, $100,000 was an enormous amount of money for a classical artist to earn for just one appearance. It was certainly more than I had made for a concert—and a lot more than I earned for an operatic performance. At the time Rudas made this offer, I was in Milan performing in *Aïda* at La Scala. Herbert phoned me and told me about the offer. I was impressed and said I would be happy to hear the man's plan. When Rudas heard what I had said, he told Herbert he would fly to Milan the next day. I was starting to like this man, even though I had never seen him. The next morning Rudas and his wife and Herbert took the first flight for Milan, and I got them seats for that evening's performance of *Aïda*.

I do not like to meet new people before I go onstage, so we planned to have our first meeting when the opera was finished. Herbert came backstage before the first act and explained to me Rudas's proposition. I had not understood correctly when he told me of the offer over the phone. I didn't realize the resort hotel was for gambling. I told Herbert to tell Mr. Rudas I was very, very sorry but I could not sing in a casino. I felt extremely bad that he and his wife had come all the way from New York, but I had misunderstood and I felt very strongly against singing in a place that is for gambling.

Herbert went into the theater, sat down in his seat beside Rudas, and whispered the bad news. Rudas asked Herbert to tell him the exact problem without any politeness. Herbert said that I was very pleased by the financial offer, but the problem was singing in a gambling casino. When I heard this story some time later from Tibor, he told me he was devastated by my message. Then, with his usual modesty, he told me what happened next.

He said to me, "That's when I had my brilliant idea." He told Herbert to go backstage one more time and ask me if I would perform *near* a casino. He would build a special tent just for my appearance.

When Herbert told me the suggestion, I was once again very impressed with this man's determination and his imagination. Of course it is nice to have someone so eager to present you that he will build a special place for you to sing—and do it just because you don't like their place. But it was much more than that. I like positive people—p.p.'s, I call them—the kind of people who don't give up, who see a "no" as a challenge. They are people who want immediately to learn the reason for the "no" and think hard and creatively about a way to remove the reason.

I had another suspicion. This tent that Rudas was suggesting would maybe contain more seats than the casino. He was trying to overcome my objections with his tent, and at the same time he would be making more money. I could see this was a very clever man. I told Herbert I would think about his idea, and I went on the La Scala stage to sing the role of Radamès in Verdi's incredible opera.

When I am performing in an operatic role, I can usually put everything else out of my mind. I must do this or I will not be able to perform. You need all your concentration just to sing; you also need concentration to act. Even if everything is going well, it is almost impossible to do both. If your mind is somewhere else, if you are thinking about a problem, you cannot do either properly. I can usually push problems from my mind, but not always. That is why, in the past, I have had to cancel performances when I have had a really big personal problem—when my daughter Giuliana was extremely sick, for example.

Rudas's offer was, of course, not that big a problem for me, but it was an important decision. I knew what people in the classical music world would say when they heard I was going to sing in

Atlantic City. Onstage I was Radamès, but when I was not on-stage, I was sitting in my La Scala dressing room thinking about singing in a tent in New Jersey. After the third act of *Aïda*, I told Herbert he could tell Rudas I would do it.

A big part of my decision was the amazing amount of money. I do not deny that. Singers have only so many years when they can earn large fees. I was forty-six at the time and tenors often start to lose their voices at fifty. As it turns out, I am one of the lucky ones, like my father; I am now fifty-nine and the voice is still healthy. But you cannot be sure. You never know when you will wake up one morning with a voice no one wants to hear. So I make no apology that the big fee Rudas offered was partly responsible for my decision to sing in Atlantic City.

But it definitely was not the only reason I said yes to Rudas. Ever since I had reached a good level of success in opera my am-bition has been to move beyond this small world and sing for as many people as possible. I believed I had something to give, but I didn't want to give it to the same people over and over. I saw the Atlantic City concert as a way of attracting more people to my type of music.

With the rising costs of operatic productions and the pressures on arts organizations like Public Broadcasting, the opera audience could grow smaller. Because I truly love opera, this possibility makes me very unhappy. Rudas was offering me not only a very large audience but a *different* audience, made up of many people who were not opera fans. That is what I wanted, and no one else had offered me that.

Herbert went back and sat down with the Rudases for the final act of *Aïda*. He whispered to Tibor, "We have a deal." Rudas later told me how happy he was and that he never enjoyed an opera as much as the fourth act of *Aïda* that night. I was very happy too, partly because of the excitement of a new project and partly be-cause *Aïda* had gone very well.

When they came backstage this man and I finally met. We were all very happy. After I got out of my costume and makeup, I took Mr. and Mrs. Rudas and Herbert for a late-night tour of Milan in my car, to show them the most important places and the places I liked best. After our drive, I took them to a favorite restaurant of mine, Il Principe di Savoia, and we all had a wonderful dinner.

During dinner I learned about Tibor. He had been born in Budapest and as a little boy of eight had sung in the chorus of the Hungarian State Opera when they needed boy sopranos. He was paid to do this, and he did it for seven years because his family was very poor and they badly needed the money he brought home. He grew up backstage at the opera and was fascinated with everything that was happening—the sets, the costumes, the lighting, the makeup. He told me that when most boys were learning geography and arithmetic, he was learning about theater. He loved it all, but when he was fifteen, a disaster hit him.

"My voice didn't change," he told me. "It went."

For the next months just getting enough to eat was a problem for him. He took any job he could find. He and his twin brother, Bandi, learned acrobatics and worked up an act that mixed acrobatics with dance. When the twins were about twenty, they added a girl to the act and gave themselves a wonderful name: Sugar Baba and the Rudas Twins. The act was quite successful, and they toured around Europe. He told me one thing about Hungarians that most people don't realize: they are all good acrobats, like the Rumanians.

In 1948 Rudas was touring Australia with his act when the Communists took over Hungary. None of the three wanted to return home, so they obtained asylum in Australia. This was not a simple thing to do. The new Hungarian government was very anxious to get all its citizens abroad to return home, especially well-known Hungarians—and Sugar Baba and the Rudas Twins were now famous in their country. But they had also become well known in Australia, and they had made friends there, including friends in the government. Some Australians were willing to hide them until the Hungarian secret police forgot about them.

After about a year, however, the three young people had run out of places to perform in Australia so they broke up their act. Now they had the problem of making a living in Australia. Tibor's twin brother, who died a few years ago, went into the clothing business, and Tibor opened up a dance school for young people where he taught his specialty: a mixture of acrobatics and dance. He soon had large numbers of young students.

But when the students finished Tibor's course, the mothers came to him complaining. "You have given our daughters this talent," they said, "but where are the jobs?" I could understand if Tibor had said to them that this was not his problem, but that was not Tibor. To make jobs for his students, he formed dance troupes and found paid engagements for them. His dancers were very young, between twelve and fifteen. Audiences loved them, and he soon had several groups of ten to fifteen dancers traveling all around Australia performing the acrobatic dance routines he had invented. By 1960 he had seven groups performing in Australia and throughout Southeast Asia. In 1963 he had eleven troupes performing as far away as the Lido in Paris.

I was fascinated by this man. At the time Tibor was presenting his troupes of teenage dancers in different parts of the world, I was beginning my operatic career in Europe. Neither of us could have imagined that one day we would go into business together.

One of the places where Rudas obtained an engagement for one of his troupes was the Dunes Hotel in Las Vegas. While he was there he got an offer to help produce the big shows. He accepted and worked exclusively in Las Vegas for a while, then later did projects for the Disney organization, for the Ice Capades, and for the Shuberts. His specialty was lavish spectacles. Eventually he formed his own producing company, which not only put the shows together but built the sets and made the costumes as well.

At dinner that night in Milan, Tibor told me he wanted to do more with me than just the one concert in Atlantic City. He was determined, he said, to put me in front of the biggest audiences imaginable, audiences larger than any opera singer had ever seen. I learned that he had already shown an interest in the larger possibilities for classical performers by presenting Zubin Mehta and the New York Philharmonic at Las Vegas.

Like me, the musicians of the New York Philharmonic did not want to play serious music at a gambling casino, but Tibor persuaded them to change their minds with another one of his brilliant ideas. He would, he told them, present each player with a hundred dollars' worth of quarters for gambling on the slot machines. They were so fascinated by the idea, they changed their minds immediately.

The ending was sad, however. When Tibor and his wife were having dinner with the Mehtas after the concert, they were interrupted constantly by players who wanted credit extended to them at the casino. The musicians lost a fortune that night, he said. Or, to say it the other way around, the casino's revenues went up a lot, thanks to the 130 players of the New York Philharmonic.

While I was listening with great interest to this man's remarkable stories, I was receiving a number of impressions. With his three years of persistence, he had already shown how determined and resourceful he could be. But now I could see his incredible drive, his original ideas, his big vision, and his powerful enthusiasm. Herbert and I worried that he did not seem to have a very deep knowledge of opera, but when we asked him about this, he assured us he loved opera.

We had already seen how sharp and clever he could be. Georg Solti, who was also a Hungarian, once told me that a Hungarian was a person who could enter a revolving door behind you and come out ahead of you. With anyone you go into business with, you must always be a little on guard. At the beginning of our relationship, Herbert and I decided the Atlantic City concert would be a good test of whether or not we were destined to do business with Rudas. As it turned out, he has been wonderful to work with over the past fourteen years. He always does what he says he will do and he treats everybody fairly. I've never gone into a revolving door with Tibor, but I don't think it would be a good idea from his point of view.

After that most pleasant evening we spent together in Milan, the first thing I learned was that when Tibor returned to Atlantic City, his bosses at Resorts International told him to forget his tent idea. They said it would cost too much and they didn't believe that Pavarotti or any other opera singer could fill such a huge place. They also said I would not attract the kind of big gamblers that they hope to attract with their shows.

Rudas was so certain his idea would be a big success that he told the casino owners he would pay for everything out of his own pocket—not only the tent but also the stage, the lighting, the sound system, four thousand chairs, and the hundred other things you need to handle a large crowd. If he did pay for all this, of course, he would keep the profits, if there were any. Watching him go into action, I saw that he was living up to my first impression.

About a month before the concert, Tibor took out large ads in the newspapers of New York, Philadelphia, and other nearby cities. When he opened the phone lines and box offices for ticket sales, all four thousand tickets were sold in less than an hour. When he saw how quickly the tickets sold out, Tibor figured out a way to expand the tent to hold another five thousand seats. Those tickets were all sold in one day. It was amazing. People stood in line for four hours to buy these tickets.

It was as if the people of Atlantic City had been waiting all their lives to hear a tenor. I was extremely pleased that the Resorts

International people were wrong about the ticket sales, but I couldn't blame them for being pessimistic about my chances of drawing that many people. I must be honest and say that before Tibor risked so much to prove he was right, I worried that maybe he was wrong and *they* were right.

By the day of the concert, the excitement was incredible. I heard that there wasn't an empty hotel room in Atlantic City. While so much excitement is not good for the nerves, I think in some way it is good for my energy and helps me do my best. For whatever reason, the concert went beautifully. The audience loved it, I loved it, and Tibor loved it. After my performances I always try to greet anyone who wants to come backstage to see me. That night I signed programs in my dressing room for over three hours. Some of the people getting autographs looked familiar. I think I signed a program for them two hours before.

It was very late when I went out to celebrate with Tibor, Herbert, and a group of friends. Tibor told me he wanted this to be just the beginning of our relationship. He wanted to present me in stadiums and convention halls around the world, to the largest audiences possible. His dream, he said, was to take opera out of the hands of the elite and bring it to the general public. He said the public had been brainwashed into believing that classical music belonged only to a small group of people. He saw me as his tool for proving this was not true. He wanted to present me in places big enough so that everyone could afford to buy a ticket.

I agree with him that a lot of people are excluded from classical music because of false ideas about who it is for. I think many people who think they do not like classical music would like it if they had more exposure to it.

After our years of successful collaboration, Tibor is now trying to do similar projects with other performers. He has assembled a World Youth Orchestra made up of players from the famous European Youth Orchestra and from Russia and America. He presented them at an enormous concert at Berlin's Brandenburg Gate in May of 1995. His plan is to take them on a tour of the world and bring about world peace. Tibor does not have small ideas.

That night in Atlantic City we were all happy and excited, and I liked everything Tibor said. He certainly had shown me that he was able to put on a large event. I love people with dreams and large ideas. I love even more people who can make their dreams and large ideas into reality. With this first concert, Tibor had shown me he could perform as big as he talked. That night a business partnership was born, and also a friendship. I have had many fantastic and wonderful experiences because of Tibor, and I have never been anything but very happy about my decision during that performance of *Aïda* at La Scala.

4
THREE TENORS: ROME AND L.A.

When Placido Domingo, José Carreras, and I did the first Three Tenors concert at the Baths of Caracalla in Rome in 1990, none of us had any idea how popular it would be. It was scheduled at the same time as the World Cup soccer matches, which were also held in Rome that year, and the idea was to celebrate the game. I think that for each of us the World Cup seemed much more important than our concert. We were there merely to show our enthusiasm for this terrific sport.

The idea for the three of us to sing together had originally been José's. Placido and I were intrigued by the idea, but we could never find a time or an occasion. But then José got sick with leukemia and miraculously recovered, and the idea of the three of us singing together seemed to be a wonderful way to celebrate his return to health.

Both Placido and I are very fond of this beautiful man, and it was terrible to think that he almost died. I have been told that I have an exceptionally strong fear of illness and death. Maybe I do, but the idea of José, so young and with so much talent, facing death because of a disease, was too terrible even to think about. When he triumphed over the disease and returned to normal health, it was definitely a cause for celebration.

There was another reason I had liked the Three Tenors idea from the first moment I heard about it. The press had made many references to bad feelings between me and Placido. This was un-true. We were completely friendly. Whatever tension there may have been in the past was long since forgotten and we had very good relations. I thought it was time for the press to forget about them also. I couldn't think of a better way to demonstrate our friendship than to sing together in a friendly, happy concert for, and with, José.

The idea of doing this concert in Rome at the time of the World Cup had come from two Italians, Mario Dradi, a talent agent, and a producer named Ferdinando Pinto who is connected with Rome's Teatro dell'Opera and with the Teatro Petruzzelli in Bari. Considering how far ahead all three of us fill our schedules, the concert was organized in a remarkably short time. Everyone told the producers it would be impossible to get the three of us together, to find us all free at the exact time of the World Cup, but they pushed ahead and did it.

I think both Placido and I would have flown from anywhere for José's sake. And of course all three of us are the world's biggest soccer fans, which gave us an additional reason to be happy to go to Rome at that time. Placido, who is Spanish, is so nuts about the sport that he will not schedule any performances when Spain might be playing a match.

We were very fortunate to get Zubin Mehta to agree to be our conductor. Despite the high spirits we were sure to fall into working together on such a happy occasion, a conductor of Zubin's high standards assured that we would stay within the bounds of musical respectability. To give us a head start, we were all able to meet in Rome in December of 1989 for a rehearsal.

Singing a concert with other tenors was a new experience for all three of us. Although I knew and admired both Placido and José, I had never worked with either of them before—not in an opera or even at a gala. In spite of the many opportunities for disagreements for this combined concert—from the first day there were endless decisions to make—we all got along wonderfully. For instance, we first had to agree on the arias each of us would sing. This could have been a problem since there was always the chance that two of us would want to sing the same aria or song. Fortunately we decided this part of the program with little difficulty.

Much more of a problem was the big medley we would be singing together. It made no sense for us to appear on the same stage and not sing together—but what would we sing? There is no music written for three tenors; no composer was ever so optimistic. So we had to commission a medley to be created especially for us. For this job, Placido wanted his arranger. This was all right with José and me, although I was not too enthusiastic about some of this man's arrangements. For one thing, I thought they were too complicated for a program that would have only a few brief rehearsals. We had several disagreements over this, but managed to work it all out so that everyone was happy.

Well, not happy, exactly. We were all very nervous about the concert, which was to take place in mid-July, and the medley only increased our anxiety. We knew we needed more rehearsal, but our schedules were locked up totally and no more rehearsal time was possible. When we returned to Rome in the spring for the concert itself, we had only two days to rehearse. All of us had been working hard at other things in the months between our one rehearsal and our arrival in Rome to give the concert.

In the brief last-minute rehearsal period it was obvious to all of us how badly prepared we were. But we worked like crazy men. Word of the novelty concert had spread, and plans had been made to televise it to an international audience. This was no longer a lighthearted celebration of José's recovery and the World Cup; it was turning into a major musical event.

I think the nervousness all three of us felt brought us much closer together. Each of us had worked extremely hard to achieve our level of success in the demanding world of classical music, and each of us understood what the others had gone through in a way that few outsiders could understand. We also understood what we were risking by performing in a sloppy, poorly rehearsed concert—a concert that was appearing more and more to be a widely publicized event.

We also had to fight off some lunatic ideas. Before the concert one of the producers thought it would make the evening more interesting if a panel of judges scored each one of us as we sang, just as they do for Olympic athletes. Thank heavens this idea did not go very far. I am all for competition. In fact, I think the atmosphere of healthy competition is what made this concert, and our later concerts together, so successful. The competition between the three of us makes us all put forth our greatest effort. And who benefits from that? The audience, of course. But giving us each a score would have taken all the fun from the event.

It would be impossible to describe that night. The Baths of Caracalla looked incredibly beautiful in the lights that had been set up for the television cameras. You noticed architectural details that you might have missed in the sunlight. The audience was filled with many very distinguished people who were in Rome for the World Cup, including the king and queen of Spain. The night was mild and delicious, the Roman air pleasantly cool.

I knew when each of us sang our first aria that things would go well. Then José blew a kiss to a jet passing overhead as he was in the middle of an aria, and I knew the tone of the evening would be relaxed and fun. Even though I could sense the audience's enthusiasm building, I had no idea how successful the evening would be until we got to the medley at the end of the program.

This was made up of light music from many different countries to suggest the international flavor of the World Cup. A lot of it was familiar music that none of us had ever sung before like "La Vie en Rose" and songs from *West Side Story*. The medley went on for about twenty minutes and had many places where we sang together and in harmony. It was not as difficult as we feared, and we all had a very good time singing these much loved songs as a team. Our enjoyment was communicated to the audience.

At the end of the medley, we sang "O Sole Mio" together and we sang it properly. But during the encores we sang it a second time and this time, with Zubin's permission, we clowned around. I led the way by holding the last "O Sole" for a long, long time, but then Placido and José echoed my joking rendition, so I was not left alone as the only ham.

At the end of the concert, the people went a little mad and were standing on their chairs—even the king and queen, I was told. For all three of us, the Caracalla concert was a major event in our lives. I hope I am not immodest to think it was also unforgettable for most of the people who were present. For many people who saw the concert on television, it was the first time they had heard José sing since his recovery. His performance left no doubt that he had returned to life and was now as superb an artist as ever. In fact, we were all in top form and sang with an exuberance and excitement that happens only rarely, I think, between artists who are performing together. We were celebrating music, celebrating each other, and celebrating life.

Because we were doing the concert for José's foundation, we all were happy to accept a modest fee for the evening. This was a flat fee with no provision for residuals or royalties from record or video sales. We had no idea the event would prove so popular or that there would even *be* a record or video. We regarded the whole thing like an operatic gala with many performers or like a concert given in tribute to a departed colleague. These occasions are always wonderful for the audiences who attend them, but they make little impact on the outside world.

We were not the only ones who didn't believe that the Caracalla concert had much commercial potential. But after the concert we all changed our minds. Even with the concert's success, however, my recording company, Decca/London, was unenthusiastic about issuing a recording, but I and some others persuaded them. As of now that record has sold over ten million copies, and it's still going strong. It is the largest-selling classical recording in history, and one of the largest-selling recordings of any type. I was told that only twelve albums have sold as many copies. It seems that our decision to accept a flat fee was not the smartest business deal any of us ever made.

The Caracalla Three Tenors concert was such a success that we immediately received many offers to repeat it. It was as if every city in the world wanted its own Three Tenors concert. I think we could have done similar concerts six or eight times a month around the world and kept busy for years. The Japanese, for instance, offered us an incredible sum to repeat the concert in Tokyo's Imperial Gardens. But we turned all of the offers down. We knew that this was not the kind of musical event that can be done often. Also, we all had extremely busy careers—as soloists.

In 1993, three years after Caracalla, Tibor Rudas urged us

to sing another Three Tenors concert in Los Angeles for the next World Cup. Being Tibor, he made us an extremely generous offer—ten times the Caracalla fee plus royalties on the recordings and videos. José and Placido were willing, but I was still against the idea.

My main fear was that we could never match the success of the first concert. I felt it would be almost impossible to equal the same mood of spontaneity and exuberance that had come out of our nervousness over working together for the first time and our happiness at José's recovery. If we did it again, people would think the idea had been commercial from the start. Not only was this untrue, it would have weakened and damaged our gesture toward José.

But of the three of us, I think José was the most eager to sing another Three Tenors. He had started a foundation for leukemia research, and his own medical bills had been tremendous. When I thought about this, I began to feel guilty for being so stubborn and uncooperative, so I agreed to a second concert. The date was set for July 16, 1994, the night before the World Cup match in Los Angeles, and the concert would be called *Encore!*

For a full year this concert dominated our thoughts. From the beginning the entire mood for this event was different. The first concert had been done in a spirit of celebration and fun; in planning the second concert, we all brought lawyers to the meetings. Caracalla had been casual and relaxed, once we were onstage, but this one was being talked about as the musical event of the century. When you have "the musical event of the century" ahead on your schedule, it is hard to keep your mind on other things.

To make us feel more secure for the big day, we arranged to do an advance version of our concert for a charity gala in Monte Carlo. This would be before a relatively small audience, and it would not be televised. For us it was like a dress rehearsal. This warm-up concert went very well and relieved all three of us to a degree about what was coming up shortly in Los Angeles. As far as size and ambition were concerned, however, there was little connection between the two concerts.

Tibor thinks very big about everything he does, but for this Los Angeles concert he was completely carried away. He got the use of Dodger Stadium for a full week because he was planning to erect an elaborate set on the far outfield. In that way, the cheapest stadium seats, the bleachers, would be the ones covered by the stage. All of the baseball field would be filled with chairs for the most expensive seats.

The design for the set was based on a tropical jungle theme, a four-story-high waterfall on either side of the stage. The stage would be set off from the jungle by thirty white pillars, which were constructed in Hungary. He also ordered a stage built that rose about ten feet off the field and was big enough to hold the thirty pillars, many truckloads of plants and trees, the Los Angeles Philharmonic, a full chorus, and three tenors.

Because some of the seats were very far from the stage, Tibor constructed a huge television screen, almost as large as the waterfalls, so the people in the most distant seats could see us clearly. Since all of this had to be done in a week, Tibor hired a construction crew of two hundred people and had the work going on twenty-four hours a day. When I arrived in Los Angeles four days before the concert, the entire stage and backdrop were already in place. We were a little worried about the giant waterfalls. The sound of splashing water is very pleasant to most people, but not to a tenor who is trying to sing pianissimo. Tibor agreed to turn the waterfalls off during the music.

When we started rehearsing with Zubin, we were able to use the new stage. As I worked with my two colleagues in the bright morning sun of California, I could look out at the empty stadium and see Tibor in Bermuda shorts standing alone and looking very small in the empty stadium. I couldn't believe how calm he looked as six hundred workers put the final touches on his enormous construction. As his three tenors and a symphony orchestra worked on our program, he spoke on his cellular phone and appeared totally cool and nonchalant. I had just heard that he had arranged to have the airplane traffic coming into Los Angeles airport rerouted so that the planes would not fly near Dodger Stadium during the concert. He is amazing.

The last few days before the concert are hazy in my memory. I stayed with my good friend Jerry Perenchio at his magnificent estate in Bel Air. (I have known Jerry for many years, and not too long ago I sang at his son's wedding.) My family and a group of my friends arrived from Italy, and when I was not rehearsing, I joined them around Jerry's swimming pool and tried to relax. I had flown to Los Angeles from Europe and was having trouble recovering from jet lag. I wasn't sleeping normally, and that was an added worry. Basically I felt okay, and the voice seemed in good shape. Still, throughout each day I would hear more and more about what a historic event this concert was going to be. Such talk does not make you more relaxed.

The concert would be broadcast live to more people than had ever seen a performance at one time. Tibor estimated the live audience would be between one and two billion people. Because we were covering the globe, our singing would be heard at every hour of the day—somewhere. It seemed inconceivable. Arrangements had been made to air the concert in *107 countries,* either while we were singing or shortly afterward. Tibor said that in the entire world there were only 120 countries. Knowing how he is, I felt sure he would worry about the thirteen countries that were *not* showing the Three Tenors concert.

At the last minute one of my colleagues wanted to change an aria. This created problems for several reasons—mainly because of rehearsal time and because the programs had already been printed. Even with the confusion caused by this change, Zubin was able to make the adjustment, and everything seemed in good shape for the actual performance.

We had also heard about all the prominent people who planned to attend the concert. Tibor had sold a block of seats in the front as VIP tickets for $1,500 each. This included a gala dinner afterward with us and all of the Hollywood celebrities who would be there.

Tibor had taken an idea from Jane Nemeth, who runs my vocal competition, for a fund-raising dinner she once held for the Philadelphia Opera. He put up a huge tent just outside the stadium but in the backstage area and set it up for an elegant dinner party for five hundred people. This meant that the people who had bought tickets to the concert and the dinner did not have to get into cars and drive to a hotel somewhere, they could just walk backstage and sit down at their table. This turned out to be a particularly good idea, since I was told that three hours before the concert began, the traffic was backed up for two miles trying to get into the Dodger Stadium parking lot.

When I was making an effort to relax at Jerry's house, I heard Nicoletta say to someone on the phone, "Yes, Luciano is anxious about the concert, but he's just as anxious about the World Cup."

She was not wrong. I was very excited, because Italy would be playing Brazil in the final match for the cup. Brazil has always had one of the best teams, so this was a very important game for all Italians. But I will not deny I was also extremely nervous about the concert as the hour got closer.

It is hard to describe how you feel when you know you will be performing live before half of the world's population. Modern communication technology means that we performers can reach many people very quickly. Because of these advances, careers no longer take years and years to get established, but can now be established in a very short time. The wonderful Cecilia Bartoli has become well known in much less time than it took me. The other side of this idea is that careers today can also be destroyed very quickly. Satellites and other modern devices can show a bad performance to everyone in the world at the same time.

Watching the concert at home on television, people just see three guys on a stage singing. What's the big deal about that? It is hard to imagine that millions and millions of people will be watching you live, that the tiniest mistake will be recorded for all time, that millions who liked you for years, more millions who maybe don't like you so much, millions who know your reputation but have never heard you sing, and millions who have never heard of you are all watching and expecting to pass judgment, be thrilled, be disappointed—or maybe watch the bull gore you. . . .

But I knew I would feel this anxiety when I agreed to do a second Three Tenors. On the good side was that we were sticking close to the plan of our first concert. The biggest difference was that instead of one medley there would be two, one to conclude the first half, another to conclude the concert. I was very happy that the medleys would not be as complicated as the one we sang at Caracalla. We would still sing together but there would not be so much singing in harmony.

Another advantage was that working together was not such an unusual experience for us as it had been the first time. Also, José now knew Placido and me a lot better, and I think he felt much more comfortable with us. Our doing a concert together in Monte Carlo in the spring had been an excellent idea for this reason too.

To give us each a place in Dodger Stadium to retreat to with all the preparations going on, Tibor had provided us each with a large trailer—a complete house, in fact. There was one for each of us and one for him. He had placed the trailers in a ring with a large courtyard in the center covered with AstroTurf. The trailers were quite a long way from the stage, so he had given us each a golf cart for traveling back and forth.

Finally it was time to go to the stadium for the concert itself. We had been warned about a possible traffic problem getting into Dodger Stadium, so we arrived three hours early and stayed in our trailers trying to remain as relaxed as possible. As different people came by the dressing room, they would give me reports on what was happening outside. I was told that Frank Sinatra and his wife had arrived almost an hour ahead of time and were already in their seats. Also in the VIP seats were Gene Kelly, Bob Hope, and Gregory Peck. Former President George Bush and his wife, Barbara, were in the audience, and so was Henry Kissinger. People coming into my dressing room told me they had spotted Arnold Schwarzenegger, Tom Cruise, and Whoopi Goldberg.

Itzhak Perlman was narrating the concert for the PBS broadcast, and he stopped by to wish me luck. With all the advance excitement of the concert, it seemed as if every journalist in the world wanted to interview us. It also seemed as if every friend I have made in the past thirty years wanted to come back and wish me luck. With all this going on, I was sitting there thinking about only one thing: would the concert go well and would I sing all right?

The time had come to take a shower and put on my white tie and tails. The excitement was getting intense when we received a phone call that two of my friends from Italy, Panocia and his wife, had arrived at the ticket gate and discovered they had left the tickets at their hotel. The hotel was in Beverly Hills, at the other end of Los Angeles from Dodger Stadium. There was no way for him to go back and get them, or even for someone to bring them from the hotel and arrive on time. I couldn't believe it.

With the temporary phone system, it was very difficult to figure out who to call to let my friends into the stadium. Also, we had to learn where they had been sitting. It was a complete disaster and one I did not need at the moment. My good friends had flown all the way from Modena for this concert, I had arranged everything for them, including very good seats, and what does Panocia do? He leaves the tickets at the hotel! Nicoletta went to work on the telephones, and she finally got the problem solved. He is perhaps my closest friend but I still could have killed him.

A few minutes later Nicoletta came back from running an errand and told me that the orchestra players were all standing in line at the concession stands to buy the souvenirs that Tibor had offered for sale. He had arranged for T-shirts, coffee mugs, even seat cushions, all with the title, *Encore,* our names, and the place and date. Nicoletta was surprised to see the Los Angeles Philharmonic musicians, holding their instruments, standing in line to buy souvenirs of the evening. What a tribute!

Because the concert was being televised live, it had to start at the precise moment. When the stadium was filled and the moment arrived, Zubin was straightening his white tie to walk onstage. He looked out at the vast crowd and turned to us and said, "There is a nice chamber-music atmosphere here tonight."

When I walked out onto that stage to sing my first aria, I cannot tell you the feeling I had. I knew that because of television, we were singing for the entire world. But with the crowd stretched out before me, it looked as if the entire world was sitting in Dodger Stadium. The newspapers the next day said there were 56,000 people present, but it looked like many more to me.

With all the publicity and pressure in advance of this concert, I was almost as nervous for my two colleagues as I was for myself. After we had each sung our first aria, however, I knew that we were all in excellent form and the concert would be a success. Just singing well does not guarantee a successful concert, however, especially at an unusual event like this. In spite of the incredible strain, you must always appear to be having fun.

You have no idea how a performance will go until it begins, whether the right mood will be there. But after we were a little way into the program, I could see the mood was there for real. By the time we reached the medley to end the first half, I was completely relaxed and could start to enjoy myself.

The first medley was a tribute to Hollywood. Among the songs was "Moon River," which we sang as a tribute to my friend Henry Mancini, who had just died. I had flown out to Los Angeles only a few months before to take part in a concert honoring this wonderful man and his incredible career composing music for films. I could see at that time that he was not well, and I am so glad that the people of Hollywood showed him their deep respect while he was still well enough to appreciate it.

As a bow to the fantastic Gene Kelly we sang "Singin' in the Rain" from one of his greatest movies, and for Frank Sinatra we sang "My Way." At the end of each song, we gestured to the star we were honoring, and both men stood up and took a bow. It was overwhelming for me to be standing on a stage in that stupendous setting paying my respects to these heroes of my youth. I couldn't think too much about it, however. We still had a lot of singing to do.

After the concert, many people told me they could see me chewing something onstage and asked what it was. They said it looked like chewing gum, but they couldn't believe I would chew gum on worldwide television. They were right. I do not even chew gum at home alone. I am sorry my chewing was so obvious, and I hope it did not distract anyone from the music. It was actually a small piece of apple which I thought would be helpful for my throat. I have tried different things to keep my throat healthy during a concert—lemons, oranges, throat lozenges, and always mineral water—but at that time I had decided the best thing was a piece of apple. I have now changed my mind. I don't think it had any effect. In fact, it was awful, and I will not do it again.

The second half of the concert went as well as the first. Throughout the evening I think the mood of all three of us was more relaxed and spirited than in the first concert. The enormous buildup certainly had us nervous at first, but as we went out onto the stage and began singing, the mood of the concert was terrific. José later explained part of the evening's success to a reporter from *Time* magazine by saying, "Audiences love things that happen spontaneously. We are all three of us Latins who like improvisation." I think he is right. And the singing was good, too.

After all the encores were over, I got in my golf cart and was driving it from the stage to my trailer. Stagehands and orchestra members were clapping and patting my back as I drove by. When I got inside the compound of trailers, the courtyard was not very well lit, but I could see Herbert signaling me to stop. He was with an elderly man who was slightly bent over and wearing a plaid fedora. I stopped the cart beside Herbert. He tried to introduce me to the man he was with, but there were so many people clustering around, clapping, congratulating me, that I just managed to hear the word "Hope," but not the "Bob." Still, even in the dim light and with that hat, the wonderful face told me who it was.

I jumped out of the cart and grabbed Bob Hope's hands and said, "Thank you, Mr. Hope, for all the pleasure you have given us." Sometimes I do the right thing.

As usual after a concert, much of what happened that night is now a blur. I only remember being very happy that it was finally over and that it had gone well. Amazingly there were no bad mistakes. A few times I made mistakes in the lyrics, but with my accent, I don't think it was too obvious.

At the dinner afterward I had my friends from Italy at my table. I had forgiven Panocia for forgetting the tickets, and we had a wonderful time. Many people came to the table to congratulate me—strangers, old friends, and people whose faces I knew from the films or television. I wanted to kiss them all. You cannot imagine my relief that the concert was finally over and that it had gone well.

The next day José, Placido, and I sat together for the World Cup match. It was fantastically exciting, but of course I was miserable when Italy lost to that one penalty kick. It was terrible to watch.

I tried to be philosophical about the defeat. I said to Nicoletta, "It's just as well Brazil won. We Italians have so much, and in Brazil they commit suicide over anything." I thought I was very sensible about it and didn't let myself get too upset. But in New York some months later I was telling friends how well I had taken Italy's loss. Nicoletta couldn't stand it any longer.

She said, "Maybe you weren't upset, Luciano, but for the next eight hours until we got on the plane to leave Los Angeles, you didn't speak a word to anyone."

Maybe I was upset, but I got over this disappointment a lot faster than I recovered from the Los Angeles Three Tenors concert. For some reason I had trouble getting back to normal. I would wake up in the morning with the same feeling of anxiety, the same feeling of worry about the next thing to do, the next place to be, the next music to sing.

I went from Los Angeles to my annual vacation at my beach house in Pesaro. Even after many days of doing nothing but relaxing, sitting on my terrace looking out at the sea, lying in my hammock, eating with my family, I continued to feel the worry that I had felt for almost a year before the Los Angeles Three Tenors. This feeling finally went away, but it took about two weeks.

The concert was a big success from every point of view. Even the critics, who are very skeptical about such big splashy events, gave us some compliments. The newspapers wrote a lot about the enormous amount of money each of us would receive for this one evening. That is true, but when people say it is too much money for one evening's work, I like to quote what Picasso said when he was criticized for charging so much for a drawing that took him three minutes: "Excuse me, but not three minutes. Thirty years and three minutes."

We are often asked if we will ever do another Three Tenors. I am all for it. Los Angeles proved I was wrong to worry about whether we could equal the mood and spirit of Caracalla. If two billion people enjoyed our singing together, and if we three enjoyed performing together, why not do it again?

5

THE PHILADELPHIA
VOCAL
COMPETITION

By the end of the 1970s I had achieved more than I
ever thought I would as an opera singer. I had sung
in all of the world's major opera houses; I had done
many of the roles I had hoped to do—not all of
them, but there was time left for the others. I had
done a number of television concerts, so I was known to an audience outside the opera world. And my records seemed to be selling
very well. I could tell myself that I had really achieved something,
but what to do with that something?

That question began to stick in my mind. As long as my voice
stayed with me, I could continue singing operas around the world,
making records, and doing concerts. I would do all of that most
willingly, because I loved it. But I also wanted to try to do something a little bit more, especially something that might help young
singers.

I had often thought about holding a voice competition. I have
never forgotten how important it was for me to win the competition in Reggio Emilia in 1961. It changed my life completely.
Until that contest I was just a young singer who dreamed of having

a career but who was no closer to that goal than thousands of others who could not get their foot inside the door.

Another reason I liked the idea of a voice competition was that I had always enjoyed working with young singers. Even today, no matter how busy I am, I always try to find time for the many young singers who are sent to me for advice. I will always listen to them, and if I have the time, I will coach them. In the summer in Pesaro, people with whom I have direct business dealings come to my house for meetings, and they get angry with me when I interrupt our meeting to listen to young singers who have arrived with their music under their arms. I feel very strongly about doing this whenever I can. With a well-planned vocal competition, however, I saw a way to help young singers in a more organized, systematic way.

One day in January of 1980 people from the Opera Company of Philadelphia came to see me in New York to ask me to sing an opera for their company. I said I'd like to perform in Philadelphia again, but I had a better idea. Why didn't we do a vocal competition instead and I would sing an opera with the winners? We could invite young singers from all over the world, and they could compete in front of me and other judges. Then when we had selected the winners, I would perform an opera with them. It would all be done under the organization of the Opera Company of Philadelphia.

The Philadelphia people were very surprised at my idea; it was not what they had come to hear. But after discussing it for a while, they agreed. I have always liked Philadelphia. It is near New York, but it is very different from New York—as Modena is different from Milan. I knew the people from the Philadelphia Opera and had good relations with them.

The city's opera house, the Academy of Music, has wonderful acoustics for singers, and that is very important for young people who are frantic to sound their best in auditions and who have enough to worry about without cruel acoustics. Philadelphia also has a large opera audience and it has an international airport. When the Philadelphia people said yes, I was very happy. Then I started thinking about what I had gotten myself into.

A wonderful woman named Jane Grey Nemeth, who worked with Margaret Everitt, the general manager of the Opera Company of Philadelphia, was made director of the competition. Jane loves singers, has great energy, and is very competent. Still, I knew myself well enough to know I would not leave everything in her hands. From the very first day I was interested in every part of the competition. This never changed. Although Jane and I agreed on most everything, I think I drove her crazy.

I don't like doing anything halfway. To me, setting up the competition, then letting others carry it out would have been doing it halfway. I guess that makes me a control freak, which I have been accused of. But I care very much about everything I do, and I particularly care about singing and about talented young people trying to fight their way into a difficult world. I could not stop caring just because we had a competent staff.

I had strong opinions about the way we should set up the competition rules: who would be eligible, how they should apply, and what we should ask them to do. But I also wanted to be involved in the smallest details, like the design for the competition's logo and the color of the application forms. I wanted to approve the posters and to read the press announcements. This would have been easy if I'd lived in Philadelphia, but when these details came up, I might be in Japan or Madrid. So it was very difficult for Jane in Philadelphia to keep me involved, but she made the big effort to let me stick my nose in everything—by long distance.

I persuaded my old friend Maestro Antonio Tonini to

become involved with our competition and give us the benefit of his vast knowledge of voice and opera. For a number of years he had been my coach, and I greatly respect his opinions about singing. I was very pleased when he agreed to work with us. He would help judge applicants and would fly to different parts of the world to hear voices when I was not free to travel.

Finally, on April 19, 1980, all of us who were now involved met at the Barclay Hotel in Philadelphia where we held a press conference to announce the competition. We explained our purpose, and emphasized to the reporters our need for publicity so that as many singers as possible would hear about the competition. We told them that auditions would be held not just in Philadelphia but around the world for anyone who wanted to enter.

We also told them of efforts we would make on our own to find promising singers. We had formed an advisory committee of very distinguished musicians who lived in different countries. We had asked them to recommend young singers who they believed should compete. We had also sent out notices to music schools and small opera companies. We had done everything we could to make sure that anyone in the world who dreamed of having a singing career would hear about our competition.

The announcement got us a good bit of press attention. Some journalists focused on me and asked if my participation meant I was retiring from singing opera. When I assured them it did not, they seemed surprised that a performer still in his career would undertake a project that took so much time. Was I making a lot of money from the competition? They seemed even more surprised when I told them I was not making a penny. Maybe that is why we got so many write-ups in the press. A tenor who works gratis must be a news story.

For whatever reason, the stories helped us spread the word that our competition was now in progress. Jane also started a campaign of writing letters to conductors and singers around the world, making sure they had heard about the competition and asking them to recommend singers who could be auditioned. Shortly after our press conference, I was about to leave on a tour of the United States with the Metropolitan Opera Company, so Jane arranged for me to audition singers in Texas, San Francisco, and Boston. She began setting up auditions in Europe.

Before long, friends in the music world were contacting us with recommendations. For example, we heard about a singer from Kurt Adler, the director of the San Francisco Opera. He was eager for us to audition a young tenor in Iceland. So I arranged to stop in Iceland when I returned to Europe for the summer. But it turned out that the young tenor had gone to Europe, where it would be easier for me to hear him.

That summer I listened to singers in London, Paris, and at various places in Italy. Jane came to Europe and talked to vocal agents, but winning the cooperation of these people proved more difficult than it had been with other music professionals. The agents all had young singers whom they were sponsoring, but they were afraid to have them "discovered" by the Philadelphia competition, perhaps for fear of losing the credit for having given them their start. Of course, they may also have been afraid their protégés would not win.

Still, we were very determined to find the best young singers from around the world, and we knew vocal agents could help us find fresh talent. Jane turned out to be very good at persuading these agents to let their singers audition. She was also good at finding singers in less obvious places. Working through consulates and music conservatories, she was even able to turn up singers in Turkey and Egypt.

In the preliminary auditions, when I listened to a singer, I concentrated very hard on the voice. That came first. But I also worked at putting the singer as much at ease as possible. I know the terrible strain of auditioning in front of people whose opinion can mean a lot to you. It is terrifying. While I believe that people who want to sing professionally must learn to conquer their nerves, I also feel that they should not be expected to have conquered them so early in their careers.

I also knew, because some of the singers told me later, that they were intimidated by me, by my reputation in opera. So I tried very hard to convince them that I was a human being who was sympathetic to all singers. Even if I did not like a singer's voice and saw little chance for a future, I would always find some bit of advice to give each person, a suggestion on how to do something differently, so they would never get the idea I was not interested in them.

That fall, Margaret Everitt of the Opera Company of Philadelphia asked me to sing a benefit concert for the competition, and I did so with pleasure. Our vocal competition was taking a lot of the time and energy of the Philadelphia Opera people. It had also cost them money, so I thought that singing to help them raise money was the least I could do.

In the winter Jane made another trip to Europe, visiting Munich, Zurich, Budapest, and Milan, always finding more singers. She went with a roll of our posters under her arm and tried to see that they were put up in any location where young singers might pass by—near theaters, in music schools, and in any other place she could think of.

By February of 1981, just under a year after we had made our first announcement, we held our European semifinals in Modena. Seventy singers from eight different countries arrived to sing in these auditions. Judging, along with me, were Margaret Everitt, Antonio Tonini, Tibor Katona, Bruno Bartoletti, and

Arrigo Pola, my first vocal coach who is still very active in Modena's musical life.

With the regional auditions that we had already held, there was a certain uniform pattern. Most of the singers were from the same country, spoke the same language, and dressed alike. But now with the semifinals, singers were coming to Modena from all over Europe, and our competition became a truly international event. Many languages were heard, many physical appearances from dark-haired Greeks to blond Scandinavians, many styles of dress.

Jane said that in the restaurants around the city, you would find the young singers all very happy and excited about having a chance to compete. The restaurant owners, and the people of Modena, were also excited to have these visitors, and made wonderful efforts to welcome the young singers. Singing is very much in the tradition of my city, and the Modenese were, I think, very honored to have an important vocal competition held there.

The pianist was my old friend, Leone Magiera. He is an excellent conductor and a brilliant accompanist who has played for some of the world's greatest singers. For these young people to have an accompanist of Leone's stature at the piano should have made their trip to Modena worthwhile, even if nothing else happened for them.

On the final day of these auditions we gave a concert with the thirty-two best singers in Modena's wonderful opera house, the Teatro Comunale. The concert was open to the public, and it was televised. We tried to include too many singers, of course, and the concert went on for *four and a half hours!* No one seemed to think that was too long. The audience was very enthusiastic and gave the young people a standing ovation at the end of the evening, which made us all very happy, especially me. Afterward I gave a dinner for all of the participants in a country restaurant not far from Modena.

By now our list of finalists was growing. This made us all

happy, even though the larger numbers meant more plane tickets and other expenses. Still, finding singers was our purpose, and we were doing this. With all of the auditions in different parts of the world, we had little idea how many singers would be coming to Philadelphia for the finals.

The semifinals for the American singers were held in New York in March of 1981. There was a layer of snow over the city, which added to the confusion and anxiety. For many reasons, I feel great sympathy for anyone who wants to sing, but high among those reasons is that the voice is such a delicate and unpredictable instrument. Snow does not make things any easier, but these singers were all very brave, and it would have taken a major earthquake to keep them from coming to sing for us.

The auditions were held in the Goodman Hall near Lincoln Center. Over the next few days, ninety singers from twenty-two states and seven countries were heard by me, Margaret Everitt, and Maestro Tonini. My good friend John Wustman, who has accompanied me for many recitals, played for singers at these auditions. As in Modena, all of the contestants, even if they didn't go on to the finals, at least had the opportunity to sing with a top-caliber musician.

We wanted very much to hold auditions in South America, because we knew that the many fine young singers there had very few opportunities to show their talent—certainly fewer opportunities than were available in Europe and the United States. Even a young Caruso in South America would have had trouble finding his way into the world of international opera. So we organized auditions in São Paulo, and Maestro Tonini flew down to hear the singers.

I was pleased and a little amused that the auditions in São

Paulo became for the city an important social event. A very distinguished audience—business leaders, politicians, ladies in jewels—came to hear the final concert given by these young singers. Maybe we were creating new interest in singing there, even if all of the young Brazilian singers couldn't win in Philadelphia.

I thought it was funny, because fancy social events are not an important part of my life and I certainly don't think of them in connection with the hard work of auditioning and competing in semifinals. But if the elite of São Paulo wanted to dress up and come to the concert to encourage these young singers, I thought it was a good thing. From the group in São Paulo, six more singers joined our finalists who were invited to Philadelphia for the finals which would be held the following month.

I would like to make a point about these preliminary auditions: even for the singers who are not invited to the finals, the preliminaries are a very positive experience. The competitors are given an opportunity to sing before local opera professionals, and that is not easy to achieve.

When I flew to Portland, Oregon, to sing a concert on New Year's Eve 1994, for instance, I held an audition for local singers. Because I didn't have much time in Portland, we asked Robert Bailey, the director of the Portland Opera, to hold auditions in advance for anyone who wanted to compete. From these young singers, Robert picked those to sing for me when I arrived. But even those who weren't picked were given an important opportunity to sing for the director of their region's opera company. I know from my early days that it is not easy to get this kind of hearing.

May 1981 arrived, and it was time for the finals in Philadelphia. It had been one year since we made our press announcement about starting the competition. Seventy-seven finalists had been chosen and were flown to Philadelphia from all over the world. Jane and the others of the Philadelphia Opera Company had arranged for the singers to stay with host families during their time in Philadelphia, each singer with a different family.

This is amazing, now that I think about it. Seventy-seven families is a lot of families. That would be a village in Italy. I think it is incredible that they could find so many families who were happy to take complete strangers into their home, often driving them around the city, translating for them, and generally looking after them. I believe this says a lot about Philadelphians, or maybe about all Americans. I don't think Europeans would be so quick to take strangers into their home, no matter how beautifully they sang.

To welcome everybody to Philadelphia, we gave a big reception on the opening day, May 17, as an official welcome, and the next morning we held a press conference for the many journalists who had come to Philadelphia for the occasion. Some of the press people and agents had traveled from foreign countries, which surprised us. When the conference ended, we got to work.

The first singer was a beautiful girl from Texas named Mary Jane Johnson. For me, she was typical of the kind of people we hoped to find. Mary Jane had a wonderful voice but had just started her efforts to have a career. Because she was married and had a child, she was torn about whether to continue. But she told me later that her husband had said he didn't want to live with her when they were old and listen to her talk about what might have been. He had urged her to compete in Philadelphia, even though it meant being separated from him and from their baby—and many more separations if she won.

I sat at a table in the center of the Academy of Music, with the theater darkened so the singers on the stage would not be distracted and made nervous by seeing me. I had a little light on the table so that I could make notes, and I had a microphone so that I could speak to the singers without straining my voice. One girl later said she found it very spooky to hear my voice come out of the darkness, telling her to sing softer or more slowly, to try it again with more feeling. She told me she felt like Judy Garland standing in front of the great Wizard. I heard so many comments about this spookiness that I now keep the house lights on during auditions.

During a long day of very hard work we listened to many contestants—about twenty-five, I think. We all agreed that we were finding the kind of singers we had hoped to find. John Rockwell, a music critic from the *New York Times* who had attended the first day's session, wrote that "the quality of the contestants seemed very high." That was terrific encouragement not just for the singers but for all of us.

The competition staff worked very hard to schedule the singers so that they didn't have to wait too long, but most of them ended up having to sit backstage for hours before it was their turn to sing. As a result they were more nervous. We tried to correct this problem, but I told them that waiting and becoming nervous were a big part of the singer's life.

When each singer was in front of me on the stage, I would work with the contestant for as long as time allowed. I have no doubt that was what made us late. I would ask the singers to try another aria, sing something a different way, or come back the next day if they didn't seem to be feeling well. I could see Jane looking at the clock.

One young baritone came onto the stage who had sung wonderfully when I heard him in Italy. But I knew something was wrong when he sang for me in Philadelphia. I asked him, "Are you feeling all right today? Perhaps you'd rather wait and take a couple of days rest and come back. We will still be here."

He got upset and said, "No, no, I assure you, Maestro, I feel fine."

But he did not sing nearly as well as he had in Europe and we did not select him as a winner. Later I was told that he was very sick with flu that day and was too proud or too afraid to admit it. Young singers often feel that this is their only chance and they must sing no matter what. I think that was very foolish. I offered him another chance, but he didn't take it. If he had accepted my suggestion, he could have recovered and, with his normal voice, been one of the winners. But I was not the only judge. I could not ask the others to vote on the voice I remembered hearing many months earlier.

We tried always to be very accommodating to anyone who wasn't feeling well or was sick, even when we suspected there was nothing the matter except stage fright. One young tenor had such a bad case of stage fright that when it came his turn, he went into a scenery storage area and hid from everybody. Jane and some others were frantic. They knew this boy had a very fine voice, so they went looking for him.

When they found him, they dragged him to a rehearsal room and made him vocalize to prove he was fine. He was still terrified and was convinced his voice was gone, so they almost had to push him onto the stage. He sang truly wonderfully and was one of our winners, but if those women hadn't gone looking for him, that voice might never have been heard again.

In one aspect, Jane and I have different feelings about dealing with singers. She is very protective of them and wants to be a mother to them. I think I am also very sympathetic. I certainly know what they are suffering. But to sing in front of audiences, you must be strong and tough. It is all right to be a mother to a singer backstage and even in the singer's daily life. But when you are out on the stage performing, you are completely alone. Even a mother can't help you. I think that a large international vocal competition is a good time to discover if you are ready to leave your mother and be a singer.

As each finalist came out, I would try to make it a personal moment between me and the singer. I would ask them a little about themselves and we would chat back and forth. I almost gave one girl a heart attack, I'm afraid, when after she had sung, I looked at my list and said, "It says here that you are a mezzo."

She said, "That's right, Maestro."

And I said, "Wrong. You are a soprano. Come back tomorrow and sing a soprano aria for us." I may sound egotistical and bossy, but I know about singing and I have very definite opinions. If someone is making a big mistake, I cannot stop myself from saying so. The girl was Kallen Esperian, who is now having an important career as a soprano.

I almost gave a heart attack to another young singer, a tenor from the Philippines, when after he had sung the aria he had chosen, I asked him to sing the very difficult aria, "Ah Mes Amis," from Donizetti's *La Fille du Régiment*. The aria has nine high C's, and is the one that brought me so much attention when I sang it at the Met in 1972, because few tenors are crazy enough to attempt it. The Filipino was not afraid, though. He jumped right in and sang it well. I get a big satisfaction from making people do more than they thought they could.

My advice to the competitors was not only about singing. One soprano was a beautiful young woman with an even more beautiful voice, but she came out onto the stage slowly, looking at the floor, and did not stand up straight when she sang. Our accompanist, John Wustman, knew this girl and I asked him later, "What's wrong with her? She looked like a sack of potatoes."

John said there was nothing wrong with her; she just had bad posture. I pulled her aside and quietly told her that, with her wonderful voice, she had to learn how to carry herself in an important way, to stand tall and show a presence. She changed completely. Her problem was such an easy one to correct, and now she has the presence of a Callas—and she too is singing in major opera houses around the world.

Sometimes all of the different languages being spoken caused confusion. I knew a particular singer could give me more than he was giving, so I got excited and yelled from the orchestra, *"Dai! Dai!"*—the Italian way of saying "Go, go," which we yell at sports events. But the word sounds exactly like the English word "die." And this young man thought I was giving him an operatic version of "drop dead." He got very upset and wanted to quit, but Jane saw the problem and explained to him what I meant.

Naturally, the singers were all nervous, but we did everything we could to make them feel relaxed and at home. I joked with them as much as I could, gave some of them pet names, and always tried to find something helpful to say about their singing. Two of the sopranos were very pregnant and I couldn't resist kidding them and asking them which was going to come first, the high note or the baby.

Listening to singers is hard work; you must really concentrate and use all of your faculties. You cannot let your mind wander for a second or you will miss something important, a clue maybe to a mistake the singer makes that affects all of the sound that comes from his mouth. Each voice is different and reveals itself in unpredictable ways. I worked hard like this every day for a full week. And they were long days, with lots of tedium, lots of boring periods for everybody.

I know that to people outside the world of opera, this sort of classical singing seems a small, very special world that interests only a few people. But when you sit there day after day, as I did, and listen to hundreds of young singers from all over the world who have sacrificed so much to come here to face maybe discouragement or embarrassment, you get a different idea. When you look at all these young people who are going to so much trouble to take big risks—and these singers are only the winners from much larger numbers of people who auditioned in their home countries—you begin to think that opera and singing are not such small matters. You get a strong feeling that this sort of music goes very deep in the human and will be with us for a long time.

Finally we arrived at the last day of auditions. The time had come to begin making our selections. From our seventy-seven contestants we planned to select about thirty to sing in a final concert on Saturday night, May 23. From these we would select our winners. The day before that concert I called together all the singers to announce which of them would sing in the concert.

Before announcing the winners, I spoke to the entire group and told them something I believed very sincerely: that everyone who had come to Philadelphia was already a winner. I also told them that those who won might not have careers and some who didn't win might have extraordinary careers. The competition is not a guarantee; it is only an opportunity.

For all my nice words to the losers, I still hate this part of competitions. But I was aware from the start that it was unavoidable. I know how painful it is for the losers, but it is also painful for us who have appointed ourselves judges. I think this may be why other established artists do not do what I was doing: they dislike making people unhappy. I certainly do not enjoy making people unhappy, but to me, the alternative is much worse: good voices will go undiscovered. I announced the twenty-nine people who were to sing at the concert the following night.

When the announcements were over and our selections had been made known to everybody, the singers who were not selected appeared to accept our decisions very well. There were many congratulations and hugs from the losers to the winners. Everybody on the stage was smiling. But I am sure we broke many hearts.

Most of the competition events up until now had been free to members of the public who were interested, but for the final concert, we planned to sell tickets. Maestro Tonini and I had worked out a program of arias to show off the winning voices and to please the audience as well. The concert went beautifully, and the singers made us proud of what we had accomplished.

But we still weren't finished with the evening's work. The hardest part was still to come. From these twenty-nine fine young singers, we had to choose immediately the final winners. As each singer came out to sing in front of the audience, Maestro Tonini and I sat at our desks in the parquet circle with our little lights on. We took notes as we made our decisions, at the same time trying to keep an eye on the reaction of the public around us.

After the last singer had performed, we went backstage for one final conference. A great deal of tension had built up in the audience. I went onstage and told the audience that Margaret Everitt would announce the winning singers. As their names were called, each should come onstage. Out of the final twenty-nine contestants, we had chosen nineteen.

The press had trouble accepting the fact that we had nineteen winners. They expected us to have one winner, or perhaps one winning tenor, one soprano, one mezzo, and one bass. Or maybe one best Italian singer or one best Wagnerian singer. But that was not what we were there to do. We were there to find the best *singers*. It would be impossible and very unfair to force ourselves to pick one and to dismiss as unimportant others who were just as promising.

Nineteen might sound like a lot of winners from the seventy-seven who had come to the finals in Philadelphia, but the journalists who complained forgot that, throughout the year of preliminary auditions, we had listened to five hundred singers, not seventy-seven. Also, if we'd locked ourselves into a rigid format, we might have been forced to select one winning tenor and one winning soprano even in a year when we heard no standout tenors and five brilliant sopranos. I know it's odd for a competition like this to have many winners, but I'm still convinced that we did the right thing. Or to put it another way, if we had done anything else, it would have been a very wrong thing.

After a year of hard work by hundreds of people—the competition's staff, those who helped us in other countries, the many volunteers and hosts in Philadelphia, and, of course, all of the contestants—we had selected nineteen singers we thought had a good chance of a professional career. We had given the other fifty-eight singers a chance to travel to another city—for many of them, a foreign city—to perform with professional musicians, to be heard by competent judges of operatic voices, and to meet and hear other young singers on their own level.

I felt strongly that winning a competition doesn't mean much unless you get a chance to perform. So, as part of the whole design of the competition, we had announced from the beginning that our winners would be given the opportunity to sing in a full opera production, with me singing the tenor role—without fee, of course. In addition, some of the performances would be aired on television.

I know the opera world well enough to know that we would attract little attention with a production that advertised a cast made up only of the winners of something called the Pavarotti Philadelphia Vocal Competition. The opera public wants to hear established names. Finding talented singers and helping them become established was our aim when we created the vocal competition. But until these young people made names for themselves, I knew they would get more attention by singing with me or with another recognized singer.

Exactly twenty-five years had passed since I won the Achille Peri Competition in Reggio Emilia, and that victory gave me the opportunity to sing before an audience and before the critics. It was important to me, therefore, to give our winners the same chance. Performing in an opera is much more important than winning a competition if you ever hope to find success in the difficult world of opera. I was repaying my debt by helping other young people as I had been helped; I like to think that sooner or later, I always pay my debts.

It took us another year before we were able to do our operas with the winners. We all returned to Philadelphia at the end of March 1982 to begin rehearsals for *La Bohème* and *L'Elisir d'Amore,* both of which would be directed by Gian Carlo Menotti and conducted by the distinguished Italian conductor, Oliviero de Fabritiis. Maestro Fabritiis was over eighty and in poor health. Our Philadelphia operas would be his last.

I can't tell you what a wonderful time I had working as a fellow performer with our young singers. The experience made me think much about that first *La Bohème* I had sung in Reggio Emilia. At that time, so many years ago, all of us were unknown. Without big reputations to protect, we could just concentrate on doing our best. We were so happy and excited at last to be given a chance to perform on a stage, just as these Philadelphia contest winners were. As we worked together, their spirits were so high that the intense pleasure they were feeling spread to me, and we had a fantastic camaraderie.

I thought how much I missed that feeling in the high-pressure world of international opera. As I worked with the beginners on that *Bohème,* I wanted very much for these young people to treat me not as an opera star but as a colleague. In some ways they did, but in other ways there was always an invisible separation, and that made me sad. Even if they could not quite treat me as one of them, just being around those young singers, most with careers ahead of them, gave me some of that same feeling of hope and expectation I had twenty-five years ago in Reggio Emilia.

The performances were good and the audiences were enthusiastic. Something else very good happened. Since in opera, it was unusual for an established singer to perform with a cast of beginners, the people at PBS decided to televise our *Bohème*. The filming was beautifully done by my friend Kirk Browning, who is perhaps the most talented and experienced television director of opera and other classical events. Kirk's television version of the opera won the Emmy Award for the outstanding classical television program of the 1982–1983 season. Even more wonderful for us was that it was the most watched opera in the history of the PBS network.

On December 7, 1983, the mayor of Philadelphia gave us an award for having won the Emmy and for our contributions to the city of Philadelphia. He expressed his gratitude for bringing international attention to the city and for reminding people of its rich cultural traditions. At that time I announced something that I think everyone had been curious about, including us: we would definitely hold a second competition.

6

OPERA IN THE
CATHEDRAL

~

For the second competition we auditioned over a thousand singers—double the number of the first. We also brought double the number to Philadelphia for the finals in September of 1985. This meant buying plane tickets and finding housing for 150 singers from eighteen countries, some from as far away as China. I sang with the winners of this competition in performances of *Un Ballo in Maschera, La Bohème* again, and the Verdi Requiem.

The finals for our third competition were held in the fall of 1988, for our fourth in the fall of 1992. Our fifth competition, with finals in 1995, is under way at the present time.

The program for our fourth competition contains several pages of photos of previous competition winners who have established themselves in the operatic world. Several, like Susan Dunn and Kallen Esperian, are well launched in important careers and have sung leading roles at La Scala and the Met. Fifty-five of our singers are mentioned in that program, and still more have made a name for themselves since that program was published. Even fifty-five is a good number of professional singers to give the world. All of us are very proud.

Everything about the Philadelphia Competition has not always gone smoothly. In fact, as we were about to present our third competition winners in a production of *L'Elisir,* something terrible happened, a disaster that threatened to prevent our winners from getting their chance to perform. The way we dealt with this problem demonstrates, I think, our determination to give these winning contestants their showcase.

The rehearsals for *Elisir* went very well, with the same excitement and energy I now expected from young singers about to have their first opportunity to perform on a professional stage. The dress rehearsal in the Academy of Music also went as we had hoped it would. Word had now spread about our Philadelphia competitions and our operas with the winners, and this year we were expecting many people from out of town. Managers, agents, and other opera professionals were coming from all over the country to hear these young people, which was exactly what we had hoped would happen.

The news media were giving us generous advance coverage, and we had been told that some New York critics were planning to attend the performances. Even a number of my friends from other cities had told me they would be in Philadelphia. I am sure they were saying, "Let's go to hear these singers Luciano thinks he has found."

With all this excitement, when the day of the first performance arrived, I was nervous for the singers, but not too much for myself. Nemorino in *L'Elisir* is one of my favorite roles. I know it as well as I know any role, so I didn't have to worry about my own performance. Also, I felt I was in good voice, and that is a welcome feeling to have when you are nervous about other things.

At about three-thirty in the afternoon of the day of the opening, Jane Nemeth and Margaret Everitt telephoned me. They were so upset I could hardly understand what they were trying to say. When I could get the story from them, the message was that the Academy of Music had been shut down and our performance had to be canceled! I couldn't believe it.

That afternoon the Philadelphia Orchestra had played a matinee performance at the Academy. While the audience was outside during intermission, it was discovered that the auditorium had a structural problem. The theater could not be used until the defect was repaired. I later learned that during the past weeks, construction people had been in the building preparing to install an elevator. The repairmen had found a crack in a beam in the ceiling. Now on this day they were up in the ceiling again while the orchestra was playing and they found that the crack had grown wider—just a tiny bit, but enough to make them feel it might cause big problems.

Immediately they decided it was too dangerous for anyone to sit in the audience until the beam was fixed. When the orchestra audience returned from the intermission and were in their seats, an announcement was made over a loudspeaker saying that everyone had to leave the Academy of Music. People left calmly, I hear, but you can't imagine what a sensation it caused. Of course, word of this spread very quickly through Philadelphia.

Jane and Margaret, as soon as they learned of what happened, went immediately to talk with the theater's management. They were told that in no way could we perform our opera in the Academy that night. My two friends went into shock. Before telling me about this disaster, the women had discussed doing the opera someplace else, but Margaret had decided that was out of the question. When they said this to me on the phone, I was silent for a moment. Then I asked, "Why is it impossible?"

They spoke about the sets and costumes and about the difficulty in telling the people who had bought tickets—over two thousand of them—of the change of theater. In addition there was no way to get word to the singers, to the sixty chorus members, and to the orchestra.

I started thinking. I love full productions with beautiful sets and costumes, and I believe they are important to the overall effect of an opera, but I don't forget that the most important thing is the music and the singing. This was particularly true for us, when our main goal was to show off new vocal talent. The critics and opera professionals were not traveling to Philadelphia to see another *L'Elisir*. They were coming to hear new voices. That was obvious.

I knew it was too late to stop them from coming to Philadelphia and to reschedule the opera for a later date. In fact, some of them had already arrived and had called to wish me well. If we turned them away, I doubted that we would get them to Philadelphia a second time. For me to sing at a later date would also be very difficult because of my own crowded schedule.

There was more to the disaster. We planned to change casts with the different performances, in order to give as many winners as possible a chance to sing in front of an audience. For some of these singers, this evening's performance would be their only opportunity. I could not accept the idea that these singers with so many hopes for this evening would not be given this chance that we had all worked so hard to give them.

I made a decision. I said over the phone, "I want everyone to be in my suite in fifteen minutes."

When all of the people involved arrived in my room—Jane, Margaret, their staffs, the director, the set and costume people, the technical director—I told them we must find another place to do the performance, even without sets and costumes. If there was no other way, we could do the opera like a concert. They said that no theater was available—they had made phone calls—and they knew of no other place big enough to hold over two thousand people.

When I arrived in Philadelphia weeks earlier, Jane had brought me up to my suite and I had admired the view up the parkway toward the beautiful art museum. Looking out my window, I had asked Jane about the large church right below me, and she had told me it was the Cathedral of Saint Peter and Saint Paul. She also told me that it was the principal Catholic church in Philadelphia, the cathedral of Archbishop Bevilacqua. I also remembered Jane telling me that Riccardo Muti recently had done a performance of the Verdi Requiem in that cathedral.

"We will do *L'Elisir* in the church," I announced to everybody.

You can't work in the theater for twenty-five years, as I had now done, and be involved in big productions with many, many people on the stage and backstage, and not know that a thousand different things can go wrong no matter how well planned things are. Some days the problems are big, and this day was one of them. But you learn to remain calm, think clearly, and work hard to find a solution. Some people are excellent in this way; others are not. I have seen very competent, intelligent people go completely to pieces in this sort of crisis. In my Philadelphia hotel suite that afternoon I could see right away that sitting around me were both types.

My friend Sandra McCormick compliments me by saying she thinks I have an X-ray mind that goes right to the heart of a problem. I don't know if this is true, but if I have any X-ray powers, I used them that afternoon in Philadelphia to see beyond all the hundreds of questions and problems that kept arriving and to hold on to one thought: our winners must have their chance to sing, and it must be that night. When I kept that thought fixed in my mind, everything became much simpler.

When we made the phone calls to get permission to use the

church, the only person we could reach by telephone was a priest who was not very high up in the church hierarchy of Philadelphia. He told us that the archbishop, along with "everyone" else, was on retreat. Unfortunately, he told us, he did not have the authority to grant such an unusual request. We discussed this with him, pleaded with him to change his mind. He asked us to wait a minute. It seemed like ten minutes had passed before he returned to the phone and said yes, he could give us permission. I don't know whether he consulted someone on this earth or a higher power, but his okay was enough for us. We went into action. It was now about four o'clock, which meant we had four hours.

My suite became the command headquarters for the operation. There were two phone lines into the suite, and they were immediately put to use to inform everyone in the production that in four hours we would be performing Donizetti's *L'Elisir d'Amore* in the Cathedral of Saint Peter and Saint Paul. All of the people we phoned were asked to phone others, and in this way the news spread quickly.

Jane and Margaret told me that even before they left their offices to come to my hotel, their phones had been ringing without stop. For the audience of the famous old Academy of Music to be told to leave the theater during a concert of the Philadelphia Orchestra was big news in the city, and it was broadcast on all the local news shows on television and radio. Programs were even interrupted with bulletins, they told me. We turned on the television in my room and saw for ourselves. We felt sure that almost everyone in Philadelphia knew about the problem at the Academy. Those who held tickets for our performance that night were telephoning to learn what would happen.

Before my decision, no one knew what to tell them, but now we could say they should go to the church. We also telephoned the radio and television news shows, and they very helpfully broadcast this information immediately. I made sure everyone was informed:

the orchestra, the stage and lighting people, the ushers. Everyone was told to go immediately to the cathedral to see what could be done to prepare for the performance.

We decided that setting up lighting would be too difficult; we would use only the lights already in the church. We also discussed setting up a platform for the chorus so that they could be seen better, but the technical people said that was too big a job for the few hours we had to get ready.

We decided to use the costumes and makeup, so trucks were hired to transport all of this from the Academy of Music to the cathedral. This was only about a mile and a half, but it was across the very center of the city, where the traffic is always heavy, and it was raining, which made our work even harder.

We were going crazy with the phones ringing constantly with everyone but the president of the United States asking us what was going on. We did not have enough phones to make all of the calls we needed to make. Our press-relations person, Carol Sargaula, very intelligently had rented her own suite in the Four Seasons Hotel so that she could handle the press in another place, leaving us free to deal with everything else.

Well, not exactly everything. One of Jane's staff members, Miriam Lewin, was sent down to the church to deal with that situation. She found a room next to the main part of the cathedral and directed the costumes and makeup equipment to be placed in there. Orchestra musicians arrived at the church with their music stands, as did the singers, chorus members, and stagehands with their gear. Finally the ticket holders began to arrive, but Miriam would not let them in. They had to stand outside in the rain.

I think now maybe Miriam had the worst job. Every ten minutes she would call us from a phone she had found in the rectory kitchen, which was in the back of the cathedral, to report that the church was turning into a madhouse of confusion. None of the people coming into the church had any idea what they should do or where they should be. Miriam and the people helping her were inventing answers to their questions. She told us that one of her problems was keeping out the press people who had learned of the plan and were beginning to swarm outside. It could have become an example of journalists coming to write about a disaster and turning it into a bigger disaster.

After a time everyone, upstairs and downstairs, had a good idea of what had to be done, and things seemed to be going along with their own energy. Catching my breath, I looked down on the church and could see people running in and out, just as people were running in and out of my room. But things seemed to be taking form, so I sat down to get calm and to start thinking about the performance.

Jane said later she remembered seeing me sitting quietly while everyone was going crazy around me. She asked me what I had been thinking. I can't remember exactly, but I know that once I was sure that the singers would be able to sing, that we would definitely have a performance, I relaxed and thought about how I loved what was happening.

I loved the way people threw themselves into doing what was necessary. They didn't wait for someone to tell them to do this or do that. They all looked around and figured out for themselves what to do. I loved how they were thinking and working hard toward the same goal, how they were adjusting to something that, when they woke up that morning, they'd had no idea would happen to them this day. For all of us, it was an exciting adventure, and I think that each one of those people running around downstairs, bursting in and out of my room, or driving a truckload of costumes across Philadelphia was loving it as much as I was.

Then another bomb fell on us. Miriam phoned from the church to say that a higher authority in the Philadelphia Catholic church had overruled the earlier decision and that we were now forbidden to perform. This authority felt so strongly about it that the church doors had been locked. No more people could get inside, and, even worse, the people inside couldn't get out. From the priests' kitchen, Miriam phoned to say she was trapped. This was not good.

It seems that someone in the Philadelphia cathedral remembered that the pope had issued an order in the last few years forbidding the performance of secular music in Catholic churches all over the world. Now, I understood that Verdi's Requiem, which Muti had done in the church, was certainly religious music. Donizetti's cheerful opera, on the other hand, is a story of young love and money. It is as secular as opera gets. I could see we had a problem. Someone asked me if I knew the pope. Actually I had met His Holiness, even sung for him, but I didn't think I knew him well enough to ask him to help us solve our problem.

We were devastated. We had already recovered from disaster once that day, but I wasn't sure we could recover a second time. No one had any idea what to do. The church people knew how important this was to all of us, to the young singers, and I think to the city of Philadelphia. If the church said no, then yes, then no again, it must really mean *no*.

But we had to make one last try. We got on the phone and pleaded with the church office to make an exception. We told them all the effort that had been made in the past hours getting everyone notified, putting the announcements on television, bringing people and equipment to the church. I even considered saying that, for lovers of Italian opera, the music of Verdi, Rossini, Bellini, Puccini, and Donizetti was *all* religious music. But I didn't want to go too far.

God obviously loves this music too, because word came that the church officials had changed their minds again. It was okay. We would be permitted to go ahead with our performance. I heard later that a board member of our competition was a prominent Philadelphia Catholic and used his influence to solve our problem. I don't know for sure how it happened, I was just very happy that it did. Miriam called to say the doors had been unlocked and everyone was back in action.

I think maybe this was the time when Jane saw me sitting quietly.

As early as six o'clock crowds had begun forming outside the cathedral. Even though it was raining, they seemed happy to stand in line and get wet as they waited for the church doors to open. We decided we must tell ticket holders three things: regardless of what tickets they held, seating inside the cathedral would be first come, first served. If they didn't agree to this, they could have their money back. But if they entered the church, they could not get their money back. In other words, their ticket was good for a refund or for entrance to the church. Once they were inside the church, they were on their own. It turned out that almost everyone chose to go into the church, and there were no problems. People were incredibly understanding and cooperative.

The time arrived for me to get into my makeup and costume in my room. But we ran into one more problem. Programs had been printed, but we had forgotten about them. They were across town in the Academy of Music, and the building staff wouldn't let anyone go in to get them. The structure was still too dangerous.

Now you might be thinking that programs are not essential to a performance, and in most instances you would be right. But in this case they were very important, because the contest winners hoped they might get representation from an agent or perhaps even an offer at some future date for a singing engagement.

Of course, anyone who is determined to learn their names

will get them somehow. But when dealing with unknown talent, people are not usually so determined. You must make it as easy for them as possible. Having the singers' names printed neatly, with the cities they live in, could make the difference between getting a call from a manager and not getting a call.

A young production assistant announced that he would go to the Academy and get the programs if he had to shoot his way in. I don't know if he used a gun or not, but he returned with the programs. We had so many heroes that day it is impossible to remember them all.

The excitement was growing. The television news was now showing the scene in the street outside the cathedral. This made it possible for me to see it on my screen or watch it from my window. The crowd was growing bigger than just our audience. It seemed like all of Philadelphia was arriving in the square down below to see what was happening.

Even with all of this media attention, we had made extra certain that ticket holders would know what was happening by putting up big signs on the Academy of Music, at the front entrance as well as the stage door, saying the performance for that evening had been moved to the Cathedral of Saint Peter and Saint Paul. I knew there was no chance we would be able to begin promptly at eight, so even latecomers arriving innocently at the Academy of Music would have time to detour to the church.

I was becoming eager to get down to the church, to see the singers and wish them well. Also, while my hotel suite had been a very busy place all afternoon—Jane called it "the war room"—the main activity was now down below, and I wanted to be part of it. I was in my costume and makeup, ready to go, but Jane said she was not yet dressed. I couldn't understand it. She is usually such an organized, efficient person; it was not like her to be unprepared. Also, she knew I was always on time and hated to wait for others.

If I have time when I am on tour, I love to visit horses. In Argentina in 1987, I became a gaucho for a few hours. OLA VERRIA

A new friend is Bruce Springsteen, whom I have visited at his wonderful farm in New Jersey. ANDREA GRIMINELLI

There were 600 people working backstage at Dodger Stadium for the 1994 three tenors concert. I think each one had a cellular phone, like my longtime manager, Herbert Breslin. WILLIAM WRIGHT

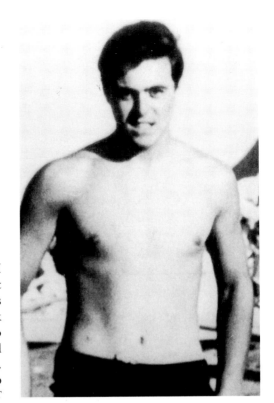

When I was eighteen, I could not imagine what would happen in the years ahead. Now, at sixty, I look out over the sea at Pesaro and still cannot take in all that has happened.

FAMILY ARCHIVES AND
WILLIAM WRIGHT

If I am not in my boat or on the phone in the summer, I am in my hammock, but rarely reading about myself as I am here.
WILLIAM WRIGHT

My mother and father are two fantastic people and have always been an important part of my life. WILLIAM WRIGHT

Bill suggested a shot of him typing and me talking, but I had a better idea: "You sing, I'll type."
BETTY A. PRASHKER

My daughters turned out to be beautiful, don't you agree? From the left, Lorenza, Giuliana, and Cristina.
WILLIAM WRIGHT

I love everything about jumper competitions—the sportsmanship, the expertise, the brave collaboration between horse and rider—even the elegance of the costumes.
CLAIRE FLAMANT

Although I had recorded
I Pagliacci and sung it
in concert, I did not
perform it on the stage
until the opening of the
Met in 1994.
HENRY GROSSMAN

The pressure for the
second three tenors
concert in Los Angeles
in 1994 had been building
for a year. By the time
Placido, José, and I arrived
for rehearsals, we were
all in tenor shock.
F. ORIGLIA

Nemorino in Donizetti's *L'Elisir d'Amore* is a simple peasant boy who wins out in the end—one of the reasons I have a special feeling for this role.
ROBERT CAHEN

Another favorite part of mine is Riccardo in *Ballo in Maschera*. The Oscar is Harolyn Blackwell.
HENRY GROSSMAN

In China, the crowds were as enthusiastic as any I have seen.
HANS BOON

Not all the Chinese were enthusiastic about me, however.
AP/WIDE WORLD PHOTOS

Even after being soaked by rain at my Hyde Park concert in 1991, Princess Diana looked beautiful while Prince Charles and I share a joke.
DOUG MCKENZIE

She came out of my bathroom with her hair a mess. I told her I was getting on the elevator in five minutes.

They told me later that Miriam had telephoned from the priests' kitchen to tell Jane to delay me, to keep me from coming down. Things inside the cathedral were still in chaos, and Miriam thought I would get so upset I might refuse to sing. I think they were crazy to worry about this. In the first place, doing our performance in the church was my idea. I knew we were moving an entire operatic production from one building to another in four or five hours. Did they think I expected no problems? Did they think I would choose a time like this to be difficult?

The scene in the street was unbelievable. Crowds of people— it looked like many thousands—surrounded the church in the rain. They still had not opened the doors for the ticket holders, so the crowd was a huge mixture of audience and curiosity-seekers. From the minute Jane and I came into the hotel lobby until we arrived at the church doors maybe a hundred yards away, we were surrounded by reporters, television cameras, spotlights.

It was something between winning the World Cup and a disaster scene—reporters pushing microphones in front of me, asking questions, which I tried to answer, always saying how confident I was that everything would go well. I was in a hurry to get inside the church. Wet and cold weather are the worst things for the throat, so I didn't want to stand outside in the rain talking too much, or maybe there wouldn't be a performance, at least not from me.

Inside the cathedral there was, to be sure, plenty of confusion, but I could see that things were getting organized. Most of the singers were in position at the front of the church. All but a few were in their costumes. The chorus was seated on neat rows of chairs behind the principal singers and the orchestra musicians had set up their chairs and stands off to one side. Everyone looked ready to go. When we were sure no one was missing, we decided to open the doors. As the crowd rushed in, I thought I would never again see so many happy, excited people—people who had been standing in the rain for hours.

Our conductor was my good friend Emerson Buckley, who lived in Miami and who had conducted many of my concerts there and in other places. Emerson died only a few years later, and at that time he was already in poor health and conducted from a wheelchair. But even in that condition that man could have conducted an opera in Times Square on New Year's Eve. His manner was always gruff and blunt, and as he wheeled himself down the central aisle, he said, "Just tell me where I should go and let's get started with this."

Sometime during the excitement of the afternoon in my hotel suite, Jane or one of the other people had said it all reminded her of one of those old Mickey Rooney–Judy Garland movies where they can't get a theater so they must put on their show in their grandfather's barn. I may have grown up in Italy, but I remembered those movies and could laugh at the comparison. To Emerson, however, this had nothing to do with Judy Garland or the movies. He was a professional with a job to do, and he would do it wherever it was necessary. A wonderful man.

As the church filled up and I knew that all of the singers, the chorus, and the orchestra were in position, I stopped thinking of everything but the performance we were about to sing, so I do not remember anything except that it went tremendously well. I think all of us sang a little bit beyond our best, including me, the music sounded fantastic in the cathedral, and the audience was very, very appreciative. It is impossible to describe the special feeling you get after you have done something like that, but I am sure that none of those young singers, even after they sing at the Met or La Scala, will ever forget the thrill of this performance. I *have* sung at the

Met and La Scala, and I certainly will never forget that night in Philadelphia.

We sang another performance in the church, and it was also a very good one, I think, but it could never equal the excitement of the first. The archbishop, who is now Cardinal Bevilacqua, returned to Philadelphia and came to hear us. He was very, very nice and said beautiful things, that he was pleased to be able to help us out of our difficulty and assist in getting our work in front of the audience. He also said he regretted all our trouble but saw one positive part of the drama: it brought all of us together.

I of course expressed my deep gratitude and told him what a fantastic experience it had been for me and everyone to sing an opera in his beautiful cathedral. I added that after getting through that first performance, I had wanted to join him on his retreat.

The problems of that production were not yet over. We had two more performances of *Elisir* to do while the Academy of Music was closed and under repair. Jane discovered that a theater on Broad Street, just below the Academy, which was occupied for our opening night, would become available. This would be much better than the church, as we could do the production as we intended, with full sets, lighting, and a proper stage.

But this was a situation in which solutions only created new problems. For instance, the theater could seat only about two-thirds as many people as the Academy. The solution was simple mathematics: we would do three performances instead of two. Also, in this way more of our singers would get a chance to perform.

I love coming face to face with problems, then figuring out solutions. I think I am good at it. I like it when friends bring me their problems and ask my advice. With a crisis like the one in Philadelphia, when you have very little time, the important thing is to remain calm and logical and above all to keep your mind on what is important and what is not. Challenges like this are good for us all and make us feel alive. They certainly get my brain working and my blood flowing. If life went along too smoothly, it would get very uninteresting.

Of course, in the life of an operatic tenor there is not even a tiny chance things will always go smoothly.

7

AN ITALIAN IN CHINA

My 1986 trip to Peking came about in a very complicated way. To celebrate my twenty-fifth anniversary as an opera singer, I had been invited to perform an opera in the city that has been my home all of my life, Modena. Shortly before this anniversary in June of 1986, I sang *La Bohème* in Philadelphia with the winners of my second vocal competition.

The Philadelphia performance, directed by Gian Carlo Menotti, was very good, so we arranged to take that production to Italy for the celebration. The singers and the stage direction would be the same, but we could not afford to transport our orchestra and chorus to Italy, so we would use the Modena chorus and orchestra. Just flying our principals to Europe was expensive and required extra fund-raising from the generous people of Philadelphia.

Each one of the Philadelphia singers was wonderful and I was very proud of my contribution in bringing them before the public. I thought presenting them to Italian audiences would be an ideal way to celebrate my quarter of a century on the opera stage. I also liked the idea of reminding my countrymen how many talented singers of Italian opera are coming from America and other countries.

Naturally, the competition winners were very excited about these plans. Most of them had never before sung on a professional stage, and now they were flying to Italy to perform one of the most loved Italian operas. While we were making plans for this European trip, which was scheduled for June of 1986, we had a much bigger excitement.

A long time before, the Chinese minister of culture had invited us to bring one of our Philadelphia productions to Peking. The China trip had been a possibility for a year, but we'd said little about it because we didn't want to disappoint everyone if it did not happen.

The details had finally been worked out, and by February it was definite that, after our performances in Modena, we would go to Genoa and perform our *Bohème* with the Genoa Opera. Then, at the end of June, we would all go to China—everybody. A jumbo jet would be provided so that we could take the entire production—orchestra, chorus, sets, costumes, and our twelve singers. There would even be space left over on the plane for family and friends. You can't imagine what an incredible thrill this was for everybody.

But first we had to go ahead with our plans for the productions in Italy. This was a big, complicated trip and, to most of us, was exciting enough. We all met in Modena for rehearsals, but you can imagine that few of us thought of much besides the trip to China.

The two performances in Modena were so wonderful for me. My native city made an enormous effort and created a lot of excitement about our opera and about my anniversary. I was very touched.

The tickets sold out quickly and many people were frustrated that they would not be able to see our *Bohème*. Because of our schedule and the China trip coming so soon, we were not able to add performances. So, to please everybody, the city had a wonderful idea. They took over many of the movie theaters in the center of Modena and televised the two performances live on a closed circuit. In addition, they set up big loudspeakers in Modena's beautiful square by the cathedral so that anybody who couldn't get a ticket could sit in the square and hear the performance free.

I thought that was a wonderful thing for my city to do. The theaters were filled, and the square was, too. I was told that during the performance, the square was as quiet as the opera house. People say that opera is dying in Italy. It certainly was very much alive that night in Modena in 1986.

Even throughout this beautiful and sentimental occasion, all of us were thinking about the coming trip to China. The more we learned about the plans, the more excited we got. Apparently, no Western opera company had performed a full-scale production of an opera in China since the Communists took over the government. I am not sure if there were any productions before. Roberta Peters, I know, sang concerts there, but I don't think there had been any full operatic productions by a Western company. We would, in many senses, be the first.

After the performances in Modena we had several weeks of freedom. Then we met again in Genoa to rehearse and do five performances before leaving for China from Genoa's airport. During those weeks before leaving Italy, I frequently ate lunch at a favorite restaurant of mine, Zefforino's, which is run by the five Zefforino brothers and their father. They are good friends, and they have wonderful food. At lunch I discussed with them the

China trip and told them of reports I had heard of the difficulty in finding certain foods there. I was worried about eating nothing but Chinese food all the time we would be there, which would be about two weeks. I like Chinese food, but I cannot eat it for breakfast, lunch, and dinner every day.

I actually knew nothing about China or about what we would find there, and I had trouble getting information. I began to worry that maybe we would run into the same food problem that Katia Ricciarelli and I had when we sang the Verdi Requiem in Moscow some years before. At the time Russia was having food shortages and even the food in our first-class hotel was very bad. We almost starved. Then a friend arrived from Italy and brought me some good pasta sauce. I prepared a big dinner in my room and invited colleagues who were suffering over the Russian food as much as I was. But I invited too many people. One of the last to arrive was my friend, the flutist Andrea Griminelli, who was performing at my concerts. When Andrea showed up at my door, I had to be rude. I told him to go away, there wasn't enough food. He is young and healthy, and I knew he would survive the Russian food. I also knew that I could make it up to him in New York or Modena.

With China, I had an even greater fear than starving: I was afraid that I might get fatter. Maybe in China I would not be able to find the kinds of food I need for my diet, the fresh fruits and vegetables that help me lose weight. I had heard that Chinese food is full of things that would make me gain weight, and that was the last thing I needed.

The more we thought about it, the more we realized that food might be a big problem. My secretary, Giovanna Cavaliere, and I would sit in that restaurant in Genoa and hold councils of war with the Zefforino brothers. They had an idea. Since we had this big airplane to take us to China, why didn't we import some food of our own? That seemed like an excellent solution, and we began making plans.

I think we were a little carried away. The first items on our list were fruits and vegetables, but as we thought about it, the list grew. In order to organize this food project, we decided that two of the Zefforino brothers should come to China with us to help cook the food in our Peking hotel room. I wasn't even sure if we would be able to get mineral water, so we decided that we had better bring that along, too. I was amazed to learn that the Zefforinos brought 1,500 bottles!

We also took large quantities of basic Italian items we were certain would not be available, things like Parmesan cheese and prosciutto. We maybe went a little crazy and kept adding things to our list. But then, we had all that space on the jumbo jet. I think we ended up with enough food to feed an Italian town for a week.

We made certain it would be permitted to cook food in our hotel rooms. Once we learned this would be all right, we had many discussions about what equipment to bring. The Zefforinos knew the pots and pans they would need, and we also ended up taking with us portable stovetops, an oven, and even a refrigerator. I began to suspect my friends were secretly planning to open a branch of their restaurant in Peking. We didn't want to get there and find we were missing something necessary for cooking an Italian dinner.

As the time approached to leave for China, there were many last-minute preparations and changes—not only about food. Every day in Italy I telephoned Hans Boon at the Breslin office asking him to bring from my New York apartment things I thought I'd need. I had invited my entire family to come to China. I was not surprised that everybody accepted except my mother, who gets too nervous even to see me in the Modena theater. Flying with me to China to watch me perform would have given her a heart attack for sure. But my father was coming and would sing the role of Parpignol in our *Bohème,* but from offstage. My wife, my sister, and my three daughters were thrilled to be making the trip.

With all we had to do, I came up with an additional project. I arranged for our entire cast to fly to Rome to receive the pope's blessing for our trip. I am very superstitious, and I believe that you should do anything you can to avoid bad luck. What could be better insurance than a blessing from His Holiness himself? The Vatican was happy to arrange this, and so we all went off to Rome. From the airport, the ladies of the company among us were taken to a convent near the Vatican and put into the hands of nuns, perhaps to make them forget about China and singing for a few minutes and get into a pure frame of mind.

I was taken into a beautiful waiting room in the Vatican. Finally we all met in an enormous antechamber and then were taken into a much smaller room were the pope was waiting for us. He started reading a blessing in Latin, but it must have been the wrong blessing: an aide took it away from him and gave him the right one. After being blessed, I presented the pope with as many of my recordings as I could find at home. He wished us a very pleasant and rewarding journey, and we flew back to Genoa.

When Hans arrived from New York the day before we were to leave, the suitcase he had brought me with my things from New York got lost in Paris and we had to make many phone calls to my friends at Alitalia to locate it. They found it quickly, and the bag arrived in Italy just in time. Finally the singers, the orchestra, the chorus, some journalists, and family and friends boarded the plane. Also on board was a filmmaker named DeWitt Sage who, thanks to Herbert, was making a documentary film about our trip. With him were his two other producers, their crew, and all their moviemaking equipment.

All together three hundred people were packed onto that 747 along with the sets, the costumes, the sound equipment for the two concerts I was to give, and everybody's luggage. It's amazing that plane could get into the air. As the huge jet began to move and built up speed, we were all looking out the windows wondering if we were going to get off the ground. We did, but I think we used every inch of the Genoa runway. We were on our way to China.

I sleep very well on planes, but I remember that at two o'clock in the morning, we landed at New Delhi. We weren't allowed to get off the plane there, but they opened the doors and the hot and humid air of India swept through the plane for a few minutes while they brought on a new crew and more food. Feeling as if I had paid a visit to India, I went back to sleep.

About noon the next day the plane landed in Peking. The airport looked like most others, but from the window I could see many people waiting—photographers, ladies holding children, others holding flowers. People clapped as I got off the plane, and there were signs saying in English "Welcome, Pavarotti." As everyone crowded around me, a Chinese woman came close to me, held up a microphone, and spoke to me in excellent Italian. She asked if I was glad to be in China. I thought how I am always glad to get off an airplane, especially after so many hours in the air, and to place my feet on any part of the planet earth, no matter where it is.

But I didn't say that because I was very thrilled to be in China. I said this to her in Italian, adding that I hoped our trip would be a success and that the people of China would like our performances. People told me later that when they saw this on television I looked groggy, as if I hadn't slept. But I had slept very well. I was just overwhelmed and dazed to be where I was.

I was taken immediately to hold a press conference in a room at the airport. I have done this many times, and I have no problems with it, but this time, of course, everything was so different—people around us speaking in Chinese, all the signs written in Chinese so we couldn't figure out which was the men's room, as you can in European countries, different fragrances in the hot July air from the flowers and trees. So often when you arrive in a new country everything looks similar to other places you have been, but in those first hours in China there were many small reminders that we were truly in another world.

We were introduced to Mr. Chien Wu, who would be our interpreter for the trip, and to a very pretty lady from the Ministry of Culture, Miss Hua. We set out for the hotel in an enormous black Mercedes they had sent for me. I was fascinated by everything I could see from the car, but one thing that struck me particularly on that first view of Peking was the number of bicycles. I've never seen so many bicycles, not even in Holland or in Scandinavia. It looked like everyone in China was on a bicycle—tiny children, young women, old men—and there were only a few cars.

We were all put up in the Fragrant Hills Hotel, which was about a forty-five-minute drive from the center of Peking in a large park that had been the Royal Hunting Grounds. The hotel had been designed by I. M. Pei and was all white. It had modern conveniences such as air conditioning and a swimming pool, both very welcome in the heat. In the coming days, the young singers would congregate by the pool when they were not rehearsing or sightseeing. I think we were the only people staying in the hotel at that time. The staff made us feel they were glad we were there, and we all quickly felt at home.

As we got settled in our rooms, and as our luggage arrived, we realized how much food and equipment we had brought. We saw there was not enough space in my room to set up our kitchen, so we had to ask my secretary, Giovanna Cavaliere, and Francesca Barbieri, who works with my wife, to move from the room next to mine that they shared. That became our kitchen. We found rooms for Giovanna and Francesca in other parts of the hotel, so it was no big problem for them.

All of our travel arrangements had been made by an Italian company called Ciao Mondo. These people set up a desk in the lobby of the hotel and helped us with any questions or problems and they would change money. They gave us not Chinese money but a certain kind of tourist money that was different. It was complicated, but they really had things very well organized, and if any of us had a problem there was always this desk where we could go and get it straightened out.

The first night our Chinese host gave a big formal reception for everybody. We were already starting to feel at home; everybody was very nice to us and very friendly, not formal, but relaxed and pleasant with us all. Adua said that the people reminded her of Italians because they were so cheerful and friendly, always smiling, laughing, and making an effort to speak to us in English.

The first day was a free day, but it turned out that DeWitt Sage and his film company had made plans for me almost every day. They had arranged for me to teach master voice classes for Chinese opera students, visit music schools, make sight-seeing trips. They knew of my passion for sports, so they also made plans for me to visit athletic events and gymnasiums and all kinds of other things most visitors don't see. This was arranged to provide interesting scenes for their film, but for me it was a wonderful opportunity to see more of China. I was fascinated by every bit of it and was very happy to do it. While I was making these visits for the film, the others of our group could take guided tours that the travel people had set up for them. Everybody was having as interesting a time as I was.

The second day, we began rehearsals, which were in the center of Peking. Often the drive took much longer than forty-five minutes. If we got behind an oxcart in our powerful Mercedes we would travel no faster than the ox. One day it took us over four hours just to travel to and from the rehearsal hall. We ran into several ox jams.

This didn't bother me. The car was very comfortable, and I was able to relax in it. Also, there was always something interesting to see from the window. The long periods in the car going from the hotel to the city gave me a chance to see a little of China and to watch the people going about their daily lives.

I was most impressed by the many tiny gardens in front of the houses. You could see that everyone was trying to get a few extra vegetables from the land. It reminded me very much of when I was a boy in Italy. In those war years we were all very poor and food was scarce. If you could grow a few tomatoes or some onions, it was a big help to the family.

Another similarity was that, when I was growing up, there were more horses than cars in my part of Italy. After the war, in the village on the edge of Modena where we lived, you would see a car go by only once every two or three hours. It was similar here in Peking in 1986. More people did their business with horse carts than with trucks. And there were a hundred times more bicycles than cars.

As we drove back and forth to Peking each day, I was a little embarrassed to see farm stands along the road with pyramids of beautiful melons. Because of our fear that we would not be able to get fresh fruit, we had brought crates of melons from Genoa. There was no room for them in our small refrigerator, and, of course, in the hot weather, they began to rot before we could eat them.

Giovanna started exploring in the vicinity of the hotel and found a little market in the village a short walk away. Every morning she would come back to the room with fresh vegetables—beautiful plums and tiny watermelons. I was fascinated by the way they would sell her these things. Instead of plastic bags, they put them into funnels, which they made out of sheets of paper. This is exactly what we used to do in Italy—another similarity to my home and my past.

We very quickly got to work on our production of *La Bohème*. Gian Carlo Menotti had not been able to come to direct, as he had the original production in Philadelphia, but his assistant, Roman Terleckyj, came to re-create Gian Carlo's stage direction. We had brought the Genoa chorus, but for supers, Roman used chorus members of a Chinese company that put on Western operas. They were familiar with *Bohème,* but even so, Roman ran into problems. Whenever he asked one or two of them to move across the stage to create a natural street scene, they would *all* move across the stage. They were not accustomed to being directed as individuals.

He also ran into problems with the official from the Ministry of Culture who attended all of our rehearsals. The problems were minor, but they said something about the differences between our two worlds. In the Act Two street scene, which Menotti had directed and which Roman was re-creating, a young boy gets into an argument with an old man. The Chinese official said this had to be changed. In China children did not show disrespect to old people. Menotti also had introduced a few prostitutes as part of his Parisian street scene. These, too, were forbidden by the Chinese official. Such women had been eliminated in modern China, and the government did not want us to remind the audience of a forbidden profession.

There was no air conditioning in the theater and it was extremely hot, but someone had the very intelligent idea to bring along some little battery-operated electric fans that you can hold in your hand. I really think these wonderful inventions saved my life. Not only did the theater and rehearsal halls have no air conditioning, they didn't have any air, either. And, as you can imagine, I am very affected by the heat. But in this case everyone else was, also. Even with the terrible heat, however, our spirits were high and the rehearsals went very well.

Little problems came up, and sometimes they were funny. Kallen Esperian, one of our two Mimis, had never been to the Far East before, and she was shocked to see that the plumbing in the ladies' room was not something you sat on but just a hole in the floor. I told her that this was very common in the Orient. Even so, she and the other young women in our company worried about their performances when they would be in nineteenth-century costumes with full skirts and petticoats.

When they managed to get past this worry, Kallen again returned from the ladies' room upset. I asked her what the trouble was. She said that the room was full of naked Chinese women. The place we were rehearsing was not really a theater—more of a school, I think. We learned that the neighborhood women come to this place to take showers at this time of day. Many things like this seemed very strange to us at first, but always there was a logical explanation.

Some of my family complained of various inconveniences and asked me if they didn't bother me, too. Of course there were inconveniences. There always are when you visit a culture very different from your own. I felt it was important that I not say anything, even when I was sure no Chinese could hear me. If I said anything negative, then everybody in the company might start complaining too. In addition, the inconveniences were all very unimportant things, especially when compared with the importance of what we were doing in terms of cultural interchange.

Like most people, I always like things in my profession done a certain way. Working in America or Europe, where everything is possible, I can make demands, but if what I would prefer is not possible, I do not gripe. I am not a griper. I either change what bothers me or I shut up about it. If the members of our company were waiting for me to gripe first, I wanted to make sure they had a long wait.

As I have said, the drive back to the hotel sometimes took more than forty-five minutes if we hit traffic, but that didn't bother me too much. One evening, however, we got stuck in the worst rain I've ever seen, and the car wouldn't go. I found myself sitting in the back of a Mercedes in the middle of what looked like a Chinese river, and I wondered if we would ever get out of there. I thought what a funny way to end my twenty-five years as an opera singer. Finally people arrived to rescue us. We got into another car and were able to return to the hotel and change into dry clothes. Amazingly, I did not catch cold. The hot weather may have saved me.

Each day when I wasn't rehearsing I was making visits in connection with the documentary film. When I taught the master classes to young Chinese vocal students, I was surprised there were so many who were studying Western operatic singing. Some had very good voices, and all of them were very serious about it and eager to hear whatever I could tell them. They were all cheerful and good-natured and seemed grateful for my comments, no matter how minor.

At one point I was taken to see a Chinese opera. This, as you know, is a fantastic spectacle where they get dressed in very elaborate costumes and makeup, then sing in a way that to our ears sounds strained and artificial. For them, however, this music is as beautiful and expressive as Puccini is to us. This tradition of Chinese opera was very interesting to me, since I spend my life performing in a similar way—and in a musical form that sounds almost as strange and artificial to some people in Europe and America. The Chinese performed a few scenes especially for me, and they did them in full costumes and makeup. When they finished, I went up on the stage to congratulate the singers, but on an impulse, I asked them if I could do it too.

I did not realize what I was getting myself into. I knew it would be a complicated process; I didn't know it would take the backstage people *four hours* to put the makeup on me and get me into one of those costumes. But once we got started, I could not turn back. Actually, I was very much interested in the process and did not want to turn back.

When I was finally ready, I looked like something that should be guarding the entrance to a temple from evil spirits. We went on the stage and performed a scene. The Chinese performers sang their pieces to me. Then I sang to them. I have a very good ear, and I think I'm a good mimic, so I improvised in their style back to them in what sounded to me like Chinese opera. When I later saw the film, someone had to tell me which singer was me. My face was covered in black-and-white makeup and I wore a headdress that made me look like Princess Turandot.

The movie that DeWitt Sage made from our entire China experience was released in theaters and was called *Distant Harmony*. It was a very beautiful film done with great artistry and imagination. It certainly captured the spirit of the extraordinary experience we were all having. For one part of the film, the moviemaker asked me to go with them into Tiananmen Square so they could shoot scenes of me in this famous place. Of course, everywhere we went, because of the big black Mercedes, crowds would form. I guess I was rather conspicuous, too. But the people were always very polite and friendly. Each time I went into a crowd, it was a pleasure to meet the Chinese people.

For one shot, DeWitt asked me if I could think of something to do in the square, some action that he could film. I told him that was easy, I'd ride a bike. He looked surprised, so I explained that I loved to ride bikes and do it all the time at my house in Pesaro. In spite of my weight, I'm very good at it.

One of the cameramen grabbed a student going by and gestured that he needed the bike. I asked him how he got the boy to just hand over his bicycle. The cameraman said, "I gave him five dollars. He'd have handed over his grandmother for five dollars."

When I got on the bicycle and began riding around Tiananmen Square, it was a wonderful feeling. I was bicycling in China! I got carried away and headed off. When I saw that DeWitt and his camera were having trouble keeping up with me, I went faster. They just wanted one shot, but I was having too much fun to stop. Everybody was going crazy trying to catch me and make me get off the bike. We were already running late, and my joyride was throwing us off our schedule even more. But I was having so much fun that I didn't care.

I later learned that when I took off this way, my interpreter, Mr. Wu, went even crazier than the film people. It was explained to me that the Ministry of Culture had made Mr. Wu responsible for my safety. When he saw me on a bicycle heading off into Peking by myself, he had a fit. Nothing bad happened, though, and my solo flight into China ended well.

Every day, even with rehearsals, I had time to do something new and interesting. My family was also having a fantastic time going on sight-seeing trips. My daughters wanted to visit the Tomb of the Thousand Soldiers, which they had read about, but were at first told that it was too far from Peking. Without our knowing it, phone calls were made and two planes were arranged to take any members of our group who wanted to go to visit this remarkable sight. That was typical of the thoughtfulness of our Chinese hosts.

While many of us were having such a wonderful time in Peking, visiting different places, meeting people, seeing the sights, others in our group were having problems. The sound equipment had been held up in customs for some reason, and our technical people were having no success getting it out. Also, during rehearsals when DeWitt Sage and his crew started to film, some Chinese men came in and said that photographing the rehearsals was forbidden. The filmmakers were floored to learn this. They explained how they had come from America to make this documentary and how important such shots were to their film. The Chinese said no, no, it was forbidden, and that was that. So the filmmaker asked if there was anybody else they could speak to about this.

They were taken into another room in the theater and brought before a man sitting on a little platform like an emperor and smoking continuously. He was the one who made the decisions. Through an interpreter, our technical people explained their problem. The official didn't seem to want to change his mind, but finally he did, in a sense. The cameramen just went on filming and no one said anything.

Another crisis erupted when our conductor, Emerson Buckley, told me the Genoa people had forgotten to bring a guitar and an accordion that we needed for the second act of *La Bohème*. I said to Emerson, "Surely somewhere in China there is an accordion and a guitar." And eventually they found these things, but little problems that could be solved in five minutes at home became big problems here.

At night I most often had dinner in my room with my family. Every day was filled with meeting people and being very sociable, plus rehearsing our opera, and by the evening, I was ready to relax. Some nights, when I still had energy, I would go downstairs to the big buffet the hotel set up every evening for our company. I learned that many of our group did not like the Chinese food they were offered. This was especially true of the Italians, who often don't like any food but their own.

I once entered the dining hall and saw a young baritone from Rome sitting at a table by himself. He had a cracker in one hand and a bottle of orange soda in the other. He looked so unhappy that I invited him to my room for some pasta. As I realized how many of our group were hungry for more familiar food, I began inviting different ones every night in a rotating dinner party. On performance nights, I made a special point of inviting the principals, as I believed they were the most in need of strength. People had kidded me about bringing food and cooks from Italy, but most of them were later glad that I had.

I also enjoyed eating downstairs with the others, and I didn't want the hotel to think I was refusing their food. The evenings when we all ate together were always a lot of fun. One night I sent our cooks from Genoa into the kitchen to show the Chinese cooks how to prepare pasta. Another night I got into a beer-drinking contest with Roman Terleckyj, our director, and some of the singers. We started singing a little, but we had some competition from some of the Genoa chorus members. The Communist Party is very strong in Genoa, and some of our company were Party members. They were singing partisan songs to show their comradeship with the Chinese hotel workers.

The mood in the dining room was usually wonderful. One night I had finished dinner down there with my sister, Lela, and some other friends. We were all feeling so happy we began singing some traditional Italian songs. The waiters stopped their work, and the cooks came from the kitchen to listen. When we finished, they all applauded like crazy. Then something incredible happened.

One of the cooks started singing a Chinese song, and everybody went silent. Although we had all sung as a group, he was definitely singing alone. We thought his colleagues would join in, but he sang only by himself. We kept expecting the song to end, but it went on and on and on. Some of my friends started talking, but I quieted them. We became more and more fascinated by this remarkable performance. The boy at one point couldn't remember the words, and he burst out laughing. Everybody cheered. While it lasted, it was a bravura performance. He had held the entire roomful of people spellbound with totally unfamiliar music. I congratulated him with sincere admiration.

During the day, when I was out among the Chinese people, I

was surprised to find that many Chinese children knew the names of the operas I have recorded! Many, both young and old, presented me with my recordings on cassettes and asked me to autograph them. I was surprised to find so many of my recordings in China and said to one of the men with us from London Records that they must sell a lot of my records in China. He said, "We don't sell any. Zero." The records I was seeing, he said, were all black market.

While I was sorry for London Records—and for myself, too, as I get no royalty on black market records—I was still very impressed that this many Chinese young people would go to so much trouble to find my recordings. Also, many brought me a copy of the first book that Bill Wright and I did together. It was, of course, in Chinese, and it was printed on very cheap paper. You read it from back to front, but it was *Pavarotti, My Own Story,* and I signed many copies of that for them.

As the first performance of *Bohème* approached, there seemed to be more and more excitement among ourselves and among the Chinese people we encountered. The crowds that would greet me as my car dropped me at the theater were getting bigger, and I saw more people wave as I went by on the road. Mr. Wu kept us informed about all that was happening. Even though many of the tickets had been given to people the Party wanted to reward, there were other seats for sale. Mr. Wu told us that people waited for hours and hours to buy these tickets. He also described the street bartering for records and books, and other things that were happening in places where we couldn't see.

Finally it was June 28, 1986, the night of the first *La Bohème.* It was so hot, I was amazed that the makeup stayed on our faces. But everything went very well. It was such an unusual sensation for me to be singing that role, which I had sung so many times for over twenty-five years and which I love very much, and to be singing it in Peking in front of an audience of Chinese. I had heard that many of the tickets had been given to workers as a reward for good work and that they had come to the theater directly from their factories on their bikes, totally hot and dirty. What a difference this was from the usual formality of opera audiences.

Since I had never sung in China and had never talked with anyone who had, I had no idea how audiences would react to my singing. I knew there were people in China who liked Western music, even Italian opera. But I also knew there would be a great deal of interest about me because of my televised concerts. Just because they were curious about me did not mean they would love my music. In the reverse situation, my curiosity had made me happy to see a Chinese opera, but it would have been phony of me to go crazy with applause at the end of it. I had also been told that Chinese audiences are by nature quiet and reserved. Whoever told me that was warning me, I suspected, not to be disappointed if I didn't receive as warm a reception in Peking as I had received in Western cities.

I was therefore not prepared for the response to our *Bohème*. The first sign of the audience's feeling was, in itself, a complete surprise. When I hit my first all-out high note near the end of my Act One aria, "Che Gelida Manina," the audience burst into applause. The aria was not finished, but they did not wait for the end. Still, they applauded as enthusiastically as at the end of the opera. The moment they heard the music continue, however, they went quiet immediately and let me finish the aria.

Throughout the opera the audience did this every time I hit a high note. Applause is nice whenever it comes, but it was especially welcome with this audience, even in the middle of my biggest aria, when I had no idea if they were loving or hating what we were doing up there on that stage.

As I thought about it later, I thought that it was nice in other ways, too. By our standards, it is not polite to applaud during a piece of music. But these people knew nothing about our concert-hall customs. They were responding in the most natural way. They heard something that pleased them so much they had to show their appreciation right away. Then, as soon as they heard that I and the other singers were continuing, they stopped clapping immediately. The result was that the music was not interrupted. For artists, there is nothing worse than "polite" applause. (Well, booing is worse, but polite applause is not much better.) Does it not then follow that *impolite* applause is very good?

Our Mimis, Fiamma Izzo d'Amico and Kallen Esperian, sang wonderfully. I particularly loved Kallen's voice. When I first heard her audition in the Philadelphia competition, I told Herbert, "You must hear her. She has a voice like Tebaldi's." Herbert agreed. After hearing her sing Mimi in Peking that night, he signed her to a contract as one of his artists. My former secretary and student, Madelyn Renée, was our Musetta, and she also sang and acted very well. While on this trip, she met the Italian journalist who had flown over to write about our visit, and they later got married.

At the end of the opera the audience went completely insane, which was an enormous relief for all of us. It had taken so much effort and expense to get us there, and we were so excited about the rare nature of our project, it would have been a huge disappointment if the response had been only polite.

Opera, when it is well done, has great power to move the emotions. But the emotions have to be in the audience to begin with; the people must have something inside them that the performance will bring out. We had no idea what emotions were inside this Chinese audience, but it turned out that the Chinese have the same things inside them as do the people in Milan, Paris, and New York. The applause and cheers we got that night made a company of three hundred Italians and Americans very, very happy.

A few days later I sang a recital, and the response was the same, even with the audience applauding each time I hit a high note. When for an encore I sang "O Sole Mio," and I couldn't believe the reception. You would have thought it was the Chinese National Anthem. I said to someone later that they applaud "O Sole Mio" like Neapolitans—maybe even more enthusiastically.

By now everyone in China, I think, knew we were there. Word came to the hotel one morning that we were invited to have lunch with the secretary general of the Communist Party, Mr. Hu Yao Pang. Our Chinese friends emphasized to us that this was a very rare and great honor, an honor given to very few visiting dignitaries. And after my bike ride, I was surprised that the Chinese thought of me as a dignitary.

The Mercedes took us to the hall where the lunch was to be held, and there were journalists and cameramen everywhere. Mr. Hu, a very short man, was very pleasant and relaxed. Like so many of the officials in China, he smoked cigarettes all the time. Lunch was a formal occasion, with many other officials, but my wife and I were very pleased to have this honor and we enjoyed ourselves completely. When we were teenage sweethearts in Modena, and Adua and I were too poor to own a car, we did not think we would one day sit in a Chinese palace being entertained by one of the two or three most powerful men in China.

For us, this lunch was enough glory and excitement, but while we were eating, Mr. Hu said through an interpreter that he was inviting me to sing in the Great Hall of the People. It was explained to me what an enormous honor this was. The Great Hall of the People is the largest hall in China. It seats ten thousand people and is the place where the top officials of the Communist Party and the top officials of the government meet to discuss matters of government. In front of all the seats on the ground floor there are desks and microphones. For the Chinese, this is one of the most important buildings in their country.

I learned I would be the first foreigner ever to perform in the Great Hall. I could tell that something special had happened to me, because Mr. Wu and Miss Hua were obviously very surprised and pleased that their government had given me this honor. On the negative side, we'd had no idea this would happen and had only a few days to change the small recital I had planned into one of the largest indoor concerts of my entire career.

Among a hundred other problems, we did not have enough time to set up the sound system, which had finally gotten through customs. In most places where I give very large concerts, it takes about twenty-four hours to set up the sound equipment. We only had six hours to set it up in a far larger hall, and one not designed for performances. During those six hours, the Chinese technicians in the Great Hall of the People were busy arranging the lighting and said our sound people could not use the stage until they were finished. That caused a head-on collision between our people and theirs, and it took a lot of diplomacy on both sides to work these things out.

And of course, tickets were a huge problem both for our people and for the Chinese—printing and distributing them in a matter of hours. But somehow everything got done. The evening of the performance, I found myself in my white tie and tails, walking, as I had so often done, from a dressing room to a stage. As I was walking past all the technicians and stage crew, I passed Miss Hua, our guide from the Ministry of Culture. I stopped and gave her a kiss on the cheek for good luck and went out on the stage to face ten thousand Chinese people.

The concert, with full orchestra, went wonderfully. The audience was fantastic, still clapping for high notes whenever they arrived and going wonderfully crazy at the end. This concert was one of the great thrills of my life. Everybody seemed to love it. It was a wonderful climax to an extraordinary two weeks. We flew out to Europe that night.

Throughout our stay in Peking, the reaction of the Chinese audiences was deeply touching to me. I don't think I have ever encountered anything like it. Their appreciation seemed so generous, so open, so without any kind of chauvinism or jealousy. Their response came from deep inside them. They seemed to open themselves up completely to enjoy what we had to give them. Even though our music surely sounded strange to many of them, they recognized what was happening on a deeper level than that of just one culture or another. It was very moving to me in a way I had not experienced before.

I was told later that because the concert was televised live, 200 million Chinese watched it while it was happening. That is inconceivable to me. Incredible.

Before leaving, we had to decide what to do with all our cooking equipment, especially the refrigerator. I decided we should make a present of it to Mr. Wu, who had been so kind and helpful to us throughout our stay in China. To our amazement, he would not accept it. When we asked him why not, he said that no one on his street had a refrigerator and his neighbors would dislike him for owning one. We were amazed and suspected there was more to it than that, but he definitely would not take it.

I have friends who kid me when I go on these tours to exotic foreign countries. I see little, they say, because I am always protected in limos and in luxury hotels. Such things are the same everywhere. "How were the limos in Hungary, Luciano?" they say. "Were they different than in Chile?" To some degree that is a fair observation. But I always try to break through this protective screen to experience the place I am in. And sometimes, as with Mr. Wu, the country breaks through to me.

The Chinese people are quite extraordinary, and they have a completely different mentality from us. All humans everywhere want to be better, to move upward in one way or another. We Italians and Americans, most of us want to have a bigger house and a bigger car, but the Chinese I met are not like that. People tell me that when I return to China in ten years I will find the streets full of cars. I'm not so sure; I'm not so sure that's what they want. They want to be better, as every human does, but maybe in their own way. Maybe not the car-and-house way.

Altogether our China trip was one of the most wonderful experiences of my life. I will certainly never ever forget it, and if that should start to happen, if the China experience begins to become a dream in my mind, I have the video of *Distant Harmony* to remind me of the beautiful places we saw, the wonderful people and the thrilling reception.

In the years since that visit, the Chinese government has many times invited me to make another visit. I have always declined their invitations. I know that no matter how successful another visit might be, it could never possibly be as marvelous and spontaneous as that amazing visit in 1986. Things like that rarely happen even once in a lifetime. They surely cannot happen twice.

8

THE PAVAROTTI
INTERNATIONAL
HORSE SHOW

All my life I have been a tremendous sports fan, almost a fanatic. I love all sports, but my favorite by far is football, which Americans call soccer. From as far back as I can remember, I played football every free moment throughout my childhood. When I wasn't in school or eating meals with my family, I was outside playing football with my neighborhood friends. I played on the high school team, and I also played with a neighborhood league.

If it wasn't football, it was some other sport. And if I was actually playing a game, I was always in motion, almost never still. I had too much energy, I think. My wonderful grandmother Giulia used to say to me, "Be careful, Luciano, you will frighten the horses."

As a football player I was not bad, but I was never good enough to think about playing as a professional. Even so, to this day, I love the sport. It is as much in my blood as music, and I follow the professional teams passionately. I might not be able to tell you who sang last week at Covent Garden or La Scala, but I can definitely tell you who won the matches in Florence or Madrid.

During the season, no matter where I am in the world, I telephone one of my friends in Italy to give me the scores. Football has even had a big effect on my singing career: it was the reason Placido, José, and I sang the first Three Tenors concert.

I also love tennis and played regularly until I began having trouble with my knee. When I could no longer move around fast enough, I played doubles for a while, but finally had to quit altogether. I am told I was a very aggressive tennis player. I used to play frequently with my good friend Renata Nash and her husband, and she would tell me that when I was her partner in doubles all I did was stand in one spot and yell at her, "Get it, get it!" Since I've had an operation on my knee, I'm hoping to be able to play tennis soon again and "get it" myself.

Another sport I am enthusiastic about is automobile racing. I particularly liked this when I was a young man, but you don't forget these enthusiasms. When I was singing in *Bohème* in Buenos Aires in 1987, I was thrilled to meet the great automobile racer, Juan Manuel Fangio. Being an opera singer and traveling around the world, I meet many famous people, but when I met this hero of my youth, I was so overcome I could barely speak. As a young boy, I had also been a big fan of two Italian racing car drivers, Fausto Coppi and Gino Bartali. These men made cycle racing popular in Italy in the forties and fifties when I was growing up. But like most sports fanatics, I admire anybody who excels at a sport. It doesn't matter which sport.

Although my first love in sports will always be football, in the last twenty years a new passion has taken me over that almost rivals my feeling for football. And that is horses. I have always loved animals. My family never had pets when I was growing up. We were too poor. Later, when I started my career and began earning money, I traveled too much to own a dog. I still travel too much; it would not be fair to the dog. They are more intelligent than horses, and they are more focused on one person. Horses are happy to see you when you come home, but they do not miss you the way a dog misses you.

In Modena I have ten horses, which I used to ride, but now only my daughters ride them. Perhaps if I can lose a bit more weight, I will ride them again.

When I was a small boy I had an uncle who lived in the country and owned a pony and a trap. I remember pleading with my family all the time to let me go and visit my uncle because I loved the pony so much. I kept on begging even when I was not so small. This uncle also bought and sold horses in the open-air markets in the nearby towns. It was always a great thrill for me to go with him and watch him examining horses and bargaining with the traders. I was fascinated to learn about the business of horses, but mainly I was happy just to be around them.

As I was starting my career and raising a family, I didn't think much about this love of horses. I had no time and little opportunity to see horses. This changed in December of 1979 when I was singing a concert in Dublin. Someone offered to take me to see some remarkable horses, and I said I would enjoy doing that. When I saw those beautiful animals, all my old love of horses came rushing back. I fell in love with all of them. Before I left Ireland, I bought two horses, and I took them to my home in Modena.

One of these horses was a four-year-old gelding named Herbie, who was an excellent jumper. I bought him mainly for my youngest daughter, Giuliana, who shared my love of horses, but this upset Adua because Herbie was quite frisky. Although he always behaved like a gentleman with Giuliana, I don't think Adua ever got over her fear of him.

Another horse I bought at that time in Ireland was Shaughran, an enormous and powerful hunter and one of the few horses I ever met who didn't mind carrying me on his back. He was a very gentle and well-behaved horse. He also had no trouble adjusting to living near a city and was not bothered by city things like traffic lights and busy intersections if I took him on that kind of route.

We originally kept the horses in a stable near our house, but eventually Adua complained about all the flies they attracted, because sooner or later the flies found their way into our house where there were better things to eat. So we built a stable farther away. In addition to my own horses, I also board a few horses for other people, so the stable is quite large. Adua looks after its administration, and we both prefer not to think of the expense, which is unbelievable.

After that first time in Ireland, when I realized how much I loved horses, I started riding whenever I could. I remember one experience with horses in London's Hyde Park that started off badly. My friend from New York, Sandra McCormick, and her husband were there with their children. When the children learned that I planned to go riding, they pleaded to come with me and said they were good riders. I told them I would take them only if their mother came riding with us. Sandra told me she was terrified of horses, but admitted she knew how to ride. I said either she comes or the children stay home. When she saw how much her children wanted to come, she agreed to come too.

First, we had trouble getting a horse big enough for me. The stable had to make phone calls, and they located this enormous horse at another stable. He was perfect, just the right size, and he seemed happy to take me. When we started out, we ran into a problem right away. To reach the park, it was necessary to cross a busy intersection with cars and buses going in all directions. The horse started across the street, but this was a new intersection for him, so he panicked and wouldn't move. The traffic stopped too, thank God. Even so, I was out in the middle of a London street on my horse and I could not get this enormous animal to move.

Cars started honking, which frightened my horse even more, and he started dancing around. He even reared a little, but I managed to stay on. It looked very bad, but I knew that we were safe from the cars because in England they would kill a person before they would kill a horse. Finally he calmed down and got us across to the park. The children loved our ride, and I think Sandra managed to enjoy herself too, but watching me dancing in the traffic with a terrified horse did not help her get over her fear.

Over the years I have been fortunate to form lasting friendships with people I have met in the cities where I often sing. When my friends in these places realize how passionate I have become about horses, they often arrange to put me in touch with horse lovers when I visit their cities. Some of my friends turned out to love horses as much as I do.

I often think about why I have such a feeling for horses, and it is not easy to explain. First of all, I see them as great, beautiful animals, noble and majestic. But I also see them as a way for us humans to get back to the natural state of things, to get away from all the artificiality that makes up so much of modern life.

Horses are so simple and beautiful. They are wonderful creations of nature. I believe they can have a very good effect on you. Just being with my horses makes me relax and realize how much in the world is wonderful and pure. When I am doing a concert or opera in a different city with much tension and anxiety, I will ask friends from that area if they know somebody with a stable who might let me visit their horses.

No matter how worried I am about the concert or opera, if I see a beautiful horse and become friends with that horse, I immediately relax inside. I can be peaceful again no matter what I face in the next days. I have heard that when people who are handicapped, depressed, or in very bad health are exposed to horses, it makes them feel better, rejuvenates them. I believe it.

I have another theory about horses that some people might

consider pretty extreme. I think that for young people, becoming involved with horses is very healthy and a very good influence. When the young, who are always looking for an outlet for their energy and enthusiasm, become infatuated with horses as I have become, they are in far less danger of falling into the bad things like drugs and crime. I believe those are things young people turn to when they are bored and have no place to put their energy and their passion. Because horses are pure and unspoiled, they make the humans with whom they have contact more pure and un-spoiled. An extreme idea, I know, but that is what I believe.

As for me, I see my love of artistry and beauty and my love of sports coming together in horses. Just to watch these animals gives me great pleasure. My enthusiasm led me naturally to the sports that involve horses. My favorite very quickly became the jumping events. For me it is something incredibly beautiful to watch one of these magnificent creatures go over a jump. You can see right away if a horse is a good jumper or not. If he is good, he looks ahead and gauges his distance and figures out what he has to do. You can actually see him making these calculations.

It's very much like a tenor when he knows that the high notes are coming. We must think ahead, test our power, and focus our energies on the obstacle that we must get beyond. I think about that comparison all the time as I watch these wonderful brave crea-tures approach a fence and jump over it. The riders, too, are very brave. This human and horse being brave together, that is one of the things I like best about jumping. By taking this risk with a horse, the rider is getting very close to nature.

To me, this sport where a human man or woman and this animal together do something very difficult and perhaps dangerous is a marvelous thing to watch. As I realized how much I liked this particular sport, I became more and more interested in the world of jumping horses, the competitions in the various countries, and of course the big international competitions. I discovered a fascinating new world, and I began following it almost as closely as I follow football.

In 1990 some wealthy and influential Mexicans approached me about lending my name to a horse show they wanted to do in Italy. They were very prominent people in the international horse world, and they had powerful financial backing. They were eager to sponsor an international show of jumpers in Europe. The only problem was that the important association that oversees these events permits only one official show in each country and all of the major European countries already had shows. This included Italy, which put on one of the most famous and important show each year in Rome. But this presented a problem. If I became involved in a show, I wanted it to be in Modena. Because of my schedule, holding it near my home would allow me to devote more time to the event.

We learned that there was no horse show in the Republic of San Marino, an island of mountainous land completely surrounded by Italy. It is not far from my summer house in Pesaro, and the people who live there are very enthusiastic about horses. We got the idea of putting on a horse show in Modena for San Marino. When we approached the people there, they were interested in the idea. In a sense, we needed a country and they needed a horse show.

When we talked to others in the international horse-show world about the plan, we found that everyone liked it. People in the horse-show business feel that the more horse shows there are, the better it is for everybody. Even the sponsors of the big Italian show were very much in favor of the idea and saw no conflict. Everyone encouraged us to go ahead.

In the horse-show world, there are three main types of shows: one is for jumping; another is for dressage, a classic form of riding where the horses perform precision movements, sometimes to music; and the third is a three-day event called combined training, which involves show jumping, dressage, and cross-country. Horse racing and polo are two entirely different sports and really have little to do with horse shows. The three major horse-show events are all Olympic sports.

The official name for the show is the Pavarotti International—CSIO San Marino. Now, I must explain that the CSIO is very important. The letters stand for a French term that means we are part of the international show-jumping circuit. The O is a most important letter because that means we are official, that we are recognized internationally as one of the principal international horse shows. Because of this O, we are able to hold the sport's most prestigious competition, The National Cup. That was why we had to find another country besides Italy; the rules say that there can be only one CSIO show per country.

In order to get permission to carry out our plan for a San Marino show to be held in Modena we had to make application to the International Equestrian Federation, the organization that makes all the international rules. I was very pleased when they allowed us to hold our horse show in my hometown. Although my main motive in doing this was to utilize my name and recognition to advance a sport I love, at the same time I saw it as a way to do something for the city I love. Because I knew the show would bring a lot of media attention to Modena and, if it went well, a lot of visitors.

An initial problem was to find a place in the Modena area to hold the show. No suitable place existed in the city, so I found some available land outside of town near the stables where I keep my horses.

Before our first show it was important to form an honorary committee. In Italy you must do these political things properly. We had to invite ministers from the Italian government and from San Marino, of course—the president of the Emilia-Romagna Council and the city council of Modena. Then I formed an execu-

tive committee made up of colleagues and people I had met in the
horse world over the years.

We had a little difficulty at first in getting the cooperation of
the city of Modena. The people of my home city are strange in one
way. They don't like new things or things that try to be a big deal.
They say that Signor Ferrari who brought the city worldwide attention with his fabulous cars became popular in Modena only
after he died. They were skeptical about the Pavarotti International
at first, but gradually they have come to see it as I do, as a very good
thing for the city.

We had a funny thing happen not too long ago at a public
meeting where I had gone to plead for more support from the city,
even some financial support. I gave my speech, and then the mayor
responded by saying how happy he was that I had chosen Modena
for the show, that it was a wonderful thing for the city and he
hoped it would continue for many years to come. When he finished, a man stood up in the audience and said, "Mr. Mayor, you
say you are happy the Pavarotti horse show is here, but what spe-
cifically will you do to help it? Mr. Pavarotti has said he needs
help."

I couldn't believe this wonderful man. He was saying everything I wanted to say, but did not say for fear of offending the city
officials. I swear I had never seen this man before in my life and
neither had anyone else on the horse-show staff. But his question
brought some results, and wherever he is, let me now thank him.

The countries that you must invite to an international horse
show are pretty obvious. You always want to have Britain, France,
Germany, Holland, and Italy. These are the big countries for
horses. As hosts, you must pay the contestants' travel expenses
within your country, plus the cost of bringing the horses to your
show. So most of the countries are happy to accept, but as with
most sports, the best people always have a very crowded schedule;
they barely finish one show before they have to fly across an ocean

to do another one. They might do a show in Canada that ends on a Sunday, and then they fly back to Europe on a Monday or Tuesday and have to come to Modena on a Wednesday for the first competition, which is held on Thursday.

We called the show the Pavarotti International, but during that first year, the Mexican organizers did everything. I merely gave them my name so as to bring as much attention as possible to the new show. I also arranged for the place to put on the show. The first year's show went well, but we had serious organizational problems, which led to serious financial problems. In the financial sense, it was a disaster.

In every other sense, though, it was a terrific success, considering it was our first. I enjoyed myself thoroughly and was proud to have had a major part in making the event happen in Modena. Although the organizers left us with many problems, I had been bitten by the bug and I wanted to continue. I realized, however, that if the show was to have my name, I had to take a far more active role.

In my years of following the jumpers, I have made many friends in the horse world. One of my best horse friends is Henry Collins, who is head of the National Association of Horse Show Foundation in New York and was for many years head of CSIO New York. Henry is a wonderful man and knows everything there is to know about horse shows, especially jumper shows. Henry advised me on everything and has been most helpful in my efforts to run the Modena show myself. I asked him to be on my executive committee and he agreed. When I am singing around the world, I always stay in touch with Henry to develop our plans for the next show and to hear what's happening in the horse world.

Putting together a show like the Pavarotti International is a project so huge, I don't know what I was thinking of. For many people, putting on an annual horse show is a year-round occupation, but I already had a year-round occupation. One of the most important things for a new horse event is to let the world know that you are serious about presenting a show each year. Because I am well known in another world, that was not too big a problem. The media were interested to hear that an opera singer would run a horse show, and they always gave us good publicity. As we got corporate sponsors, we were able to build more permanent facilities on the showgrounds, which we called Club Europa.

Even more important for a show than publicity is money. Horse shows are extremely expensive, and one way to raise the money is to persuade business owners to support your show in exchange for publicity. Naturally it's easier to involve business people who have a special interest in horses. We were fortunate in this way. As it turned out, many business people were as crazy about horses as I was.

In the nearby city of Parma is a company called Parmalat, which was rapidly becoming a large international company with a process they had developed for processing milk so it would stay fresh for six months when stored on a shelf, not in the refrigerator. These people were eager to make their name known internationally, and we were very happy to win their support.

We found another important sponsor in A. Testoni, a high-quality leather company in Bologna. This company was in the process of expanding to become another Gucci or Hermès. Because they wanted to publicize their name, they also gave us generous support. Our contact at the Testoni company was an attractive young woman named Silvia Galli. She impressed me so much with her ideas and organizational ability that I later asked her to be the permanent director of the Pavarotti International shows. Silvia's husband was a veterinarian, so she knew a lot about horses.

Finding sponsors and raising money were new activities for me, and I turned out to be very good at both. Henry Collins once said to me, "Luciano, I've been raising money for horse shows for years. How come you're so much more successful at it than I am? What is it you're you doing that I don't do?"

I told Henry the answer was simple: I sing.

He said, "Well, maybe I should start singing, too."

"It wouldn't be the same," I told him.

Henry would not give up. "How do you know whether I can sing or not?"

"It is something about the way you speak," I said.

Another reason I was successful in raising money is that I would promise to support my sponsors' activities in return for their supporting mine. For instance, when the Testoni shoe and leather company recently opened a store on Fifth Avenue in New York, I was happy to go to the opening to show my gratitude for their financial help. The Parmalat people asked me to make commercials for them. I think they have a very good product, and I was glad to reciprocate their generosity to my horse show.

Without the help of the Mexican organizers who were very experienced with running horse shows, I needed someone to run the shows. Henry Collins strongly recommended an Englishman, Raymond Brooks-Ward, who was very prominent in the horse world. He ran all of the big shows in England and did a lot of events for England's Princess Anne. When I met Raymond, I liked him very much. We thought alike about many things, especially about horses, and we got along extremely well. With Raymond in charge of everything, I felt confident that I could turn my attention back to my profession—singing.

Because I had not worked with Raymond before, I asked my friend Henry Collins, who knew him well and always had other business to discuss with him, to make sure everything was going along smoothly for our Modena show. Also, because Henry had been involved in setting up our show, he knew exactly how I wanted things to be. As it turned out, Henry spoke on the phone from New York to London with Raymond Brooks-Ward almost every day, and I was, as I said before, frequently in touch with Henry from wherever I was in the world. In this way the three of us kept in constant touch.

Then, in August, about five weeks before the show, I was in Italy enjoying my vacation when I received a telephone call from England with horrible news. Raymond had suddenly died. He was about to leave for Princess Anne's house and had dropped dead from a heart attack. I was completely stunned. He was such a wonderful man, and this news was very painful. But I was also upset because of my horse show. It was only a month away, and who would run it? I called Henry in New York. Because it was the weekend, I got him at his country house. All I could do was stammer out, "He's dead, he's dead, he's dead." I was so upset I didn't even think to tell Henry the name of the man who had died. But I finally got it out.

Henry was marvelous; he immediately made telephone calls to learn what had happened. He called Princess Anne's house, and they gave him the sad details, which added little to what we had heard from the beginning: a sudden heart attack. Henry came back with some encouraging news. He told me that Raymond's son, Simon, had worked very closely with his father and had, in fact, done a lot of the work on our show. Because of Raymond's well-run organization, his son was completely familiar with our operation. Henry said that Simon Brooks-Ward was willing to step into his father's place and take over the running of our show.

As it turned out, this worked very well. Simon did an excellent job, and the show went as smoothly as I could have hoped. At one point during the closing ceremonies, we gave a beautiful tribute to Raymond, but the success of the show was the best tribute. Raymond's sudden death gave me a taste of the disasters that can happen when you're running something as complicated as an international horse show. As with an opera, hundreds of people are depending on one another, but all are depending most heavily on a few people. If one of the principals gets sick, has an accident, or dies, it can be a calamity for the others. At times in my career I have gotten sick and caused a calamity for others. Now I had experienced the kind of disaster impresarios sometimes experience.

In the five years we have been doing shows, our facilities have grown a lot. The first year we had arenas for the jumping events, some stable space, and temporary stands for spectators. Almost everything else was in tents. Now the facility has grown to include two large stables, five arenas—two grass, the others sand—horse walks and paddocks, three clubhouses, permanent stands for four thousand spectators, several parking areas, office buildings, and several restaurants for light meals and snacks.

I never had any idea how expensive these shows are to produce. Henry told me that the CSIO New York now costs two million dollars—that is for each show. In Italy it is even more expensive, and of course each year we have had capital expenses as we've expanded our permanent structures. As an example of the horrible costs, we recently had to change all the dirt in the arena where the horses jump. We changed it completely—took up all the old dirt and put down new dirt. There was no other way to make it right for the horses. Do not even ask how much this cost.

In building this sports arena and compound for our horse show, we set it up as a separate business where other events could be staged during the year, where people could take riding lessons, and where horses could be stabled. This was a way of helping us recoup the cost of building the complex. There was already a very good restaurant at this location, and we incorporated it into the Club Europa complex. We call it Cesare's. If I can be a little immodest, I think it's the best Italian restaurant in the world.

Each one of the international horse shows has a distinctive characteristic, and I wanted to give mine special qualities as well. From the very beginning I did not want my show to be exclusively for horses, but a broad general celebration focused on the horse and the jumping events. I also staged art shows, commercial exhibits, and some events for children—anything to make the show more of a general fair, but all of it in honor of the jumping horses.

I think a goal of mine has always been to take my enthusiasms, whether for horses or for opera, to a much wider audience, to try to make others love these things as much as I do. One way you can reach more people, find fresh converts, is to mix things people already like with the new things you want them to consider.

From the beginning I had hoped to stage a concert in connection with my horse show. My idea was to do a concert in which I would sing with many other well-known singers from every musical field. No other horse show has a concert, and certainly not a concert like the one I envisioned that would mix opera with popular ballads and rock. I knew we had a good chance of getting such an unusual musical event televised, and that would bring even more publicity to my horse show.

Naturally I was enthusiastic about the idea of a concert because it would combine my two loves—horses and music. But even more than that, because it would be a kind of concert that had not been done before, it could further my ambition of drawing new people both to my music and to my horses. Horse lovers might hear music that was new to them, and music lovers might become interested in the horses.

I invited the great British rock singer Sting to perform at our concert. I knew him and liked him, and when he accepted, we were all very excited and pleased. We also invited two of the best-known singers in Italy, Zucchero and Lucio Dalla. I loved the idea of performing with these very popular singers. I knew their audiences and mine were completely different, but I didn't see why this had to be. I believed that if their fans listened to our concert and also heard me sing, some of them might come away with an interest in my traditional type of music. Even if it was only a hundred, or even fifty, of the thousands of rock fans who heard us, it would help break down these walls, which I so dislike. Also, some of *my* fans might decide that rock was worth listening to.

I sometimes think I was crazy to take on this horse show. Last summer from June until the show in September, we had meetings every day, often starting at 6:00 A.M. and sometimes going till three in the morning. Singing operas and concerts is already hard work. In the summer I am supposed to relax and rest up for the next season of singing. Instead, I have chosen to kill myself with a vocal competition and a horse show.

I usually manage to succeed in accomplishing everything I start. But with the second show in 1992, my habit of putting too much on my schedule got me in trouble. That was when I lip-synched at the horse-show concert with the pop singers. It was not the proper thing to do. I feel very bad about it and would like to explain how I came to do such a stupid thing. Like many criminals, I started out innocently, but little by little I got into serious trouble.

That year had been as busy as any in my career. When in the summer I finally had free time in Pesaro, we scheduled rehearsals for that year's horse-show concert. Gildo Di Nunzio was there, and Zucchero came to teach me the song he had written for me. Lucio Dalla had also written a new song that I was to sing. My part of the program was not only music I had never sung before; it was, for me as a singer, a new kind of music. I was happy to do it, but the unfamiliarity made me nervous.

I can remember going with these rock-and-roll stars to a small town near Pesaro where we rehearsed. It was a lot of fun, and I was interested in the free and easy lifestyle of these musicians with their friends and beautiful women around them. We were all professional musicians, but they were working in a different universe than I was. On an Italian hillside, theirs looked like an enjoyable universe. In that relaxed atmosphere, we recorded all of the music, and I think I sang the songs very well.

In September just before the Modena horse show, I was in London singing performances of *Tosca* at Covent Garden. There were so many last-minute problems and crises with the horse show that I was on the telephone constantly to Modena and New York. Between the horse-show problems and the problems of Cavaradossi and Tosca I had little time to think about our pop concert.

I arrived in Modena four days before the show was to begin, and I think all of the people in town except the archbishop had to talk with me immediately about their problems. It was total madness. When the important horse people began arriving, I had to perform the duties of the host. And of course the sponsors and their families expected me to spend time with them, which I was glad to do, but I was also obliged to take part in the opening ceremonies and throughout each day I had master-of-ceremonies duties. Also, I was expected to watch the jumping events I had gone to such trouble to present. But of course, I wanted very much to do this.

Throughout it all, I was becoming more and more afraid of the concert. I was not sure if I remembered the songs, and there was no time to rehearse. One other thing, usually in the days before I sing an opera or a concert, I take care of myself as if I were a sick baby. I avoid going outside, and when I do go out, I bundle up like an Eskimo. When you see a picture of me with a hat down over my face and a scarf around my mouth, I am not being mysterious or cute; I am protecting my voice.

Taking care of myself in this way was not possible during the horse show. It was necessary for me to be outside all the time, and I couldn't protect myself; I had to dress like a normal person. I say all this not as an excuse but merely to explain what led me to my bad decision.

As the time of the concert approached I remembered the recordings we had made of the program. I asked if my part could be played on the recording while the musicians and the other singers performed live. They told me that, from the technical point of view, this was no problem.

And that was how it happened. I was corrupted by fear and technology.

I was also corrupted by another thing. I was certain I could appear to be singing live. I thought I could move my mouth in time with the music so that no one would notice that my singing had been done a month earlier. This was the stupidest part of my decision. The concert was televised live in Italy, and I'm told that a four-year-old child could have seen that I was not singing, that the music was not coming from me. When they made a videotape of this concert, the editors had mercy on me and took out the places where the four-year-old saw through my fraud. For the live television version, everyone in Italy caught on.

I think every newspaper in the world wrote about the scandal. I was the O. J. Simpson of the concert world. A price of being famous is that when you do something wrong, everyone is twice as fascinated. The newspapers wrote about my crime for days. I deserved the criticism, I admit. The public always has the right to expect that when you appear in a concert, it is really you singing *at that moment*. I was focusing instead on their right to hear me sing the music correctly and well, but I understand that is not the most important thing.

I have only one complaint with the press criticism. In almost all the accounts of this lip-synching scandal, they only referred to it as "a Pavarotti concert": "Pavarotti Caught Lip-Synching a Concert." My friends in England and America and in other parts of Europe tell me that the newspapers never mentioned that it was not an ordinary Pavarotti concert. They did not write that it was an unusual concert for me, one made up almost entirely of popular music, music that was completely new to me.

I think that makes a difference, and I wish the newspapers, in their eagerness to write about this, had made that distinction. Using the recording was still wrong, I do not deny it. But it would have been far worse, in my opinion, if I had lip-synched a concert of the kind of classical music I usually sing. If I had done that, they would have been right to put me up against the wall in front of the firing squad. As it was, many still wrote my obituary.

If I had lip-synched songs from my standard repertory, songs I knew well, that would mean I did it for one reason: I was afraid I wouldn't sound good enough when I performed live. If singers could get away with that, we could all go on "singing" for years after we have lost our voices.

I have sung hundreds of times in hundreds of places since then, so I don't think anyone now believes I used a recording because I no longer had a voice. The episode is forgotten, I hope, and I have learned my lesson. But I still regret doing it for another reason: the Modena concert was wonderful in other ways, but this was overlooked because of my mistake.

Zucchero and Lucio Dalla performed marvelously, as they always do. Sting was incredibly nervous about singing with me César Franck's "Panis Angelicus"—he said I would make him sound terrible—but he was actually fine in a type of music that was different for him, and the audience loved it. Aside from how well I sang his music or he sang mine, we both created a spirit, I think, of respect for each other's music and a sense that the walls between classical and popular music do not have to always remain impenetrable. I am afraid that the scandal over my lip-synching distracted from these wonderful performances and from this wonderful aspect of the concert.

For the fourth show, in 1994, we managed to bring the British rock star Bryan Adams to sing in the concert. In making this mixture of singers and musical styles, there is usually a wonderful mood of cooperation and experimentation. Because we are all coming together from different fields, no one behaves like a prima donna. But there was one exception.

We opera singers are supposed to be difficult and give management a lot of headaches. I don't think I'm like that, and neither are most of my colleagues—only a few. But even so, I tasted what it was like to be management when I staged my concert in Modena. Most of the time, everything goes pretty well despite the usual small problems. But in 1992 a singer came who was so difficult that she made me have more sympathy for managers than I've ever had before. She was a famous French singer of popular music, but I do not want to say her name because she will accuse me of writing about her for revenge. (Besides, I can't pronounce it.) When she arrived in Modena, she did not like the hotel we put her in, so she moved to another place, and then she did not like the new one; she moved again. She changed hotels three different times in two days. She also refused to come to rehearsals: she said she knew what she was doing.

We had arranged for her to sing a song with me, and then she was to sing with one of the other pop singers. She refused to sing with the other singer and said she would only sing with me. Then she decided she did not like the song that she and I were singing and refused to sing it. She got more and more difficult until we had a big drama in her dressing room before the final rehearsal. She had just told me she wouldn't sing the duet with me, so I went to her dressing room with the manager of the horse show. We tried to persuade her, but she said no, she wouldn't do it. We pointed out to her that the programs had been printed and the show was to be televised and everybody was expecting the program to be as it had been announced.

Still, she refused. I told her I thought she was being unprofessional. She told me I was being unprofessional to ask her to sing this song. We continued to plead with her, but nothing we said made any impression. Finally she said, "I insist that you leave my dressing room."

I don't know what came over me, because I'm usually very polite; but I said I would not leave her dressing room. She had made me very mad.

Then she said, "I want to see if I understand the situation correctly. I have asked the gentlemen to leave my dressing room and the gentlemen refuse?"

We said that was correct. Then she got up and pushed past us and left the room. She went directly to her hotel, packed, and left Modena. We never heard from her again.

I don't think I have ever behaved that badly with any manager—not even close. But for whatever I have done to make a manager unhappy, God sent this lady to punish me.

9

SOME RAIN
MUST FALL

~

In one important way my life is like every other life. I
have problems, professional and personal. You think
when you succeed in a difficult profession, your worries
will be over, but of course that is not true. Your financial worries might be over, but you soon learn what a
small part of life money is—unless, of course, you have none.
Then it is everything. But once you get past financial problems
and gain a measure of security, you quickly find that many more
problems are waiting for you.

One of my biggest goals as a performer and a vocal artist is to
make people happy. I frequently get letters from people telling me
how depressed, miserable, and even suicidal they were. Then they
heard me sing on television and felt better. For maybe a few minutes they felt good about life. You can't imagine how wonderful it
makes me feel to hear such things. To be able to help, even a little,
strangers in trouble or in despair, is fantastic.

I know that many people want only that from me. They do
not want to hear that I have troubles too. But would that be a real
life? It certainly wouldn't be mine. In case, however, you are one
of those people who only want to hear the happy, upbeat part of

my life, I have put most of the bad things into this one chapter—
some of the crises, the sad things that happened, and the many
things that did not go as I wished. I have put them together in one
sacco di quai, a sack full of troubles. If you only want to hear about
happy things, the things that go well, you can skip this chapter and
move on to the next.

The worst things that happened to me were personal, mainly
the serious illness of my youngest daughter, Giuliana, and the death
of one of my oldest friends, Emilio Coughi. But I also had professional problems such as the disastrous *Don Carlo* at La Scala and the
lip-synching scandal at the concert in Modena that I spoke about in
the last chapter. These were the problems that got into the press
and I tell my side, not necessarily to make excuses for myself but to
correct some exaggerated impressions created by the newspaper
stories.

There is another reason I want to discuss these bad things.
Too often books like this become long lists of triumphs, one
success after another: "And then I had them cheering in Barcelona. . . ." These accounts become boring, and they usually tell
only part of the truth. Nobody's career is perfect. Neither is anyone's life. If a book pretends that they are, who will believe it?

First, the problem when I got booed at La Scala in 1993. For a long
time I had wanted to work with Riccardo Muti. I think he is one
of our greatest conductors and certainly one of the very greatest
conductors of Italian opera. When I was singing in Vienna in the
spring of that year, Muti was also there and we arranged to have
dinner. He told me he was scheduled to conduct Verdi's *Don Carlo*
at La Scala and why didn't I sing the title role in his production?

I was very excited with the idea. Not only would this give me
the chance to work with Muti, but this was a role I had never sung

and was eager to learn. At that time, my secretary, Judy Kovacs, was accusing me of getting lazy and was always pushing me to take on new projects, to work harder. There was unfortunately a big problem with Muti's proposal. At the time of the *Don Carlo,* I was scheduled to sing *Lucia di Lammermoor* at the Metropolitan Opera with James Levine; the contracts were signed, the cast was set, and all the plans were made.

Still, that engagement was still four months away. I phoned Jimmy Levine and told him of the opportunity I had been offered and asked if he would release me from my *Lucia* commitment. He was very understanding and agreed! Maybe what happened at La Scala was my punishment for treating the Metropolitan Opera this way.

As usual, I got myself too busy during those four months. I had many singing engagements. During the summer in Pesaro, the quiet period when I planned to study the role, most of my time was taken up with meetings about my horse show in September. I arrived in Milan for rehearsal not well enough prepared, and as a result I got into vocal trouble on the opening night.

The newspapers said my voice cracked on a high note. This is not true. I admit I did something bad—*uno strisciamento.* I don't think there's a word for it in English, but it means that the voice gets away from you, and for a note or two you sound like a chicken being strangled. But it did not happen in a top note. Those were okay. And it is on the high notes, for better or worse, that most people judge tenors.

I cannot deny it is something that should not have happened. But I say it was a result of inadequate preparation for a new role rather than the condition of my voice at that time. You might ask what is the connection between an imperfect knowledge of the score and making an ugly sound. I can hear someone asking, "If you make a mistake in the score and sing a wrong note, that doesn't mean you have to sing the note badly."

I say there is a big connection between your musical preparation and the quality of the sound that comes out. Every singer
knows this. If you are unsure of where you are going next—if you
are uncertain about the precise notes you must sing—this uncer-
tainty has a strong effect on the voice. The insecurity in your brain
becomes an insecurity in the throat.

I do not say this to excuse my bad singing that night. The
loggonisti, the people who sit in the top balconies at La Scala and
other opera houses, the people who live for opera—they were correct to boo me. They had paid good money to hear me sing. When
I did not give them good singing in return for their money, they
had every right to complain. If I want them to cheer, I must sing
well; if I sing badly, I must expect the reverse.

My only complaint is with the critics who announced this as
the end of my singing career. Such things do not happen to me
very often, thank God, but they have happened a few times since I
first started singing, and they will happen again. Some years ago an
interviewer from *Playboy* magazine asked me how many times a
year I cracked on high notes. Two? Three? I said that if I cracked
three times a year I would be world famous as a cracker.

Actually, I can honestly say that I almost never crack. If I
think it is a possibility, I do not sing. It happened, though, during
my second performance at the Met after my 1968 debut in *La
Bohème.* I had Hong Kong flu at the time and could not sing in the
top register at all. I have since learned not to sing when I am in
poor health. I learned this lesson another time when I was singing
Rigoletto with Herbert von Karajan in Munich. After the second act
I said I could not continue. Maestro von Karajan came to my dressing room and told me if I didn't continue to sing, we would have
to return almost a quarter of a million dollars. I got the message and
went back out onto the stage, but I made a bad noise in "La Donna
è Mobile."

Now, because I have this big reputation, I am not allowed to make such a mistake, not even once. Newspapers around the world told the story of my difficulty at La Scala as if my temporary vocal problem was a major international event. The critics forget that this happens to all singers from time to time and at every stage of their careers. When you are said to be one of the best in your profession, the critics act as though they never heard of a professional singer hitting a bad note, and when it happens to you, they announce the end of your career.

Fortunately, opera professionals and managers know better. I have sung in many places since the La Scala difficulty—operas at the Met, Covent Garden, San Carlo; and concerts in the United States, Mexico, the Far East, and South America. I am happy to say none of the audiences or critics in those places said I was finished. But I know that in opera, as in many professions, you must prove yourself each time you appear. Your reputation is based on your last performance, or on the performance you are singing at the moment.

Because the press makes such a big issue of my mistakes, maybe people will understand better why I am such a fanatic about the two things I can do to keep such things from happening in front of an audience: I try to know the score as well as the man who wrote it, and I protect my throat like a crazy person.

Throughout my career, the press has been very generous to me. If the critics help raise you up, they have the right to pull you down, too. In recent years, however, there seems to be a greater eagerness to do this. We live in the day of the attack. There is a certain level of success that is particularly vulnerable to attacks. Once you reach this level, you find that many people are waiting to cut you down. I know this goes on between the press and celebrities all the time, and in a way, I am flattered to be included in this process.

In interviews, you worry all the time that you are going to say something that will give the wrong idea, that you will be misunderstood. When you possess a famous name, you can be misunderstood even without saying anything. For example, I was once singing an orchestra concert in Naples in 1987. Just before going onstage, I made my usual search of the backstage area for a bent nail, which I always do for good luck. On this night I could not find a small nail, so I had to settle for the only one I could find—a large nail maybe six inches long. I put it into my pants pocket.

When I was out on the stage singing, the nail got caught in the fabric and made my pants stick out. I could see it when I looked down. I thought to myself, Good God. Some reporter is going to notice this and assume something terrible. They will write about it, and it will be in newspapers everywhere.

I don't think I am paranoid, but sometimes the press makes you that way.

Problems concerning my singing career become totally unimportant when compared to problems of health. I have heard people say that if you have good health, nothing else matters. I would add to this: as long as your friends and family have good health, too. Probably the worst thing that has happened in the past fifteen years of my life occurred when my youngest daughter, Giuliana, got very sick in 1984. One of the most difficult aspects of this catastrophe was that for a long time we had no idea of the nature of her sickness.

For almost a year Adua and I grew more and more worried about Giuliana. We knew something was very wrong with her. When she woke up in the morning she would be bright and alert, as she always was. Then, as the day went on, she would start to slur her speech. By six o'clock at night, we could barely understand her; she sounded drunk. Finally she would talk gibberish, and we could make no sense of what she said.

We had no idea what was causing this. Naturally we took her to a doctor in Modena. Our family doctor had died and this was a new doctor, a man we didn't know very well and who didn't know us. This doctor did many tests and examinations, but he remained completely puzzled about what was wrong with Giuliana. We consulted other doctors in Italy. None of them had any idea what might be wrong with her. We took her to two major neurological institutes, one in Switzerland. No one offered any ideas about what was wrong.

The problem was getting worse and worse and Adua and I were more and more frustrated and uncertain about what to do. To be more accurate, we were growing frantic. We went back to our first doctor and told him he must do something. He said that he and the other doctors had done many tests, had examined Giuliana thoroughly, and had found nothing wrong with her. They all agreed that there was nothing wrong with her physical condition.

Finally he said something that made me very angry. He suggested we take Giuliana to a psychiatrist. I was furious. I knew that our daughter was very sick with something physical, something in her body.

I told him, "I think *you* should see a psychiatrist." Then Adua and I left his office for the last time.

I was about to go to San Francisco to sing and I knew a very good doctor there named Ernest Rosenbaum. He was a big opera fan and an old friend of mine. In fact, I had met him when I first sang in San Francisco in 1968. At that time I got a beautiful letter from his daughter, who told me she loved pop music, especially the Beatles, but she also loved opera. She said many nice things including that she thought I was the greatest tenor in the world. Since she was only seventeen years old, I didn't think she had heard all the tenors in the world. Still, I was very touched by her letter, since I was not well known back then and I did not get many letters.

Also, I knew no one in San Francisco at that time and I needed company. I telephoned the girl's house and spoke to her father, Ernie. I said to this man I had never met, "Would you let your daughter meet an Italian tenor?"

He told me to wait a minute, then came back and said, "I say yes, but my wife says no." I asked to speak to the wife. Would she let me meet her daughter if she came along as a chaperon? In that way she would see that my intentions were proper.

They must have heard some things about Italian tenors, because not only did the mother arrive with the girl, the father arrived, too. That is how I met Ernie Rosenbaum and his wife, Isadora. They were protecting their daughter from me.

I had invited the family for drinks at the Huntington Hotel where I was staying. After talking for a while, we began to become good friends. We made a date to see each other again, and soon we fell into a routine. The mother and daughter would come in the afternoon and we would watch movies on my television together. Burt Lancaster was our favorite, but we also loved John Wayne. I had always been a nut for American movies, but more so at this time when I was trying to improve my English. Sometimes we went out to the movies, but eventually we were watching movies together almost every day.

Knowing the Rosenbaums was wonderful for me, like having a family in America. Because I was just learning a new language at that time, I needed friends who were patient and understanding about my bad English, so I was very grateful to have met them. To this day, whenever I sing in San Francisco, I see this family, and Ernie always treats me when I have medical problems while I am in California. He is an excellent doctor and has become the unofficial doctor for the San Francisco Opera.

When we were so worried about Giuliana in 1984, I was scheduled to go to San Francisco to sing *Ernani*. I decided to take Giuliana with me and have my old friend Ernie Rosenbaum look at her. This plan had a problem: Giuliana was very sensitive about her illness, and I was afraid to tell her the reason I wanted her to go with me to San Francisco. But if I took her to a doctor's office, she would right away understand my plan. I was afraid it would hurt her feelings; she might think I had tricked her or only wanted her along on the trip to get her to an American doctor. Her condition was now so apparent that I thought Ernie would learn a lot if he could just see her. He agreed, and I arranged for the Rosenbaums to have dinner with us one evening at Lanzoni's, a very popular restaurant near the opera house.

During dinner we talked about everything but Giuliana's illness, but all the time Ernest was observing her as a doctor. He could see that she was having trouble chewing. When she was not talking or eating, her mouth hung open. She really was not able to close it. At the end of the dinner, Ernie pulled me aside and said, "I think I know what's wrong with your daughter, but before I say anything, I want to talk to some other people and I want to look up a few things. I'll call you tomorrow."

Some time later he told me that he telephoned his brother, Arthur, who was a top neurologist and a professor at Harvard Medical School. Ernie described to his brother the symptoms he had seen at dinner and told about other symptoms I had described earlier to him, such as Giuliana's double vision and the fact that she sometimes could not swallow. He told his brother he believed she had myasthenia gravis, a rare disease of the nerves which causes a loss of control of facial muscles.

Arthur Rosenbaum thought Ernie was probably right. All of the symptoms fit his understanding of that disease. To make sure, he suggested that Ernie look up the symptoms in the standard medical textbook by Cecil and Lowe. When Arthur read about the disease and the list of symptoms, he felt sure that he had found my daughter's problem.

He called me and said, "Luciano, I'm ninety-nine percent

certain your daughter has myasthenia gravis." This disease, he told me, could be cured.

After all these months of watching our daughter fall apart, you can't imagine how Adua and I felt to know at last the problem. Then, too, to learn that it was curable made us unbelievably happy. I had always been convinced that there was something physically wrong with Giuliana. People don't develop such strong physical symptoms unless there is a physical reason. Now these medical men were saying the same thing—but, more important, they were giving the reason.

I have always been interested in medicine and enjoy reading about new treatments and discoveries. I was especially interested since Giuliana had become sick. I had some books with me, and I was able to look up this disease. As soon as I read the description, I had no doubt at all that Ernie was right. For me, the books were not describing an illness; they were describing Giuliana. I was very excited. Thanks to Ernie, we might finally be able to solve this terrible problem.

I called Ernesto back to tell him about what I had read and that I was sure he was correct. I asked him what we should do now, and he told me he would find out for me. First, he called a friend of his at the University of California, Dr. Robert Lazer, who was a top neurologist and an expert in muscular disorders. Ernie told his friend that I was in town for only a short time and that we had been going crazy for a year over this. Ernie asked Dr. Lazer if he could see Giuliana right away. He said he would be happy to.

I had to sing a concert that evening at the Hollywood Bowl and had to catch an early flight to Los Angeles in order to be there for the rehearsal. Adua and Giuliana stayed behind to see Dr. Lazer. With Ernest and Isadora Rosenbaum, they drove to the University of California, where Dr. Lazer had his office. After examining her, he confirmed that he felt quite certain she had myasthenia gravis. There was another test he said he could do, but he saw little reason to do it, especially since it was a complicated test. He was so sure that their diagnosis was correct that he didn't believe another test was necessary.

During their visit to this wonderful doctor, Adua and Giuliana learned more good news. Lazer said there was a medicine in pill form that was very helpful to sufferers of this disease. It doesn't cure the illness, but it reduces the symptoms. Luckily they were able to find this medicine at the hospital. Giuliana took some of the pills and immediately there was an improvement. She felt much better, and her symptoms were reduced to half what they had been.

She and Adua were so happy that they got on a plane and flew to Los Angeles in time for my concert at the Hollywood Bowl. I think I sang better than usual, and afterward we celebrated. That was a very happy night for the Pavarotti family. We called home to tell my parents and my other daughters the good news.

I called Ernie in San Francisco to tell him how happy I was about Giuliana's improvement. But the problem was a long way from solved. I told him he was a genius. He said he wasn't a genius. "When doctors examine patients, sometime they go to sleep," he said. "To be a diagnostician, you must be awake. With Giuliana, somebody was asleep at the switch."

I told him that many people in several different countries had been asleep at the switch, but I would be forever grateful he had been awake during the dinner with my family at Lanzoni's.

When we got back to San Francisco, Ernest brought Dr. Lazer to our hotel for breakfast and we talked for about an hour and a half. They told us there were various options for treatment and explained them all to us. The doctors said the most promising treatment was an operation in the throat. The surgery wasn't that major, they said, but it did not have a hundred percent chance of curing the disease. They also told me that the best surgeon to do this operation was in New York. I told them as soon as possible I was getting Giuliana to New York to see this doctor.

In spite of this doubt, I was thrilled that at last the problem had been located and we had a plan to fight it. Even if the operation was not guaranteed, any attempt at curing Giuliana was a fantastic step forward. We had spent a year with doctors who could do nothing more than shake their heads and watch her grow worse. Of course, I hated and feared the idea of Giuliana having an operation, but my entire family was in agony over this illness and my daughter's life was being destroyed by it.

I couldn't think of anything else except dealing with Giuliana's disease and the surgery she was about to have. It was one of those times when I was too worried to even think about singing. I canceled a performance of *Ernani* and flew to New York with Giuliana to see the doctor that my friends in San Francisco had told me about.

When we got to this doctor's office, Giuliana was given the second test to see if she had myasthenia gravis. This was the test that Dr. Lazer had mentioned but felt was unnecessary. We decided she should have the test, but this decision turned out to be a big mistake: Giuliana had a very bad reaction to the test and went into shock. Although she recovered, it was a very bad time for us all. To be honest, I was terrified, and this test going badly only reminded me of how serious her illness was and how vulnerable her condition.

By the time Giuliana finally went into surgery at Columbia Presbyterian Hospital, I was a wreck. We had not told most of our friends what was happening, but many found out, and they were wonderful—calling, sending notes and flowers. Placido Domingo came and was very concerned and called often. Placido is like me: his family is the most important thing in his life, and he understood completely what I was going through.

Giuliana's surgery went very well, and the doctors were optimistic that she would recover completely. After a few days they were able to test her to see if any traces of the illness remained. They could find none. She would have to take a certain medicine indefinitely but aside from that, she was completely cured. The operation was as successful for her as it can be for anyone.

You can't imagine how happy I was, how relieved we all were. Giuliana is now a happy, healthy, good-looking young woman. She has taken advanced courses in physical therapy and has also trained to teach physical education, as I once did. She does not like to talk about her illness and prefers to put it behind her. But I will never forget it. For a time I was convinced that my daughter was dying and that we were doing nothing to save her. That is a terrible feeling for a parent to have, surely the worst feeling.

I will also never forget what Ernie Rosenbaum did for us. Of all the doctors we had seen, he was the first to recognize her symptoms. The experience has made me a big enthusiast for American medicine, and not so big about the medicine of my native country, or of Europe in general, where no one had any idea of the real problem.

Even before Giuliana's illness I was fascinated by health and medicine. (Some people tell me I am too fascinated by my own health.) For as long as I can remember, I have read articles about new treatments and cures and have read many books about medicine. Ernesto kids me about my interest, and when I was in San Francisco one time, he got some friends of his at the University of California to work up a phony diploma, which they all signed and presented to me. It made me an honorary doctor of medicine. It wasn't for real, of course, but I called him a month or two later and told him I thought we were all in trouble: I had taken out someone's appendix and the patient had died.

~

A terrible blow to me in 1994 was the death of one of my oldest and dearest friends from childhood, Emilio Coughi. Emilio was a wonderful man. As boys we played soccer together, and we both loved music. Throughout the years we remained close. An important part of Emilio's life was Modena's Rossini Chorus, a group of music lovers who get together to sing and put on concerts. They are a marvelous group and a fine example of the Italians' continuing love of traditional singing. When I have had the time, I have sung with them. Emilio was one of the most active members of that group.

By profession he was a barber. If I could possibly avoid it, I would allow no one else to touch my hair. But Emilio was more than my barber and my close friend. He was a communications center for Modena. Adua called him the Figaro of the city because he was interested in everybody and always knew what was going on. He had hundreds of friends, and they all loved him. He was one of my favorite kind of people, always very upbeat and optimistic. Like Tibor, he was a p.p., a positive person.

When he contracted cancer, he remained cheerful even though it became clear to everybody, and I'm sure to him, that he was not going to survive for very long. I hated the idea that my old friend was dying, and I thought about him all the time. Some of my feelings were selfish. He was part of my youth and an important link to my non-operatic, non-famous life.

Every time I returned to Modena I would drop by his shop to say hello and catch up on the news. If anything interesting happened while I was away, I could be sure Emilio would know about it. After singing in Peking or meeting the queen of England, I would go into Emilio's shop or his home and I would feel like a normal person again. So I felt very bad for myself when he fell ill, but I also felt very bad for his wife and family and for all of the other people who loved Emilio.

In the last year of his life, even though I was very concerned about Emilio's condition, I made a point of not telephoning him more often than I usually did when I was away from Modena. I didn't want him to suspect that I knew he was dying. He was only in his late fifties, and his death was a terrible blow for everyone who knew him. We will all miss him very much.

We had just finally gotten over the scare from Giuliana's operation when my mother had to have surgery. For years she had been suffering more and more difficulty with arthritis in her knees. Finally it got so bad that she decided to have a knee operation. When the doctors examined her, they thought the best thing would be to operate on both knees at once. This is a major undertaking for an older woman. And it was a big thing for me, too. I had to see another member of my family experience surgery. Other people might accept operations as part of life, but they terrify me.

As with Giuliana, we were lucky with my mother. She came through the operation very well. After long periods of therapy, she's now walking. My daughter Giuliana used her knowledge of physical therapy to work with my mother a lot. Also, my father was always there to help her take her walks in those first months after the operations. She walks with a cane, but she walks very well and most of all of her old pep and sparkle have returned. She is not as lively as my father, who is older than she is, and I think this bothers her. She is very aware that she is growing old, and it makes her angry that my father, who is eighty-two, refuses to grow old with her.

Finally I, too, had to have my knees operated on. For several years I had been having trouble with one knee. The problem was growing worse, and it made walking very difficult. It was getting close to the point at which I would not be able to perform on the stage. So I finally agreed to have the operation early in 1994. The surgery helped me a great deal. I move much better and with much less pain, and my knee seems to get better all the time. People tell me that in my *Pagliacci* at the Met in the fall of 1994, I moved on the stage more quickly than they had seen me move in years. I hope to play tennis again before too long, but even if I can't, it is enough that I can still perform on an opera house stage.

10
TELEVISION, MOVIES, AND OTHER GAMBLES

D oing concerts broadened my range as a performer by a lot. Television broadened it even more. My first major television project was the performance of *La Bohème* I was part of that was broadcast from the stage of the Metropolitan Opera for PBS in 1977. This was the first opera of the Live from the Met broadcasts. It was a wonderful experience for me to sing an opera I love so much, not for the few thousand people in an opera house but for many millions of people across the country.

A short time later I did a concert of Christmas music in the cathedral of Montreal. PBS made a television show of this, and it was shown every Christmas for years afterward. I made a few other specials and appeared on talk shows. Pretty soon friends started to kid me about how often I was appearing on television. Some people said I was doing too much, especially for an opera singer, and people would get sick of seeing me. Even Rudolf Bing, who had brought me to the Metropolitan Opera, said something cruel about being tired of seeing my face everywhere.

My answer is that once you make a television show, you have nothing to say about how often it is repeated. If people see me on television, they might be seeing a show I made four years ago. If the television viewers don't happen to know this, they have the impression the show is on the air live at that moment. Well, they might think that as long as too many years have not gone by. The Montreal Christmas concert was shown for so many years that it finally became obvious to everyone that this heavy singer with the full head of hair was a much younger Pavarotti.

As with concerts, I like trying new things this way, but when I do, I always feel less sure of myself than I do when I'm performing in opera. I have been well trained in opera, coached by the best people in the profession, and I have performed on the operatic stage for thirty-five years so I know what I can do and what I cannot do. Making films is a different area, however, and I still rely on professionals to guide me. But even with people very experienced in this field, you must make sure that when they get carried away with artistic inspiration they do not make you look ridiculous.

For instance, one time when I was in Buenos Aires a European director was making a television film with me. He had heard about some singing nuns who were very famous in Argentina. He took me out to their convent and had me sing with them. This part was fine, but he brought along fog machines and he had the nuns and me singing in the fog. The effect was very strange and arty. Then he had me handing one of the nuns a rose through a screen. Was I trying to lure her from the convent? I am not sure.

Back in the city in a public park this director found a pond he liked. He put me on a boat and had me singing an aria from *Lucia.* Here again this man wanted fog. The machines were set up, and my boat appeared in the mist with my voice singing Edgardo. As far as I know, Edgardo was not interested in boats. There are no boats of any kind in *Lucia.* I finally put my foot down, but not soon enough.

I suppose my biggest mistake was my one Hollywood film, *Yes, Giorgio,* which I made in 1981. Not too long ago during a press conference, a reporter asked me about the movie and said, "Isn't it true that some of the critics were a little negative about it?"

I said to him, "You are wrong, my friend; they were *very* negative about it. In fact, they murdered me."

I agree with the critics in their opinion. The movie was not good. The humor was corny, too obvious. The character I played, Giorgio, is false, not real. They tried to make him like me, but he was not really like me. For instance, I would never do a food fight as we did in the film. I love to joke around, but I would never throw food at someone. Never. And that was a big scene in the movie. The character of Giorgio was a little like me, but only in superficial ways. He was different in important ways.

In my opinion, they should have made the character very much like me or else give me a completely new character to play. We should not have done something close to the person I am but different enough to make me seem false and phony. I think the producers had very good taste in the production, but very bad taste in the script. Also, at the time of shooting, I was very, very heavy— at my worst, I think—and I am sure that hurt the movie with the public.

In some ways, though, the movie was fun to make. Like everyone who makes movies, I had to get up very early every day and I worked long hours. But I did not have to sing, since the sound track was made separately. So the entire experience was, for me, like a vacation. Even if it did not turn out well, I'm glad I did it and that the film was made. Will I try again? I am not sure, but maybe. I have been presented with some ideas. One or two of them have possibilities, but I know one thing for sure: I will not throw food.

Some of the television shows I made have been long interviews, like the conversation I had with Peter Ustinov at my house in

Pesaro. Other times they are actual filmed specials like the documentary on our China trip, *Distant Harmony,* or the PBS show *Pavarotti Returns to Naples.* Still other shows have been a mixture of both. This was the style of the show, *The Italian Tenor.* In that I was the narrator and I sang a little, but we talked a lot about great tenors of the past and showed rare film footage of singers like Gigli, Schipa, and Caruso.

I enjoy making television films, especially the ones in which I do not have to sing, as that takes far more preparation. This was true of the Naples show because we used recordings I had already made of traditional Neapolitan songs. For the film, I only had to be photographed in the Neapolitan settings or while talking about Naples. In many shots I neither talked nor sang; the camera just showed me exploring the city. For this sort of project, I don't have the pressure of worrying about how I will sing. In fact, a week or two of work like this gives my voice a good rest.

When I arrived in Naples in May of 1987 to film that special, David Horn, the producer of PBS, and Kirk Browning, the director, had already been there for several weeks making the preparations. They had a script, which Bill Wright had written. Bill had lived in Naples for a year when he got out of the army and knew the city well. All three of them had selected the locations. I only had to show up at the right place properly dressed and do what they told me to do.

This wasn't always as easy as I hoped, however. The second morning my car and driver brought me to one of the locations they had picked. It was high up on Posillipo, the scenic peninsula on the north side of Naples, which has spectacular views across the gulf to the city with Mount Vesuvius in the background. We arrived on time at the spot where we had been told to meet the others—I always try to be on time—but no one was there. No camera crew, no lights, nothing. We sat in the car for a few minutes wondering what to do. Then Kirk Browning came running up to the car.

"Come on, Luciano," he said with the enthusiasm he always has. "We have found a terrific spot to film this scene. It is just down a walkway a few hundred meters."

I got out of the car and looked where Kirk pointed. A paved walk zigzagged a long way down the side of the cliff to a terrace over the water far below. I could see the camera crew had set up their equipment on it. I could also see lots of steps. My knee was quite bad at that time, and I was having trouble walking on level ground. Steps were a real problem. It was obvious there was no way to get a car any closer.

I told Kirk I was sorry but I could not manage all those steps with my knee.

He told me if I stayed on the paved walk, I could avoid the steps. I looked again, but could see this made for a very long walk, and returning to the car would be uphill all the way.

I told him, "If I go down there, you will have to bring me back in a basket, and then you will have to take the basket to the hospital."

Kirk was unhappy. "But, Luciano," he said, "the spot is fantastic. You can see all of Naples with Vesuvius in the background. It is the view that people think of when they think of Naples. We have everything all set up and ready to go. It will only take twenty minutes."

Couldn't we find another spot? They had looked, he said, and no other spot was as beautiful. Nowhere near. Couldn't he film the scenery, then show me looking out of the car window? No, I had to be in the setting. As Kirk and I were arguing in this way, a crowd was forming. Neapolitans are always ready for a little excitement, and some of them had recognized me. A boy on a motorbike was particularly curious and had come very close to where Kirk and I were talking. He was sitting on his bike, just watching us. I got an idea.

I turned to the boy and asked him if he would rent me his

motorbike for an hour. I would pay him 20,000 lire which was then about $12. He looked very surprised, but said okay.

Kirk's mouth hung open as I got onto the motorbike, tested the accelerator, and took off down the walkway. People think I cannot do these things because of my weight, but I am very good on a bicycle and on motorbikes. You could not grow up in Italy when I did and not be completely at home on a motorbike or a scooter. I did not go down the hill very fast, and I was extremely careful on the turns. I made the trip with no difficulty.

Someone must have gone ahead and told the others that I refused to come down. From a distance I could see how unhappy they all looked and then how their faces lit up when they saw me approaching. They looked happy and totally surprised. You would have thought I was riding an elephant from the looks on their faces. The last stretch of walkway as I approached the terrace was long and straight so they had time to line the sides and greet me with applause as I came up to them. A cameraman got a shot of me driving onto the terrace, and we used it in the film.

Kirk came running up after me and was hugging and kissing me. I was glad he was happy. I know that, because of my physical problems, I can make difficulties for directors. But I think I am very good at solving them. The car could not have gotten me to the location spot, and I could not have walked there under my own power. I only had to think of another form of power to transport me. It was easy.

I just wonder about the boy who owned the motorbike. He was not only trusting me to bring his bike back, he was trusting his bike's strength to hold up a very heavy tenor.

My schedule gave me only five days to shoot this entire television special. In spite of the rush, we had a lot of fun. The weather was wonderful, and we spent each day working at a different setting in Naples, all of them beautiful and *caratteristico*. Southern Italy in the spring, when all the lemon trees are in bloom and the sea becomes blue again, must be one of the world's most beautiful places.

Our driver was a Neapolitan man in his sixties named Giuseppe. He did not work for a company but was the owner of the old white Mercedes in which we traveled around Naples. Giuseppe was a great character, a little mad but always cheerful and talkative. Three of us rode with him every day: me, my secretary, Giovanna Cavaliere, and Judy Kovacs, a Hungarian girl raised in Vienna whom I had recently hired to help me diet and do therapy on my knee and who later became my secretary.

Very soon we all had grown very fond of Giuseppe. He told us a lot about Naples and its sad, terrible history. This was remarkable for us to hear because we could see from the car window how alive and happy everyone in the streets appeared to be—as *vivace* and *allegro* as Neapolitans are expected to be.

Bill told me that when he lived there and the weather was cold and rainy, the people looked grim and unhappy, but when the sun came out "the Neapolitans lit up like a string of Christmas-tree lights." The lights were definitely on when we were in Naples that May.

Sometimes as we drove around Naples to the different locations, I was so carried away by the beauty of the city and the magnificent sunny weather, I would burst into one of the traditional Neapolitan songs that were part of our television special. Giuseppe would always nod his head to show he knew the song I was singing, but he never gave any sign of pleasure. In fact, he usually looked concerned. Finally I asked him why he never said anything complimentary. Did he not enjoy the free concert I was giving him?

He said to me, "Maestro, you are a great singer, but you don't know how to sing our Neapolitan songs."

"Tell me," I said. "What am I doing wrong?" I knew he was being sincere, and I wanted to hear his criticism.

Giuseppe then began to sing the songs for me as he thought they should be sung. He had no voice, but he was fantastic. Of course he knew every word, and in several places he pointed out phrases where I had mispronounced the Neapolitan dialect. I wish I could say my pronunciation was the only problem in Giuseppe's eyes. He put much more emotion into each phrase than I had, he knew exactly which notes to emphasize, which to hold a little longer. His singing was a revelation to me.

These Neapolitan songs have been sung by all the great Italian tenors—Gigli, Schipa, Caruso. My favorite recording of them, I think, is by Giuseppe Di Stefano. But I know the truest interpretations are from Neapolitan men who sing in restaurants and cafés. Most of them, like Giuseppe, have no voice. And now he was confirming this for me. Because these singers do not have a beautiful sound, all of the feeling must come from their interpretation.

There is an entire school of such Neapolitan singers. They are such proud artists, they give the impression they believe that a beautiful voice gets in the way of a true interpretation, that a beautiful voice distracts from meaning and feeling. I suspect many of these men had good voices when they were young, but the voices have gone. This leaves only the passion.

It is something quite remarkable to hear, and this sort of singing goes on every night in Neapolitan restaurants along the sea, especially the restaurants of Santa Lucia in front of my hotel. Also at the restaurants in that fishing village that is so romantic to Neapolitans, Marechiaro. When these singers die, there will be no one to replace them. A great Italian vocal tradition will die with them. It makes me very sad.

Naturally, one of the scenes of our Naples special was shot at Marechiaro, which is the subject of one of Tosti's greatest songs.

Kirk's idea was to film me up on the terrace of a building over the sea yelling down at some fishermen who were setting out in their boat. Kirk had found the fishermen earlier in the day, and they were all waiting a few meters offshore when I arrived at the terrace. When I saw them, I waved down and they waved back.

Kirk explained the shot to me and told me what to say. I was to look down, see the fishermen going out in their boat and yell, "Hey, *ragazzi,* I want to go fishing with you!" I was not to say it in English or Italian, however, but in Neapolitan dialect. The dialogue man told me how to pronounce the words, and I said them a few times until I thought I was ready.

With the cameras going, I waved down at the fishermen and called out my line. They were supposed to smile and wave back at me and say things like "Why not?" and "Come on!" Instead, the young men in the boat said nothing and looked stunned. Then they all started laughing. They began laughing louder. Kirk stopped the cameras.

Other members of our crew were in a boat near theirs, just out of camera range. They rowed over to the fishing boat and asked the fishermen what was going on. It turned out that my effort at dialect came out not as I wanted. I had said, "Hey, guys, I want to piss on you." The Neapolitans like a joke, but they have their limits too.

Some of our scenes took us into the heart of Naples. When they told me to walk through an open market near the central railroad station, I went crazy looking at all the beautiful fresh fish and produce on display. The men and women selling were terrific. They all recognized me and said something friendly in greeting, but they did not make a big fuss, as some people do. They were there to sell fish, not to go crazy over an opera singer.

Bill and Kirk wanted to film a shot of me walking down the Spaccanapoli. This is the famous street, more of an alley, that slices through the heart of Naples and is full of shops and open stalls.

After the war, it was the center of the black market, and it was said that the police didn't dare enter this street. Even now it has the reputation of being a little dangerous. Kirk and some of the crew worried about our wandering around that area with expensive video equipment.

Word came to us not to worry. Our group had made arrangements with the city government people to shoot the various scenes during our work in Naples. But there was another man who was with us at every location who apparently represented another government. Because of this man, we were told there would be no problems in the Spaccanapoli or anywhere else during our stay. *Napoli è sempre Napoli.*

The last day of the shoot was in Sorrento, the incredibly beautiful town high on cliffs at the south end of the Bay of Naples. We were going to film the scenes for two songs that I sing frequently in concerts: "Torna Surriento," one of the most famous of all Neapolitan songs, and "O Sole Mio," probably the most famous of all. Our week of shooting had gone very well. I had started a new diet, and I felt I was already seeing some results. So I was feeling very good—except for my knee.

Because of this problem, it was decided I would not drive to Sorrento with the others. The trip took over an hour because much of the road winds along cliffs with many sharp curves. You cannot go very fast, and when a truck is coming the other way, you must stop altogether. If I had to stay in a car for long periods, I would not be able to move my leg, and the knee would get worse. David Horn said he had arranged for a boat to take me directly across the bay to Sorrento. It would take half the time.

About an hour after the others had left, David, Judy, Giovanna, and I arrived at the boat dock in Santa Lucia ready to leave, but there was no boat. David was very upset and tried to get an explanation from the men at the waterfront, but each person he talked to gave him a different story. The boat was broken, the owner had a family emergency, there was no fuel available. There are moments when Naples can become very mysterious. David tried to hire another boat, but no one wanted to make the trip to Sorrento. David said going by car was out of the question because it would make us very late and we could run into traffic.

I felt very sorry for him. He was paying cameramen, extras, and a large crew. All of them were in Sorrento ready to work, but they could do nothing until I arrived. We only had a few hours left to shoot because I had to sing a concert in Naples the next day; then I would leave for London the following morning. No schedule change was possible. The sun was moving toward the horizon, and we were sitting on a wharf in Santa Lucia harbor without a boat.

David told us to wait in the shade and he would see what he could do. We waited about an hour and then saw this large boat pulling into the harbor and heading toward us. It must have been fifty meters long with upper and lower decks. It was one of those party boats they use for young couples to spend an evening on the water to have dinner and dance. David was at the bow waving at us to get ourselves together. He yelled, "Party boat for Sorrento now boarding!"

We got on board and found that the boat had a bar, a restaurant, and a small ballroom. It could easily have held a hundred people, but now, with only four passengers—David, Judy, Giovanna, and me—it left immediately for Sorrento. David had telephoned ahead to Sorrento to let the others know we were finally on our way, although the boat did not seem to be going very fast. David kept asking the captain if he could go faster, but the boat was for lovers, he discovered, not for people in a hurry.

Because of all the trouble about a boat, we were very late

arriving at Sorrento. Kirk Browning and the crew had been waiting at the Hotel Excelsior Vittoria for us to arrive. We had several
scenes to shoot, and I knew they must be going crazy because I was
not there. When we pulled into the dock, Kirk came down to
meet us and said that, yes, they were all going crazy waiting for us.
He told me which clothes he wanted me to wear for the first shot
and asked me to change in the elevator that takes passengers from
sea level up to the hotel terrace. I would go up alone with my
secretary, who would help me change. Kirk and the others would
go up in the car.

I changed my shirt and hurried to close my pants. I had just
finished when the elevator doors opened. Standing there to greet
me was the hotel owner, and behind her was a big crowd, mostly
guests of the hotel who had been hearing for three hours that I was
coming at any moment. They applauded as I walked from the elevator, and a cameraman filmed my entrance. If all this had happened a few seconds earlier, it would have made an interesting
scene for our television movie: Pavarotti closing his pants as he
stepped off an elevator with his pretty secretary.

The hotel owner was an attractive lady who was very excited
to meet me. She told me she was especially happy that I had come
to her hotel because Enrico Caruso had often stayed there. In fact,
she said, she had preserved his room as a museum. I asked if I could
see it. David and Kirk got very upset and told me there was no
time. With only two and a half hours of sunlight left in the day we
had to shoot two big scenes.

I later learned that they had pleaded with the owner, and with
everyone else, not to tell me about Caruso. They knew how much
I worshiped Caruso and they were afraid if I learned this hotel was
a part of his life, I would do something to delay our work.

They were right, because I was determined to see the room. I
might not come to this place again. But before going to see it, we

got to work on the first scene, which was shot right where we were standing—on the terrace. I already had on the correct clothes, and I didn't have to talk on camera, so it didn't take too much time.

All I had to do was walk across the hotel terrace to the edge overlooking the gulf. It was a sunny day, and the vista was magnificent. There was a little haze, so you couldn't quite see Naples, but you knew it was there. You knew the world was out there, too, but from this incredible combination of mountains, cliff, and open sea, you felt it was very far away.

Then we went up to the suite where Caruso had stayed. When I saw it, I was so moved that I told Kirk and David I wanted to shoot a scene there—not singing, but just me walking around looking at the Caruso photos, the piano he played, the programs and other mementos of his career.

They got very angry with me. There wasn't time, they pleaded; the sun was sinking fast and we still had to shoot "O Sole Mio." Any more delay, Kirk said, and it would be "O Luna Mia." I promised them I would be very quick with the Caruso scene and would allow plenty of time to shoot the final scene. They agreed, and Kirk immediately started filming me walking around the Caruso suite while David and the others went down to the waterfront to prepare for the final scene.

Between takes, Kirk explained to me the plan for the next shot, our last scene in Sorrento. When I heard what he was planning, we ran straight into an even bigger problem than the sinking sun. Bill Wright's script put me out in a small boat, rowing myself alone in the bay of Naples while I sang "O Sole Mio." I knew Bill was protective of this idea because he said it was for him the ultimate symbol of Neapolitan song: the solitary fisherman out on the water making beautiful music by himself—no orchestra, no guitar, only the human voice. Months before, I had read this in the script, but that was before my knee came to be such a problem. I had forgotten I would have to get into a small boat.

There was another problem, too. The next day I was singing a concert. I was afraid if I went out on the water, I would make problems for my throat. Damp air on the throat is almost as dangerous for a singer as cold air. I didn't want to take the chance.

I told Kirk I could not do this scene. He told me I must do it. Today was the last day to film. I was leaving Naples after the concert and would not be able to come back. The scene was the climax of the film. He told me it was essential. I told him no way. The air was not warm, with the sun almost down, and being in an open boat on the water would give me a sore throat—for sure.

Kirk is usually very easy to work with. If he sees you have a problem with something, he works hard to find a way around the problem. I like to think I am the same. He usually succeeds very quickly at this, or I figure a way to accommodate him, like with the motorbike on Posillipo. But today he was different. Kirk looked at me hard and said, "You are going to get in that boat, Luciano."

This was not his style. I looked at him and said, "Why am I?"

"Because," he said very slowly, "you love me."

I knew he was kidding and that this was his way of telling me how important the scene was to him. But not getting sick was very important to me, too. When it is a question of protecting my voice for a performance, I can be very unreasonable. Many people were depending on me to sing well the next night. If I didn't protect the voice, no one else would protect it for me.

I didn't smile at Kirk or say anything. We went on with our work and Kirk filmed everything for the Caruso scene that I asked of him. But I could see he was getting more and more anxious. Neither of us said anything about what was coming up next, and I was trying to decide what to do.

I hate being so afraid for my voice all the time. My nature is to do things on the impulse of the moment—I am Italian, after all. But too many times, I have regretted very much some of my impulses that resulted in my having to cancel a performance—like the

Bohème in Buenos Aires. Still, Kirk looked so unhappy, and David Horn would be unhappy, too, and Bill would be the unhappiest of all if I would not do his scene.

I reminded myself that this television special had been planned long before we arranged the concert, which really came about after I arrived in Naples. To me live performances take precedence over everything, because they cannot be postponed, but it was not fair to use this last-minute concert to damage a film that had been planned for six months.

When we finished shooting the scene, I left the room immediately while Kirk stayed to make some close-up shots of Caruso items. I went down to the hotel parking lot and found a crew member getting into a car. I asked him if he would drive me to the port. When I got to the pier, David Horn showed me the little rowboat. He told me all I had to do was sit in the boat by the dock for a close-up shot. They had found a double they had dressed like me and would use him for the distant shots out on the water.

I love boats, though, and I love the water, so I got into the boat and told David to forget about the double, I would do all the shots. I got a cigar from my jacket and lit that, too. If I was going to take chances with my throat, I might as well have all my forbidden pleasures at the same time.

I rowed the boat a little out into the water with the cigar in my mouth. I looked up to see the car and driver they had hired for me coming too fast down the road to the pier from the hotel. It drove out onto the pier. I thought it was going into the water, but it stopped suddenly and Kirk and Bill jumped out. When they saw me in the boat, they began to run. Kirk yelled at his cameramen to start filming. I waved at him and rowed out into the open water. He shouted, *"Grazie,* Luciano. *Grazie, grazie."*

It was dark when we finally got back on the love boat to return to Naples. Everybody was happy because we had filmed everything we needed. Mitch Owgang, the associate producer from PBS, had arranged for a buffet to be served on board. Almost everyone came back with us on our big party boat.

We ate the food and drank the wine. It turned into a real party. Hanging from the ceiling was a ball with pieces of mirror on it, and someone switched it on to make it turn slowly and throw lights around the ballroom. Many in our group started dancing. I sat in the stern with Bill and David and some others, enjoying the wonderful breeze and looking at the lights of Naples getting closer. I was in too good a mood to worry about damp air.

David Horn asked me to sing something. I said no, my contract said I didn't have to sing for this special. Instead I asked him to sing. He agreed and sang a Frank Sinatra song, "Strangers in the Night."

"Not too bad," I said, "Now it's my turn." I sang "My Way."

David responded with "Foggy Day," and we were off on a Sinatra duel. We each had to get through one chorus of the song and not miss any of the lyrics. The first person to miss a lyric was the loser. This was easier for David, as he was born in America. For me English is a foreign language—but I still won. Frank Sinatra is a friend of mine, but that was not why I won the duel. I am older than David and I knew all these songs long before I knew Frank. I learned Sinatra before I learned English.

It was still over a month before this television special was finished. In New York, David and Kirk spent many days editing the footage. I was told that they had to return to Naples to take more background shots. Finally Bill Wright and Kirk Browning flew to Pesaro to show me the finished film. As we sat down in my living room and put the videotape in my VCR, I could see they were both anxious about my reaction.

In general, the film was wonderful. Most of these Neapolitan songs are so familiar that it is hard to build a film around them and avoid seeming too obvious. But I think Bill and Kirk succeeded in making something fresh and interesting. The shots of Naples were spectacular, and I didn't look too terrible as I walked around the streets and parks.

Only one thing bothered me: the opening sequence. It was the song "Chista Paese de Sole" (This is the Land of Sun). Bill had constructed the scene from the song's introductory lyrics about a man returning to Naples after many years and getting more and more excited as his train approaches the city. Kirk had filmed me on a train looking out of a window at beautiful views of Naples—the landmark buildings, the bougainvillea, the lemon trees, the bay with Capri in the distance.

I didn't know what it was exactly, but something about the scene bothered me very much, and I said I wanted to cut it from the film. Kirk looked as if he wanted to kill himself—or me.

"But why, Luciano? That scene is one of the best."

I told him I didn't know why, but it just didn't seem to work. He explained that the film was just the required length for a one-hour special. If we cut anything, there would be a big problem. I would have to return to Naples to shoot something else to fill the gap. I told him I wouldn't be free to do that for a year and a half. We were getting nowhere, but I knew that scene was not as good as the rest of the film.

I told Kirk and Bill to go have lunch in a restaurant while I thought about it and looked at the scene again. They went off and I played the opening sequence two or three times. Then it came to me why I didn't like it: I did not like the way I sang the song.

Maybe it was something my driver Giuseppe had told me or something I had picked up just being in Naples. But my rendition of that exciting song sounded false to me. I also realized that for the film we had used a recording of the song I had made for London Records long before we shot the special. I had approved the recording at the time and it had been released. I knew it wasn't fair to hold up the film just because I had changed my idea of interpretation.

When Kirk and Bill returned, they looked grim. They told me later the lunch had been miserable. Neither had eaten much or spoken much.

"Cheer up, *ragazzi,*" I said. "The film is okay. It's just I don't like my singing in that scene, but it won't be the first time."

11
THE ROAD
TO SINGAPORE
~

When I go on concert tours to foreign countries, there are always problems and inconveniences. No matter how beautiful and luxurious the hotels, they can never be like your own house, where your television set is exactly where you want it and you know where every pan and pot sits in the kitchen. But there are also many wonderful aspects to traveling the world, even when you move from one place to another very quickly, as I do. The good things more than make up for the small inconveniences.

First, for me, is always the people. I genuinely love people. And with my tours, when I am always seeing differences—strange clothes, unusual customs, exotic traditions—I realize more and more how similar we all are. I see this when I meet the people directly, but I also see it when I sing for them. I thought that if any people were truly different, it would be the Chinese. Not only are they Orientals, a completely different race, but they live under a strict Communist government. This makes their way of life profoundly different from ours. But when I sang "O Sole Mio," the Chinese turned out to be just as Italian as I am.

They say music is a great leveler, that it brings us all together. I say that from the start we are all level and together. Different cultures and different traditions push us apart and make the differences more pronounced. Great music is the opposite. It finds and brings to the surface the qualities that all humans share. For me, the most beautiful thing about singing around the world is the proof I see that in important ways humans are the same. If I sing a concert in Portland, Oregon, a few days later in Mexico City, then in Lima, Peru, I experience a great similarity in the way the audiences react. I get the same feelings and emotions, the same thirst for something beyond the everyday events of their lives.

I know some people will say, "Yes, but this is entertainment you are talking about. The differences that you can see are about more important things—customs, traditions, nationalism." I say that maybe those things are not more important. What I am receiving from these audiences—the flood of emotion at music and beauty—maybe that is more important. Whatever part of these audiences is responding and making me connect with, that part might be more basic to our human character.

I know very well that some aspects of human nature are not so wonderful, but I work with music, and music makes people happy, so I see mostly the wonderful aspects. Fortunately there is enough of this goodness, and it is so powerful that it makes me less afraid of the bad and allows me to be more optimistic about the future of humanity.

Seeing all these different people around the world as one people, this is for me the best part of touring the world. But there are many smaller pleasures as well. When I travel to interesting new places, I have the opportunity to see wonderful things I would never see at home.

For instance, when I was in Lima, I was taken to the home of a wealthy Italian, Enrico Poli, who has a fantastic collection of Peruvian art. Most of the art is from the Inca civilization, but he also has other ancient artworks that date from before the first Europeans. There are magnificent gold pieces—vases, weapons, plates, jewelry—with beautiful designs and fabulous workmanship. To be in a room with these treasures, to be able to hold them and admire them, it was an amazing experience for me. You cannot see these things in a museum, I do not believe. You must be in Peru and you must be admitted to this collector's home. I feel very fortunate to have visited him.

So you see, when I travel the world I don't only look at horses.

When I arrive in a new country, there is often much publicity about my concert. Asian and South American countries, for example, are always excited to receive European and American artists. The newspapers write a lot about our visits, and the television news programs film our arrival, our rehearsals, and so on. Often I am given the opportunity to meet important people in these places and I am sometimes entertained and treated with great honor.

When I was in Peru, for example, President Alberto Fujimori invited us to have lunch at the Presidential Palace in Lima. Herbert Breslin, Tibor Rudas, and Nicoletta also went to the lunch. It was very nice—good food and relaxed conversation. But I sometimes worry that such honors are wasted on me. I know nothing about Peruvian politics and very little about the country and its problems. While I was sitting there eating with the president, I kept thinking how many people who lived in Peru would like to have this opportunity to sit and talk with their leader.

In Peru my concert was held in a racetrack. This was the largest place that Tibor could find. When I first heard this plan, I was afraid of Tibor's imagination. I worried he might ask me to sing from a truck going around the track so everyone could see me. Tibor does not have bad taste like that, but sometimes he gets carried away with his enthusiasm, and I have to stop him.

When I travel on a tour for Tibor Rudas, we usually go in a private jet, which is, I confess, a wonderful way to travel. In our group is my secretary, Nicoletta, and a number of people from the Rudas organization. In the 1995 South American tour there was our conductor, my old and good friend Leone Magiera, and a wonderful young American soprano, Cynthia Lawrence, who comes from Colorado but now lives in Minnesota. Cynthia was one of the winners of our Philadelphia vocal competition, and she is already having a good career in America and Europe.

Also in our traveling group are our driver, Martin, who also acts as a bodyguard, and Thomas, who looks after our living arrangements. Thomas makes sure that the hotel is all right and that the management has placed in the rooms the things that we need, like mineral water, fresh fruit, and other food items because I like to cook for myself. That is the only way I can stay on my diet; if I must eat in restaurants, I am finished. Thomas makes sure there are the basic items: arborio rice, Parmesan cheese, butter, fruit, mineral water, and maybe some chicken.

When we arrive in a new city, two of Tibor's men, Shelby Goerlitz and Ian McLarin, have already been there for a while making sure that all of the arrangements for the concert have been taken care of. They do a lot of the preparation a long time before the concert, either by telephone or during earlier trips. Even so, they always arrive in the city several days before I do to make sure all of their plans have been carried out as they wished. By the time I arrive, everything is done and I don't have to worry about anything except singing.

Throughout South America on our 1995 tour, the crowds were incredibly enthusiastic. In some places the enthusiasm was so great that I could not leave my hotel. One time I rebelled against being a prisoner. I made a plot with our driver, Martin, to sneak me out of the hotel so I could do some shopping in private.

We planned to do this without telling the special police who had been assigned to accompany me whenever I went out. This was the local government's idea; in fact, they insisted on it. It is very nice they want to take care of you so well, but security men can cause problems themselves. For instance, when the local people see these security men in the streets, they know somebody interesting is behind them and they rush to see who it is. Immediately you find yourself in the middle of a big crowd. The security men are supposed to protect you from crowds, but they often help create the crowds.

I do not want to have a Pavarotti festival every time I go out my door, but that's what happened in South America. I tried to figure out a way to go out into the city without the guards all around me. In the different hotels I stayed in, these uniformed men generally waited for me in the lobbies. As soon as they saw me get off the elevator, they jumped into security action.

I very much wanted to go out in one city like a normal person. So we made a plan. To avoid the guards, Martin, Nicoletta, and I left the room and went down a back staircase used only for fires, I think. We succeeded in arriving at the street without the security guards knowing I was gone. For a few minutes I felt free. But it was only a few minutes. When we went into a shop, our plan failed. We were only there a very short time—we had not yet bought anything—when the guards came rushing in.

I don't know who told them I was in the shop, but they found out right away. They were very upset with me that I had not told them I was going out. Of course, when they came running into the store, very excited, crowds of people came running in behind them and hundreds more were waiting outside. I surrendered to these uniformed men like a criminal and returned to the hotel without buying anything.

In other countries when I attract crowds, I think maybe some of the people are just curious; they want to see this tenor that others are making such a fuss about. Maybe they don't even know there is a tenor and are curious about anybody who makes other people curious. But in South America, the crowds' reaction was too strong to be called curiosity. They went a little bit crazy with their affection.

It finally reached a point where I thought maybe I should stop feeling grateful for this enthusiasm and start to worry about the danger. One day in Chile we went to the horse races and the situation got very bad. As we were walking from the car to our seats, the crowd pressing in on me became so passionate and excited that I was, for the first time, really afraid. I had heard about people being crushed to death in crowds that got out of control at rock concerts and football games. I was afraid that was going to happen to me. Usually I don't mind the inconvenience or the delays when many people come out into the street to see me, because I appreciate the affection they are showing. Also, it makes me happy to see the great thirst people have for music, sports, art—all the things that a few people do well enough to excite the others.

Generally, I am not afraid, even in very large crowds. I know these people have come to show their love and that they wish me no harm. Because of this, I feel uncomfortable about all the security and bodyguards the governments in South America believed were necessary. One time during our 1995 tour, we were driving through the downtown of one city—I won't say which one—and the security guards were riding in the car in front of us.

Now, I know these men all carry guns, small automatic rifles, and I understand the need for them with all of the political unrest and perhaps terrorism that exists in some of these countries. But the truth is, I hate guns. They frighten me. They are ugly machines that can make a beautiful life end in an instant. Although I understand the security guards' guns were there to protect me, I still dislike having these terrible weapons around me.

Once when we were driving to a rehearsal, all of a sudden the car carrying the guards stopped very suddenly. We stopped also, and so quickly that we all got thrown from our seats. The security men jumped out of the car with their guns. I don't know what caused their excitement, but they were circling around our cars pointing their guns in every direction, even toward us! I didn't know what was happening, but I thought they were going too far. It was actually very frightening. I opened the window and yelled at them to stop, to calm down.

They didn't like me interfering in their work, but I didn't like having loaded guns pointed at my face. Martin jumped out and spoke with them, and they got back in their car. He told them not to point their guns at me anymore. They said they would try not to, but they said we did not understand the situation in their country. They were under orders from their superiors to do whatever was necessary to protect me. Their attitude was that they were going to save my life whether I liked it or not. I still don't know what upset them so. Maybe they jump out of the car like that every once in a while for practice.

One other thing besides guns makes me nervous. That is elevators, especially old elevators. I have a terror of getting stuck in an elevator. Once on an earlier tour of South America we were taken to a rehearsal hall. It was an old building, and we were put in a large freight elevator that should have been in a museum as an exhibit. It started up and went slower and slower. I said to Martin, "This elevator is not moving. We must do something."

He said, "No, Luciano, it is just moving very slowly."

Then the elevator stopped between floors. I started yelling for help. Right away it started up again, moving very slowly. We got to our floor. When we got off, all the security guards were there with their guns out. They had heard me yelling and thought somebody had attacked me. I got off the terrible elevator, but I was immediately facing my other fear: loaded guns. There is a lesson here, I think, about one fear producing another, but I don't care. If the elevator stops too soon, I yell.

Some of the problems on that tour, I caused myself. The worst was in Chile when I spoke to an enormous crowd and said how happy I was "to be here in Peru." A roar went up from the thousands of Chileans, but it was a roar of laughter, thank God. They understood that I was moving quickly around South America and sometimes didn't know where I was. Bad as that was, I don't think I make mistakes like that too often.

In exotic foreign countries, you must be ready for anything. Some form of Montezuma's revenge—Pizarro's revenge, the Incas' revenge, somebody's revenge—is always waiting for you in the food or water. Even though we try to be careful about this, it usually gets some of us. In Bogotá toward the end of the tour, I found I could not breathe. The city is very high—over a mile, I think—and I got so out of breath that they had to give me oxygen. Not during my concert, thank heaven.

Sometimes when I am driving through a foreign city, very nice things happen. In Mexico City they had given me an enormous black Mercedes, which Martin was driving. As we passed through a poor section, I saw a little boy on the side of the road selling bread. He looked so small to be selling things—not much more than five or six—that I was moved. And maybe I was also hungry. I asked Martin to stop the car and to give me some local money. When the little boy walked over to the car, I put down the window, held out the money, and reached for the bread. When the boy looked at me, an amazed expression came over his face and very slowly he said, *"Pavarotti!"*

It is wonderful to have a stadium full of people shouting your name. It is also nice when the country's president invites you to lunch. But this little boy, so poor, with a dirty face and so incredibly *young*—to find that he knew who I was meant more to me than anything.

I like to shop when I am traveling in different countries, but I must be in the mood. Even if I am in the mood, I don't shop like a normal person. Very often the impulse to buy things comes over me without warning. And I sometimes grow very attached to these impulse items. One time I saw a Hermès scarf I liked very much in the Paris airport. It was incredibly expensive, but I bought it and wore it every day for years. My secretary at that time, Giovanna Cavaliere, knew how much I liked this scarf, and she washed it for me every night in Woolite. I was desperate to have that beautiful scarf clean and waiting for me every morning.

I remember another bizarre shopping experience I had that was, in a way, typical. I was making an American Express commercial in New York, and it was being filmed in Abercrombie & Fitch, a store I had never visited. It was down in lower Manhattan near Wall Street. The store's management and the film people wanted us to be in the store in the evening after the customers had left. Because I was performing at the Met, we didn't go until midnight when not only the store was empty but so were the streets.

As soon as I was inside this wonderful store, I saw many things I wanted to buy, terrific sports clothes and other beautiful things. At that hour, of course, the cash registers were closed, but the manager was very nice and didn't seem to mind opening them up for me. I bought so many things that I think I drove the film people crazy with my shopping madness. I don't shop often, but when I do, it is often in unusual circumstances like this.

Frequently I see things I want when I am driving. I don't

know why this is, except maybe I am not thinking of a hundred other things when I am looking from the window of a car. Or maybe because it's one of the few times I am not in a hotel room or a concert hall, places where there is no shopping. When I get a glimpse of the normal world, I want to buy a piece of it.

One time I was driving to the London airport and I was in a hurry. As the car passed through a neighborhood at the edge of the city, I caught a glimpse of some fabric in a shop window that looked as if it might be incredibly beautiful. I had the car stop, and I went up to the window for a better look. I was right. I had never seen a fabric like it. The store was open, and I bought enough to make myself two caftans. I still made the plane and left England very pleased with myself.

I am not always so lucky. When I want a particular item, I always have that item in the back of my mind. I owned a pair of low-neck boots which I had bought in London. I liked them very much for both style and comfort, better than any shoes I ever had. Because I wore them all the time, these wonderful boots were almost finished after a year and I wanted to buy several more pairs. I was unable to remember exactly where I had bought them, so when I returned to London to do a recording with Joan Sutherland for Decca Records, I looked everywhere for the boots. I went to all the stores I remembered going to before, but with no success. I was very frustrated.

One day when we were not recording, I had been invited into the country to visit a friend. A car and driver had been sent for me, and I was riding in the back of this large Bentley with my secretary. The car passed through a village, and in the center of town there was a shoe-repair store. I have very good eyesight, and in the store window I saw the exact pair of boots I had been searching for.

I told the driver to stop the car. Giovanna said I was crazy. How could I know if they were the same boots? I told her I was certain. Then she said, "But, Luciano, it is a repair place, and the shoes are probably not for sale."

"Then why do they put them into the window?" I asked her.

She said she had no idea, but she insisted this was not a place that sold shoes. I am stubborn, I know, but so are the people around me usually.

I got out of the car and went to the store. I was right. The boots were exactly what I had been looking for. They even appeared to be the right size. I was very excited, but was horrified to find that the door was locked. This was unbelievable because it was late morning on a Thursday. I may be an opera singer, but I know that every store is open on Thursday. Giovanna pointed to a sign that said: Closed Thursdays. Once again, she told me to forget about the shoes.

She was asking too much of me. I was so close to the boots, just inches away, and I wanted them so badly. I knew I would never see them again. This may sound childish to you, but then, you don't know how most shoes hurt my feet.

I peered into the dark store and thought I saw a light in the back. I felt sure someone was there. We knocked for a while, and finally a man came to the door. He opened the door only a little and said the store was closed. I explained that I was from Italy and would not be back this way for a long time. I told him that the shoes in the window were the exact ones I had been looking for for weeks. Were they for sale? He said yes! Even more amazing, they were the only pair he had and they were my size.

But the most amazing part is still to come. He said he could not sell them to me. Why? Because it was Thursday. Can you imagine? I offered to pay him double. He wasn't interested. Nothing we could say would make this man change his mind. Is there a religion that celebrates Thursday? We were totally frustrated.

In the end, I got the boots, but if you think I persuaded the man to change his mind by singing for him in the street, you would be wrong. I am always determined to get what I want, but I am too serious about singing to use it in such a way. Also, the man did not ask me to sing. My method for getting the boots was much simpler. Before driving away, we wrote down the address, then, back at the hotel that evening, Giovanna wrote the man a letter with a check. He mailed the shoes to me in Italy.

Even though I now make plenty of money, I still have habits from the days when I was poor. For example, I hate to waste anything. Over the years, I have driven my secretaries crazy by insisting that when we leave one place and go to another, they pack up and bring the food we did not eat. I don't do this too much on a fast tour like the 1995 circle around South America, but if I am going to remain in a place a long time—that is, as much as a few weeks—I love to stock the refrigerator with twice as much food as we need. When we are ready to leave for the next place, there is always food left over. I hate to leave anything behind.

Several times this has placed me in trouble. One time we were returning to New York from Europe as part of one of Tibor's tours. We were in a private jet, but the customs people at New York airports are too busy to bother with private planes, so it was necessary for us to go through customs in North Carolina. The customs people in New York see me so often, they know me and know I am not a criminal. The officials at the North Carolina airport, however, were not so sure.

As we waited in that airport to take off and complete our trip, I couldn't understand what was taking Nicoletta and my other assistant, Larisa, so long. They were in another room talking to the customs people, and I was trying to sleep on the plane, but I was anxious to get to New York and into a real bed. It turned out that the customs people were curious about two large cardboard boxes that were taped shut. They asked my two assistants what was inside the boxes.

Larisa, who also is a masseuse and works on my bad knee, told them the box contained her massage equipment. The men told her to open the boxes. When she did, they could see that the boxes were full of food. When the inspectors saw all the fruit and vegetables we had brought from Europe, they went crazy. We didn't know it, but you are not allowed to bring even one apple from Europe into America, and we had two large boxes of this type of food. They were even more unhappy about the meat that we had brought, mostly prosciutto and salami.

The customs men got very angry. One of them picked up a pear and said, "Do you know, young woman, I can fine you $100 for this?" He was talking about $100 for *each* pear, and we had maybe two dozen of them.

Nicoletta was terrified and said the food was not theirs. Larisa helped her and said she was completely surprised to see these things and that she had no idea how the food got there. Trying to help the customs men solve the mystery, she said the food must belong to people in the Rudas organization, maybe Mr. Rudas himself. These clever women are very loyal to me. Tibor has his organization and I have mine.

Nicoletta and Larisa's plan did not succeed. The customs men took all of our food away. Since what we did was against the law, we now know, they were really quite nice about it and didn't fine us. Before letting my assistants go, however, the customs men gave them a lecture about bringing dangerous bugs and diseases into the country. I really was not aware of that danger and felt bad that maybe I was bringing a new plant disease into a country I love very much. I am not that well informed about these things. When I look at a peach, I see only a peach.

It's not just fresh food that can get you into trouble with customs inspectors. Sometimes I carry with me food items that I am afraid I will not be able to find in other places. That is particularly true when I leave America, because so many of the wonderful new products don't arrive in other countries for years. One of these is powdered cream for coffee, which I like and think is very convenient. I bought a lot of this product and poured it into large plastic jars, which I thought would be safer and would travel better.

I don't have to tell you what the customs inspector thought he had discovered when he saw this white powder. He believed he had captured the biggest drug criminal since Manuel Noriega. The inspector must have been new to this business, because when he tasted the powdered cream substitute, he *still* thought it was cocaine. I couldn't believe it. Maybe he didn't really know how cocaine tastes and was just pretending that he did. Whatever he thought, he became very excited and made a big fuss. It took a long time to convince him I was not transporting dangerous drugs. Apples and pears are one thing, cocaine another.

There is always some catastrophe or adventure when I travel on concert tours. One of the worst happened when I started on my Asian tour in 1994. For some days I had been having trouble sleeping. Usually, I am a very good sleeper and sleep longer than most people, but at this time I was unable to go to sleep. The long jet trip across the Pacific made the problem worse. Also, I think at that time I was coming down with the flu or perhaps a cold. When I made my Metropolitan Opera debut in 1968 I was almost destroyed by Asian flu, so it seemed only fair that I should now bring American flu to Asia.

After crossing the Pacific and before starting the concerts, we stopped on the island of Bali for a few days' rest. Even with nothing to do on that beautiful island, I was feeling worse and worse—and not getting a normal sleep. With the concerts approaching, I began to panic.

Tibor is as concerned with his health as I am with mine, and he always has lots of pills with him. He also is very interested in my being rested and in good voice for my concerts. Seeing my problem, he offered me some sleeping pills that he had brought with him and that he said were very special and effective. In desperation I took his pills, and it was a total disaster. I slept for three days, and even after that I could not stay awake.

It was terrible. One night we had to go to a performance of ceremonial Balinese dancing. The performance had been arranged just for me, and many important people were present. I kept falling asleep—right in front of everyone. It was a disgrace, but I could not help it. Nicoletta would punch me to wake me up, but as soon as she forgot about me and became interested in the dancers again, I would go back to sleep.

The same thing happened the next day when we went to a big luau that was given in my honor. It was incredibly beautiful with exotic flowers, huge platters of food, and flaming torches. I was seated next to one of the most important men in the islands. As this distinguished gentleman was talking to me, I kept falling asleep. At this party, Nicoletta was sitting across from me. She saw what was happening, but she did not want to make a scene and interrupt when the important man was talking to me. The poor man was talking to a corpse and didn't know it.

I was aware I was sleeping in front of him, and I kept waking up. I also knew it was terrible of me, very rude, but I didn't know what else to do. The only other thing I could have done was to have gone to my hotel room and slept. That was what I wanted more than anything, of course, but that would have meant getting all of my group to leave as well, since we had only one car. If I had done that, it would have totally disrupted the beautiful feast and been even worse manners. I was miserable—and I don't think I made my hosts very happy.

When the concerts began, I was able to sing, but for the first part of that trip I did not feel healthy. It wasn't a full case of flu, but I could not stay awake, and I didn't feel right. It was like a long sleeping-pill hangover that would not go away. In Malaysia our hosts were sympathetic to my problem and sent me a Chinese doctor, a man they recommended very highly. As it turned out, he was quite wonderful, both as a doctor and as a person. He gave me some-thing that made me feel a lot better. And I stopped falling asleep at dinner.

While we were still in Malaysia, I had some days free between concerts. A very rich man invited me to be his guest at a resort he owned on an island in the Indian Ocean. There was nothing on this island except the hotel, and that meant no doctors. This wor-ried me, because I still had not completely recovered from those sleeping pills and my own illness. In case I should get sick again, I asked my Chinese doctor to come with us, and he said he would be happy to have a few days off.

The first bad thing happened when we arrived at the airport nearest the island. Our host had arranged for a helicopter to take us over to his island. I must explain that I am very afraid of helicop-ters, worse than elevators, which at least have some cables. In fact, I try never to fly in them, and I tell the Rudas people who make our travel arrangements, "No helicopters."

I don't think I am unreasonable about this. It is bad enough I am always in airplanes, but I try to draw the line with helicopters. I read about too many accidents. Also I hate what they do. You are sitting on the ground, and then you go straight up. You hang there in the air for a few minutes as if you are deciding whether or not to drop back down again. Finally you move off to your destination, but by that time I have already turned to jelly. That is one of many reasons why I don't want to be president of any country. It would mean flying in helicopters.

The resort was wonderful, though, quite luxurious even though it was simple and rustic. The private island it was on was very wild and beautiful, mostly dense jungle with wonderful birds and flowers. We were told that a tiger lived on this island. Our doctor told us that the Chinese have an ancient expression: "One hill, one tiger." He explained that the expression is talking about the ecology, that one hill has enough food to support only one tiger.

This worried me. Surely when the hill tiger needs company, he can go down into the valley. What does a tiger on an island do? He must get very lonely. And that probably puts him in a bad mood. I was thinking about this island tiger's bad mood when Nicoletta insisted we go for a walk. They had some roads into the jungle from the hotel, and everybody said that if we didn't go too far we would be safe. I can assure you, we didn't go too far.

Our host had given our party adjoining bungalows away from the main buildings and surrounded by jungle. The rooms were very comfortable, with large beds covered with mosquito netting. After an excellent dinner with our friend, I went to bed. There was a beautiful scent of flowers in the warm air. I think it was jasmine. Sometimes flowers with a strong smell can give me problems with my throat. There is a certain kind of lily that I react to very badly; roses, too, can affect me. The wrong flower can destroy my ability to sing. So I must be very careful about flowers.

But I knew this wonderful smell was not the kind to give me trouble. I lay there listening to the jungle noises outside—birds, beetles, four-legged animals—but it didn't bother me or make me worry that one of the noisy animals was going to come into my room. It is bad enough to be afraid of flowers; I was not going to be afraid of animals too. I lay there surrounded by rich natural beauty. I had gotten over my scare from the helicopter ride and my fear of the tiger. I felt very much at peace with myself and with nature. I went quickly to sleep.

About six o'clock I woke up. I generally sleep soundly for a long time, especially after those pills, but I was very thirsty and I think that is what woke me up. There was a small refrigerator in my bungalow, so I turned on the light beside my bed and went into the kitchen to get a drink of mineral water.

To my horror, on the floor beside the refrigerator I saw a snake. It was not a huge snake, but not tiny either—maybe two feet long. He was moving very slowly along the floor, so I knew he was alive.

Now, more than helicopters and tigers, I am afraid of snakes. I admit I went into a panic. I was lucky I didn't have a heart attack. The snake did not come toward me, so I very quietly backed away from him until I reached the telephone. I picked it up and dialed very slowly so I didn't upset the snake. The man at the front desk who answered had a British accent. "How may I help you, Mr. Pavarotti?" he said cheerfully.

"You must come quick," I said, trying not to scream. "There is a snake in my room."

"What color is it?" he said, now not so cheerful.

"Black and yellow," I told him.

I understand that in emergencies such as this, it is the job of the hotel people to calm down the guests, even if the problem is serious, so I was prepared for him to play down this snake. I couldn't believe what he said instead.

"Good God!" he yelled. "That's the worst kind! They are very poisonous. Don't move. I'll send people right away!"

I called Nicoletta to tell her what was happening, but told her not to come because the snake might bite her. When she said I was exaggerating the danger, I elaborated a little on what the desk man had told me. "Nicoletta," I said, "this snake is so poisonous, he just looks at you and you die!"

A number of people from the hotel arrived with snake sticks. They looked everywhere in the room, but they couldn't find him. They said he must have gone back outside. I insisted they continue looking everywhere—in the closets, under the bed, in my shoes, in the shower—any place a snake might hide. Finally, I was convinced the snake had gone away, but I was a nervous mess.

The hotel people were very apologetic and said that it was most rare for any type of snake to come into the rooms, but especially this super-poisonous guy. I guess what they said was true. Otherwise, they would not have too many guests returning—or leaving either, maybe.

I phoned Nicoletta again and asked her to come to my room to help me make it snakeproof. She thought I was being ridiculous, but I made her help me put towels under all the doors, shut the windows, plug up any place a snake might find a way into my room. Finally I went back to sleep, but this time I was less enthusiastic about beautiful nature.

I managed to have a good time the rest of my visit, but I never stopped worrying about that black and yellow snake. Any time I saw anything on the ground that was either black or yellow, I thought, "There he is again!"

To enter my bungalow I had to walk across a veranda that separated two parts of the building. The central section of this veranda was open to the sky. Each time I returned to my room, I didn't want to walk under this open part because I was afraid the snake was waiting up there to jump down on me. Nicoletta told me I was being foolish.

"If you are so sure I am foolish," I told her, "then you walk first in case I am also right."

On the 1995 South American tour we had some problems finding good hotels and restaurants. I'm sure they have plenty of excellent ones, but we were unlucky more than once. And the worst was the last city we visited, a Chilean city—not Santiago—and the food was terrible. Not only did it not taste good, it made us sick. Everybody got sick. Then when we left Chile to fly north for my Miami concert there were too many people on the private jet and we all felt like survivors on a life raft.

When we finally arrived in Florida, for the big concert on the beach scheduled for January 22, 1995, my friend Judy Drucker, who lives in Miami and who was organizing the concert with Tibor, met us at the Miami airport and took us to the place she had arranged for us to stay. It was Fisher Island, a very exclusive resort island in Biscayne Bay quite close to Miami Beach but separated by water. You must take a little boat to get there; they are not allowed to build a bridge because all of the big ships sail in and out of Miami harbor through this water. But because people want to go back and forth all the time, every fifteen minutes a ferry goes across with people and their cars.

We crossed the channel and drove our car from the ferry into a fantasy. We were entering a different world of tropical perfection—beautiful broad lawns with palm trees, a golf course, a lake, and the ocean in the background. The buildings were far apart and all built in a tasteful Spanish style. I told people how beautiful I thought the island was and said it must be the island where Bill Wright lived in the winter. Herbert said I was wrong. Bill lived in Key West, which was one hundred miles away.

Fisher Island is not exactly a hotel, more a complex of luxurious condominiums and villas, some of which are available for rent, even by the day, which makes it like a hotel. Frank Weed, the manager, had provided fifteen of these suites for our group. My villa was spectacular, a low building right on the ocean. Outside the glass doors there was a broad terrace. From there, you could walk on a lawn for a little way and the open ocean was right there.

My living room was large, with a fantastic view of palm trees and ocean. It had two pianos, a Yamaha grand for playing and an antique upright for looking at. The room had fresh flowers, baskets of fruit, oil paintings. Everything looked shiny and new. I went into the kitchen and found the most modern appliances that looked as if they had never been used. I opened the cupboards and found all of the pots and pans I needed to cook my risotto.

I was very pleased at how beautiful and organized everything was. This place was the opposite of what we had been finding in South America. Then I opened the refrigerator and saw that Judy had filled it with food—fruits, cheeses, all of the things I like. I was overwhelmed and went out into the living room where Judy and the others were waiting to see how I liked my Miami home. I threw out my arms and sang full voice: "God bless America . . ."

12
ON THE BEACH

~

Judy Drucker is one of my oldest friends in the United States. I have known her since my first appearance in America when I sang Donizetti's *Lucia di Lammermoor* with Joan Sutherland for the Miami Opera in 1965. That was thirty years ago. Unbelievable! The tenor who was scheduled to sing Edgardo in this *Lucia* had canceled at the last minute, and they were desperate for someone to replace him. Joan Sutherland and her husband, the conductor Richard Bonynge, had heard me sing at Covent Garden. They liked my singing very much, and Joan was also pleased that I was taller than she was.

But Miami wasn't interested. They wanted a well-known tenor to sing opposite the world-famous Joan Sutherland. I was just starting out in Europe, and no one in Miami had heard of me. No one anywhere had heard of me. Joan and Rickie worked hard to persuade them to give me a chance. When every other tenor had turned them down, the management had no other choice and decided to hire me.

I didn't know any of this until Bill Wright started researching our first book to help my memory. All I knew was that I was in Europe and got a phone call from Miami asking me to come to sing for them. Believe me, at that point in my career, I didn't worry very much about *why* they called me. I was thrilled and pleased.

When my Miami debut was a success, no one remembered that they hadn't wanted me. Joan Sutherland was too nice to tell me how she struggled to get the job for me. But she told Bill, who insisted we tell the story accurately. That is how I found out. I did not want to seem ungrateful to the people who hired me in Miami, but I think the true story makes an important point. It shows how hard it is for unknown singers to get the opportunities that are so necessary. Even with a great and respected singer like Joan Sutherland pushing for me, I still was given my first chance to sing in America only because all the established tenors were unavailable when Miami needed a replacement.

At the time, I didn't care why I was offered the job. It was a wonderful experience. You can't imagine how exciting this was for me to make my first trip to America to sing in a masterpiece opera opposite one of the great sopranos of all time. Everything was new and interesting to me—the tropical climate, the beautiful city of Miami, the overhead highways, the mixture of Cuban and American people.

Looking back now, I now laugh at my ignorance. For instance, coming to rehearsal one day, I watched members of the chorus arriving in the parking lot. I could not believe the expensive cars: Cadillacs, Lincolns, Mercedes, even a Rolls-Royce. In Italy I could not afford any car at all until I sang my first lead in an opera and began getting other jobs as a soloist. And that car was the cheapest one of all—a Fiat 500 or, as we called it, a *topolino*.

I said to someone, "I've never seen so many beautiful cars. Do they pay chorus people so much in the United States?" They told me that the chorus was made up of volunteers. Many of them were lawyers, doctors, and business people. Chorus work paid them nothing.

Even though I spoke very little English, everyone was very nice to me and I had a fantastic time. Because of this wonderful introduction to America, and because the city gave me my first opportunity here, I have always had a special feeling for Miami.

We worked very hard on *Lucia,* and during the rehearsals I became friendly with some members of the company. That was when I met Judy. She had studied voice at the Curtis Institute in Philadelphia and was singing in the chorus for our opera. She was very lively and enthusiastic and loved to laugh—all things I like—so we became friends. And we have remained friends for thirty years.

As I was building my career as an opera singer, Judy was building a reputation as an impresario, one of a very few lady impresarios in the United States. She brought some of the world's top artists, including Vladimir Horowitz and Jascha Heifetz, to perform in Miami Beach. When I became well known in America and could fill a concert hall, I was happy to be one of the artists that Judy brought to her city as part of her concert series. I have sung many concerts in Miami for Judy over the years, and it has made me very happy to watch her have one success after another.

Early in 1994, long after I had started doing big concerts, Tibor Rudas and Herbert Breslin told Judy about Tibor's idea for a very unusual Miami concert. This concert would not just be *in* Miami Beach; it would be *on* Miami Beach. Yes, Tibor wanted to do a concert right out in the sand. His plan was to do an event similar to the Hyde Park concert in London. He would sell seats in the front, but in the open space behind those seats, on the sandy beach, anyone who wanted could sit and listen for no cost. They just had to bring a blanket.

He also had the idea to do the concert at four o'clock on a

Sunday afternoon, which is an unusual time for a concert to begin. We would start in the daylight when everyone could see the beauty of the Miami Beach oceanfront hotels and the ocean itself. As the concert progressed, it would grow dark, and there would be a completely different effect. I'm telling you, Tibor is fantastically creative.

Tibor had already discussed the idea with me, and I liked it very much. I liked especially the idea of many people being able to come for free. Tibor estimated that about 150,000 people could see the concert, but he would sell tickets to only about 5 percent of those people.

Please don't think I have anything against selling tickets. I understand the need for this. Someone must pay for the stage, the lights, the orchestra, the chorus—even the tenor. But I dislike that so many of my performances in opera houses and concert halls appear to be for rich people, for the elite. Except maybe for my voice, I am not part of any elite and I don't think that way. The cost alone of live performances makes them for a financial elite. I know how much they must charge for tickets to an opera at the Metropolitan or Covent Garden. That is why I like very much doing television. I can reach all of the people, whether or not they have money.

But live performances are very expensive. They become more expensive each year. Tibor's idea seemed to find a way to solve the problem. He would make enough money to pay for the concert by selling tickets to people who wanted to sit in chairs close to the stage, then let everyone else sit on the beach right in the sand and hear the concert at no cost. Tibor is a genius. Most people have to deal with the realities of a situation. Tibor is not limited that way. He creates his own reality.

In January of 1995 when I was flying around South America singing concerts in opera houses and concert halls, I would hear little bits about the preparations going on in Miami Beach. I would hear these things from people in the Rudas organization who were traveling with us, and sometimes Judy would phone me to tell me how excited she was about all that was happening.

The concert would be on the beach at Tenth Street, which is in the middle of Miami's South Beach section where all the restaurants and sidewalk cafés have appeared in the last few years. The beach is very wide at that place, and there would be space for our nine thousand folding chairs and room left over on either side for people to sit free of charge. Tibor and Judy would use the same stage that he had built for the Three Tenors concert in Los Angeles. I asked him if he was going to ship the waterfalls, too.

"We don't need waterfalls in Miami," he told me. "We've got the ocean."

The stage was enormous—big enough to hold a full symphony orchestra, a huge chorus, palm trees, other decorations—and three tenors. There was only one problem: Zubin Mehta liked the stage so much that he had borrowed it for a big outdoor concert he was doing in Bombay with the Israeli Philharmonic. But there was time enough to get the stage sent by ship from India to Miami after he was finished with it. I liked this idea of a concert stage traveling across the oceans, going from one huge audience to another.

Then Judy called me sounding very upset. Environmental people in the Florida government had told her she was planning to put the folding chairs too close to where the turtles make their nests. I was fascinated to learn that some turtles make babies and have their families on Miami Beach. Later, Judy said the problems had been solved by moving the seating areas a little.

Judy phoned me again awhile later and said, "Boy, Luciano, your friend Tibor really takes care of you."

"What do you mean?"

"His people phoned me today with the dimensions your trailer must be. The living room must be so big, the bathroom so big . . . Really, Luciano!"

"I am glad to hear it, Judy," I said. "Do you really want me to get stuck in a tiny trailer when a hundred thousand people are waiting to hear me sing?"

During those weeks before going to Miami, my mind was completely on the concerts I was singing in South America. As we went from Peru to Chile, from city to city, however, I was hearing more and more about the preparations in Florida. I heard that the construction people in Miami had found it necessary to place a plywood floor on the beach for the nine thousand folding chairs. The wood alone cost $50,000. Incredible!

Judy said that was nothing. There was to be a dinner after the concert, which would also be held on the beach. The tent for the dinner would cost $80,000. The reason it was so expensive was that they needed to construct steel supports under the wood floor to hold the weight of the tables, chairs, and people. The dinner would be a fund-raising event for Judy's Concert Association of Florida. A wealthy Brazilian developer, José Isaac Pères, had offered to pay the cost of the dinner, which was at least a quarter of a million dollars.

That meant all of the money Judy took in by selling places at the dinner would go for her concert series. Mr. Pères also offered to allow the dinner to be held on the site of a condominium development he is planning to build on the beach, which he calls Il Villaggio. All this money floating around being spent on the concert must surely have been good for the city and for many people who work there.

The next thing I heard from Miami was that the city officials insisted that Judy and Tibor hire lifeguards to be placed along the beach between the spectators and the ocean.

"Can you believe this, Luciano?" she said. "The officials think people will become so excited by your singing, they will throw themselves into the ocean and drown."

She was making a joke, of course, but Judy was thrilled by all the new things that were happening and was getting more and more excited as the beach concert approached. So was I.

Then the city decided that the streets near the concert could not possibly handle all the cars that would come, and there would be no place for people to park. They set up a bus and jitney service from parking lots all over the area—not just in Miami Beach but also in Miami, which is several miles across the bay. People would park their cars at one of these lots and take a bus to the concert. The streets of South Beach would be closed to traffic so that the buses could arrive at the concert area with no problem.

With the lifeguards, the parking lots, and the traffic strategy, it was obvious that many, many people were giving a lot of thought to this concert. They were all working hard to make possible a musical event in a totally unusual setting. Because this had not been done before, they had to anticipate all of the things that might go wrong, and to create new ways of avoiding problems.

I got another call from Judy while I was in my hotel in Santiago, Chile. "Well, I have your stage, Luciano," she told me. That day she had gone down to the Miami docks where the big ships come in and had claimed the stage. She told me she said to the men at customs, "That's my stage. Give it to me!"

When they put the stage together and were setting it up on the beach, the engineers predicted trouble. They believed that with the orchestra and chorus, the stage would sink into the sand. Judy called Tibor, who was in California, and told him they had a crisis. Something had to be done to hold up the stage and stop it from sinking into the sand. Tibor disagreed. She was worrying too much, he told her. Judy tried to convince him there was a problem, and they argued about it. Judy told me Tibor finally yelled at her. "I staged the Three Tenors concert in Dodger Stadium and you're telling *me* about stages?"

The best thing was when Judy called to tell me she had spent all day "auditioning" portable toilets.

"Which was the winner?" I asked her.

"Oh, it's one called the Crowd Pleaser," she said. "It has eight stalls and is air conditioned. It's fabulous!"

The company did not have enough Crowd Pleasers, though, so she also got seventy-five Porta Pottis. Judy told me she was now an expert on outdoor toilets and they didn't teach her anything about this at Juilliard.

The last week before it was time to fly north, I began to think I was already in Miami because of all the reports I was hearing about the concert preparations. But when we all got sick in Chile, we could think of very little else.

Everything bad went away when we arrived in Miami, however. As soon as we all had a good sleep in the beautiful quarters Judy had found for us on Fisher Island, we got back to normal health and began enjoying ourselves. On my first day in Florida I did little but rest and go over the concert program with Leone Magiera. But I soon had harder work to do. Tibor had arranged a press conference, and also we were holding auditions for my Philadelphia vocal competition.

Judy had set up the audition in the Dade County Auditorium, which is a good distance from Fisher Island. It also serves as Miami's opera house—until Judy builds the new one she is planning—and it's a good place to judge voices. Many voices that sound beautiful in a smaller space could not succeed in a large auditorium. This location for our audition had an even greater

significance for me. It was the same theater where I had made my
first appearance in *Lucia*.

As I walked down the aisle to the desk that had been set up for
me in the middle of the auditorium, I thought how strange it was
that thirty years ago I had stood on that same stage about to sing
and be judged for the first time by an American audience. Now I
was sitting on the other side of the footlights, about to judge young
singers just starting out, as I was then. It is the memory of my own
struggle for recognition that is my motivation for the vocal competition.

Sitting in this Miami theater in January 1995, I felt this motivation with great power, because I remembered all the terrible fear
and hope I had felt when I first walked out onto this stage—the
same hope and fear these young people waiting backstage were
feeling now, I was sure.

As the singers began, I did what I always do: when they finish
their arias I try to give them a word of advice, perhaps ask them to
sing something different. Sometimes I do not make any comment
at all, and merely thank them and go on to the next singer. People
have asked if no comment means I do not like the singer. Not
necessarily. It only means I do not hear anything wrong or anything I think I can improve. I have selected many singers for the
next level of competition without saying anything but "Thank
you." Usually, however, I try to give a word of advice or encouragement. I want them to be glad that they came to the audition.

When Jane Nemeth held preliminary auditions before I arrived in the city, she had asked for help from two wonderful operatic singers from the Metropolitan Opera who now live in the Miami
area: the great baritone Thomas Stewart and his wife, the top soprano, Evelyn Lear. They agreed to help Jane screen singers, and I
understand the three of them worked very hard for a day listening to
dozens of singers from all over Florida and from other southern
states.

They did a sensational job. As I listened to these young people, I couldn't believe how many good ones there were. Years ago, when we first started the Philadelphia competition, I told my old friend Emerson Buckley, who lived in Miami, that I wanted to have auditions in his city. "What for?" he said. "There are no singers there."

Well, Emerson is gone now, but he would admit, I am sure, that he was wrong. I was fascinated to hear that many of the promising singers auditioning for me that day were students of Emerson's widow, Mary, who had sung at the Metropolitan as Mary Henderson.

Jane and I have noticed that certain places in the world have better vocal talent than others. This usually means that there is a very good coach in that area, someone who knows how to get the vocal talent out of the singer so the rest of us can hear it.

I think it took about three hours to listen to all the singers. As they sang, I gave each of them a grade. I knew that any singer graded above a certain level would be invited to the semifinals in New York. I called them all out onto the stage, and the twelve young men and women lined up along the footlights. I told them I would call out the names of the ones who had been selected to go to New York. As I looked at them all standing up there, I thought to myself how brave and wonderful they were.

I called out the first names, and I could see the others reach out to shake their hands and throw them a smile. I read the next name, then the next. With my terrible English I had trouble pronouncing some of the names, and I must admit that I was exaggerating my difficulty to add to the suspense. Finally after the fifth name, I said, "And all the rest!"

You see, without even looking at my list, I knew each one of these fine young singers had a good enough grade for the invitation. But I thought it would be more fun to make them anxious for a few minutes longer. Or to say it the other way, it would not have been fun to say, "Everyone is invited. Good-bye." Also, for young singers to stand up there on the stage wondering if their names would be called is, I know, an agony. But such agonies are part of a singing career. The more experience you have with them, the better off you are.

The next day was Saturday, one day before the concert. I asked Bill Wright to come to my hotel where I would cook him lunch. Bill had arrived the day before from New York, and I had seen him at the vocal competition, but we did not have a chance to talk. When he arrived at my villa, we sat out on the terrace for a while enjoying the warm sunlight on the ocean in front of us. Then we went into the kitchen so I could start cooking the risotto. Bill complimented me on looking well. "Why not?" I said. "I have lost weight, and I feel wonderful."

Bill told me about all the preparations for the concert. He had gone to the beach to watch them building the stage and setting up the lights and sound system. "They are rebuilding Dodger Stadium right there in the sand," he said.

He said that while he was there, a number of small airplanes had flown along the beach with signs saying "Welcome, Pavarotti," and then the name of a hotel or restaurant. I could see these planes from my terrace, and it made me feel very good. I have a wonderful life, but airplanes don't say hello to me every day.

Bill told me that all of South Beach near the concert site would be closed to parking and traffic, that all of the bars and restaurants along the ocean had agreed to quiet their music, and that the airplanes coming into Miami airport would be told not to fly over the beach. Fifty refreshment stands were being set up, and a hundred extra police would be in the concert area.

Everywhere he went in Miami and on Miami Beach, Bill

said, there were large posters for the concert. He also told me the mayor of Miami Beach had said on television that he thought the concert would be the most important event in Miami Beach's history! Not just cultural event, but any event. I couldn't say these people were not enthusiastic. I was very pleased and interested to hear what Bill was telling me, but of course it made me nervous, too.

When we sat down to eat lunch, Nicoletta joined us. She and I told Bill about the concerts in Peru and Chile. As we were finishing our food, Herbert arrived to take us to the orchestra rehearsal, which was being held in a hall at the Convention Center. Herbert had already eaten lunch but sat with us at the table as we talked.

Suddenly, I felt very strange. Something was not right. I said to the others, "I don't feel well."

Bill, Nicoletta, and Herbert looked as though I had said "I am now going to kill myself." Well, maybe not Nicoletta. She is very calm and has heard me complain so many times that she doesn't react. Instead, she waits quietly to see what I will say next. I told them I was not joking; I really did not feel well. I asked Nicoletta to bring a towel to put around my shoulders. With the towel around me, I got up from the table and went to sit on one of two sofas that faced each other. Bill asked if I wanted to be left alone to rest, but I told him no. We had to leave for the rehearsal in a few minutes.

Bill and Herbert sat on the sofas facing me and didn't speak. I closed my eyes and prayed that whatever was going on inside me would pass. In my mind, I saw an airplane fly over Miami Beach with a banner that said, "Don't Get Sick, Pavarotti!" Then I think I went to sleep for a few minutes, and soon I heard Nicoletta telling me it was time to go. I got up and put on my jacket and scarf and went to the car. I still felt very strange, but I couldn't say exactly what was the matter.

When we got to the rehearsal hall, I walked into a large room in which they had packed the entire Florida Symphony Orchestra and the University of Miami Chorale. Judy told me that the parents of these student singers were flying in from all over the country to hear their children sing with me. As I entered, they all applauded and greeted me warmly, which made me feel not as sick.

The rehearsal went very well, but I sang only mezza voce as I usually do for rehearsals. On the high note at the end of "O Soave Fanciulla," however, I sang full voice to make sure I was okay. The note sounded pretty good. I was in good voice and good spirits—I just wished I didn't feel so strange. It was like having a huge sword hanging over my head. And to make things worse, I felt the sword was hanging over the city of Miami as well. They divert the air traffic for you, go to so much incredible trouble, the whole city is waiting for you to sing. What do you do? You get sick.

At the rehearsal, when we got to "O Sole Mio," I was feeling almost normal again. In the second verse, when I am quiet and the orchestra plays alone for a few bars, I stopped Leone Magiera and said, "Why not have the chorus sing here?"

Everybody looked confused and worried. Someone told me that they had not rehearsed this song and did not know it. I told them, "Of course they know it. Everybody knows it."

Then they said, "But they don't know the words in Italian."

"Well," I said, "just have them sing la-la-la. It's the music that is important."

The chorus did what I asked and seemed to love it—they were all smiling—but I think it upset their director. He wanted to make copies of the words and give them to the singers so they could learn them by the next day. I did not mean to upset this man, but the song sounded so pretty and natural with them all singing. I don't like doing everything in a fixed and rigid way. Also, this little variation in our program had helped me forget about how I was feeling.

When the rehearsal ended, however, I still felt bad. I went

into the dressing room they had given me, and I asked for Herbert and Judy to come in. I told them how bad I felt. Because I was having pain in my chest, I was frightened. When you are as heavy as I am, you must always worry about your heart. Judy said she would get me a doctor.

With Judy at the rehearsal was a prominent Miami attorney, Stanley Levine, who sits on her board. He said he knew a very good doctor, Stuart Gottlieb, who is one of the city's best. They made the phone call. Because it was Saturday afternoon, Dr. Gottlieb was on the golf course, but they got him right away. Thank God for cellular phones and beepers.

When the doctor agreed to meet me at my villa, I insisted he not tell anyone where he was going or whom he was going to see. In addition, he should not carry a doctor's bag, but instead carry whatever equipment he needed in a beach bag or a briefcase. I didn't want anyone to know that a doctor was entering my villa. Because of my fears about my heart, the doctor said he should bring a paramedic and an EKG machine. I said all right, but that the paramedic should not wear a uniform, just normal sports clothes.

The media were already writing so much about the concert the next day, and I thought how excited they would be if they thought I had been taken sick and would be unable to sing. Things going wrong are more interesting to newspapers than things going right. I wanted to get over whatever this was without causing a big sensation.

We returned to my villa on Fisher Island, and I got into bed. The doctor arrived not only with a paramedic but also with his wife and the assistant fire chief for Miami Beach. Dr. Gottlieb checked me for everything. I told him I had pains somewhere between my stomach and my chest and was either having a heart attack or indigestion. "It feels like the whole world is sitting on me."

"Are these pains unusual?" he asked me.

I admitted to him that they were not so unusual. "Look at me," I said. "I love to eat."

I told the doctor I also believed I might have a fever. The doctor had forgotten his thermometer, so I told him to touch my face. His wife was standing next to my bed and said, "I am a mother. I'll kiss your forehead."

She gave me a long kiss then said, "A little bit warm."

The doctor agreed I had some fever. He was sure my problem was a mild flu and said he would give me antibiotics. I told him I had my own antibiotics, which he said were all right with him. He also gave me something for stomach upset. I had no trouble going to sleep and slept well.

The next morning I woke up and immediately remembered I had to sing an important concert that day. Then I remembered that I had been sick the day before. How did I feel? I asked myself. I checked my chest, my stomach. No pain at all. I couldn't believe it. I felt terrific. I immediately called Dr. Gottlieb to tell him, and to thank him. In addition, the sun was shining and there were no clouds.

I, of course, did almost nothing until it was time to drive to South Beach, where the stage had been set. Some weeks before, I had asked Judy what she would do if it rained. Without any hesitation she said, "Kill myself." The weather forecast had said it would be cool for this time of the year but it would not rain. The rain, the forecast people said, would come the next day. That seemed to me to be very close to today. I would have felt better if they'd said the rain would come next month.

But the day was incredible. It was only cool in the shade; in the sun where the audience was sitting, it was perfect warm Florida weather. But I had to sing in the shade, and I was afraid I would get sick again. That can happen. You go out on the stage feeling fine; then during the performance you start to feel bad. You never know when the bad feeling will hit you or how fast it will take over.

So I decided I would dress very warm. This meant I could not wear the traditional concert clothes of white tie and tails, even though I knew Leone and the orchestra and chorus would be in formal clothes. Also Cynthia Lawrence, the soprano, had bought a very nice long white dress especially for this concert. I wore an all-weather parka, a Gucci woolen scarf, and a porkpie hat. I knew that these clothes were absurd for a concert performance, but staying healthy enough to sing the entire program was more important than looking proper.

When I went out onto the stage I faced a sight I will never forget. An incredible crowd of 9,000 people sat on folding chairs in front of me. Beyond and to either side of them was a crowd of 100,000 to 150,000 people who would watch the concert for no charge. It looked like a sea of people as far as I could see, and to make it even more dramatic, right beside this huge crowd was the real sea. The stage pointed north, so the sun was behind me and lit up this amazing sight and made the ocean a vivid blue. In the front row I could see Tibor, Herbert, Bill, Judy, and Nicoletta. I had been told that the governor of Florida was coming and the Nobel Prize winner, Elie Wiesel. Also, Sylvester Stallone was there and Gloria Estefan.

The crowd greeted me warmly, and I gave back my usual greeting by throwing my arms high in the air. When the crowd finally went silent, I felt I should make some explanation for my strange clothing, so I made a gesture like I was cold, pulling my collar up and hugging myself and said into the microphone: "It's cold." The audience applauded and cheered.

When I began my first aria, I knew my voice was all right and the concert would go well. I was so relieved to be in good voice, and also so relieved not to be sick, that I think I sang better than I usually do. And the audience seemed to feel this too.

Cynthia sang marvelously, as she did throughout our South American tour. It is always fascinating for me to hear the audience reaction to a very good singer they do not know. At first they are polite, but not very enthusiastic. I understand this. After all, they have come to hear me, not a soprano they have never heard of. But it is the same as when you introduce a friend to other friends. Because they like you, they want to like the new person. But they are not going to do this right away. They wait until they have listened to the new person for a while. With Cynthia, after her second aria, the applause was fantastic.

We finished the first half with the end of Act I of *La Bohème*. I sang "Che Gelida Manina," and Cynthia sang "Mi Chiamano Mimi" and we did the duet that finishes the act, "O Soave Fanciulla." My high C at the end felt so true and secure that I think I held it longer than I was supposed to. The crowd was very happy, Cynthia was very happy, I'm sure Tibor, Judy, and Herbert were very happy, but I was happiest of all.

After the intermission, the sun was almost behind the hotels on the waterfront, and twilight fell as the concert's second half progressed. The light became more and more beautiful, especially over the ocean. The scene was so fantastic that I found it difficult sometimes to keep my mind on the singing. As the sun went down, the stage lights came up. This changing light added a wonderful visual drama to the music. Cynthia, Leone, and I and the others were working hard to make our kind of beauty while nature was working right along with us to make her kind of beauty.

In the second half we got away from the Italian repertory for a while when I sang Franz Lehár's "Yours Is My Heart Alone" and Cynthia sang another Lehár song, "Villa," from *The Merry Widow* and "My Man's Gone Now" from *Porgy and Bess*. I brought us back to Italy with two arias from *Manon Lescaut*. By the time we got to the encores, it was completely dark and almost as beautiful with the lights from the restaurants and hotels along one side and, on the other, the spotlights making long reflections on the ocean. When I sang "O Sole Mio" as my second encore, the chorus sang their part as I had requested, but only with "la-la-la." It sounded terrific and I don't think anyone noticed they were not really singing the words. I guess the singers were afraid of the Italian pronunciations and preferred singing la-la-la correctly rather than the Italian words wrong.

After I sang the last encore, I put up my arms to silence the crowd, then gave a little speech to say what an incredible occasion this concert had been for me. I wanted to thank the entire world, but I thanked the city of Miami Beach for inviting me and making it possible to do the concert on the beach. I thanked Judy Drucker and the Rudas organization for planning and executing all the difficult arrangements. And I thanked the audience for making me feel so welcome. Then it was over.

As I came off the stage, there were already so many people in the backstage area that it was difficult to reach my trailer dressing room. Sylvester Stallone had sent word in advance that he wanted a few minutes alone with me after the concert. That was fine with me, but I knew many people would be waiting to come to greet me and would want to come in. For Stallone, that was no problem. He had his bodyguards stay outside and protect us while we talked.

The after-concert dinner Judy arranged was done in the same spectacular way Tibor does concerts. The tent was lined with what looked like white silk, and there were even chandeliers. Each table had a tall display of flowers with a fat, bearded man in the middle wearing white tie and tails. This gave the people of Miami a chance to see how I look when I come out on the stage properly dressed.

There were about eighty tables for the patrons and a long table that was raised up a few steps for me, Judy, Tibor, the governor of Florida, the mayor of Miami Beach, and various other dignitaries. I spoke again very briefly and so did Judy, the mayor of Miami Beach, Judy's board chairman, and José Pères, the host for the dinner.

After a day when everything had gone amazingly well, something now went very wrong. Immediately after the concert, Tibor got mad at me because I had not thanked him personally from the stage. He was so angry that he would not come to the dinner. When Bill interviewed Tibor the morning after the concert for this book, he heard a lot from Tibor about what a terrible, ungrateful person I am.

I felt very bad about that, because the entire concert had been Tibor's idea from the beginning. Also, he was the only one who'd had experience staging events on this scale, as Judy willingly admits. Tibor had told Judy what needed to be done and she had done it very well, but he was the one who knew and understood how to create these enormous outdoor events. I'm sure Judy could do it on her own next time, but the first time, she needed Tibor's experience.

So he should get the largest portion of the credit and thanks for this concert and he was right to be angry with me. Thanking a person's organization is not the same as thanking the person. My only excuse is that it is difficult to say everything exactly as you should when you are speaking without notes to many thousands of people. I was glad that Tibor forgave me after a few days. I think he knows how I really feel.

Tibor certainly got appreciation from one person, if not from me. Backstage at the end of the concert, the mayor of Miami Beach ran up to Tibor and said to him, "You must forgive what I am about to do, but you have done so much for our city, I must do it." Then the mayor grabbed Tibor's head, pulled it down, and kissed him on the forehead.

The morning after the concert, Monday, January 23, we woke up and packed our suitcases to leave for Rio de Janeiro. Judy came to say good-bye and gave me a beautiful Gucci scarf as a present. I had no feeling of bad health and was ready for the long flight to South America. It seemed we had just arrived in Miami, and then I was looking down on it from the air as the city got smaller and smaller. Then there was nothing below us but ocean.

When we were settled in our hotel in Rio—Ipanema, actually—Judy phoned to say that the chief of police for Miami Beach had gone on television to say there was not one arrest during the concert, not one misdemeanor, and not one instance of drunkenness. He said this had never happened for a large concert in public. I think that if you bring 113 extra policemen to an event, you expect *something* to happen.

Judy also said that the people sitting in the sand reached back for half a mile. Instead of the usual beer and pretzels, they had brought wine and cheese—maybe because I am Italian. Also, the people cleaned up after themselves. The sixteen trash collectors Judy hired to clear the beach the next day did not have much work to do. Not only was there no trouble, but at the back of the audience, far up the beach where people were so far from the stage they couldn't see much, the crowd during our singing was absolutely silent. The papers wrote about this the next day.

Judy drew a wonderful conclusion from this. She said that the crowd's beautiful behavior proves that the arts have a civilizing effect. That is one of the things I like so much about Judy. She thinks and reflects about what is really going on. She knows that with an event like our concert on the beach, more than just a concert is happening. Judy is a philosopher.

She is very happy about another thing. She told me that the city of Miami Beach believed she was the one who got me to come—which is partly true, even though holding the concert on the beach had been Tibor's idea. To show their gratitude the city had named February 15 Judy Drucker Day. Fantastic!

Bill also phoned to say that Miami was still high from the concert and that the entire city was trying to recover, to get back to normal. He told me, "They've stopped thinking about Hurricane Andrew, Luciano. Now they talk about Hurricane Pavarotti." I'm just glad I didn't stay sick, thanks to God or Dr. Gottlieb.

13

MY WONDERFUL
FAMILY

~

When I am interviewed, I am frequently asked about my personal life. On television especially, you don't want to refuse to answer, as that can sour a conversation that many people are watching. My way of dealing with questions I think are not too polite is to joke about them. For instance, at a press conference in Miami, a reporter raised her hand and asked me, "Mr. Pavarotti, is it true that you are divorced and available?"

Now, I am not stupid enough to misunderstand that question. I know I am often seen in the company of pretty women, and I flirt with every woman I meet, from seventeen to seventy. At the same time, I've been married for many years. I said to the reporter, and to everyone else, "I am not divorced, but I *am* available." That was not what she expected me to say. I suspect that she asked her question in order to confuse me, so I tried to confuse the reporter.

One question about my fan mail is asked frequently. There is a rumor that many women write offering to make love with me. I think maybe this is a fantasy journalists have about famous people. A reporter asked if it was true that I get as many propositions as a rock star. I said, "If I do, then I feel sorry for the rock stars." I was being a little coy, actually. Sometimes I do receive such letters, but they are not often so bold and obvious.

A woman might write that she loves my singing so much that she would do anything for me in return. Now, "anything" can mean many things. If I telephoned to accept her offer in an improper way, the lady might be horrified. Or she might say that lovemaking was exactly what she had in mind. I don't ever plan to find out which she meant. In this way, it can remain a matter of sweet mystery.

Others are always pointing to the attractive young secretaries I usually have with me. It is true that I like having women around me. If they are intelligent and good-looking, that is all the better. When I grew up, there was nothing but women around. I was the only little boy in the sixteen families in our apartment building, and the men were off working all day. The women all made a big fuss over me, so from as far back as I remember, I was the king of my own private harem. It is a very nice way to live, and I am afraid that I got used to it.

In a sense, I owe everything to women. So many have been important in my life—my mother and sister and my wonderful grandmother, Giulia. Adua, of course, and my daughters have always been central in my life. But in my career, many women have been extremely helpful. Mirella Freni showed me that a young person from our simple background could make a success in the world of international opera. Joan Sutherland taught me so much about singing and Joan Ingpen brought me to Covent Garden, which gave me my start in major-league opera.

Another reason I like having women around is that I believe women generally have keener sensitivities than men. For an artist, that is important. Women are quick to understand. They know what is on your mind without you telling them, and in the performer's high-pressure world, that is most valuable.

Women also protect you. A man might feel that because I am also a man, I do not need protection. But this is not true. Women see this right away. When they see that you need protection, they protect you like crazy. Women won't let anyone get at you or hurt you. For protection, I'd pick a woman over a man any time.

For a man like me who relies very much on the women in his life, there is one thing he must be careful about. Women are very good at getting the upper hand over a man and making him do what they want him to do. In Italian we have an expression about women breaking two parts of the body that are very important to a man. It is a very good expression because some women know how to treat a man so that he doesn't feel like a man anymore. When that happens, you must ask them to please not break these parts.

I am happy to say that my secretaries don't often make that effort. They are very nice with me and have become a very important part of my life. They organize my activities, help me diet, and stay up till 3:00 A.M. playing cards with me. They must sometimes wake me up two hours earlier than usual to catch a plane or attend an important meeting. They must help me deal with my clothes and see that, when I go in front of ten thousand people, my hair is combed and my shirt buttoned.

These young women and I go through so much together. They help me through my agony when I think I am too sick to sing. They see me running down the back stairs of a hotel to get away from a crowd. When I am traveling, my secretaries are my managers, my bodyguards, and my companions. They also become my family. People can make of that what they want.

The secretaries' job is to concentrate on my life and make sure I do what I am supposed to do. But I want to know about their lives, too. I take a very big interest in the boys they are dating, the problems of their families, and anything else that concerns them.

These young women are very much a part of my life. Not

I know I am not the greatest actor, but I work hard to portray my characters' emotions with more than my voice.
THE RUDAS ORGANIZATION

Riding my bike is a favorite form of exercise. In the summers at Pesaro I make daily laps around my house. WILLIAM WRIGHT

My friend Tibor Rudas is a fantastic impresario who for twenty years has produced my large concerts like Hyde Park, Miami Beach, and the Los Angeles Three Tenors.
HENRY GROSSMAN

During a rehearsal, I am not being rude to the conductor, just reacting to a bad note I had sung.
HENRY GROSSMAN

I sang at Sting's Carnegie Hall benefit for the Amazon Rain Forest, and he kindly sang with me at my horse show concert in Modena.
SYGMA

I forget what Joe Volpe, the Met's General Manager, was telling me, but I don't think I had been bad. When working, I always try to be professional.
HENRY GROSSMAN

It is like an injection of hormones to work with great conductors, and I regret I did not sing more often with Leonard Bernstein.
HENRY GROSSMAN

Riccardo Muti is another
conductor who always
makes you see things in
a fresh way.
HENRY GROSSMAN

When I first heard Kallen
Esperian audition at my
Philadelphia competition,
I thought she had a voice
like Tebaldi's. Here the
three of us are at my
house in Pesaro.
GIOVANNA CAVALIERE

I enjoyed very much singing *L'Elisir d'Amore* with the remarkable soprano Kathleen Battle, which we also performed, as shown here, in Tokyo.
JUDY KOVACS

I was so afraid of catching cold at my concert on Miami Beach in January 1995, I wore my windbreaker instead of white tie.
CLAIRE FLAMANT

For all of us in opera, it is so wonderful to have the friendship of the great stars who came before— like Licia Albanese.
ROBERT CAHEN

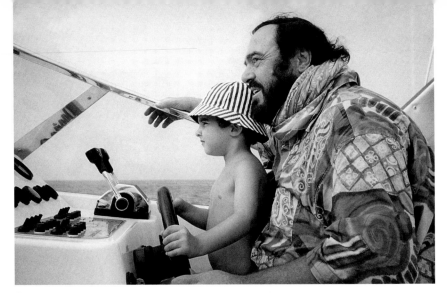

In the summer, my sister-
in-law's grandson, Nicola,
doesn't just run the boat,
he runs everything.
WILLIAM WRIGHT

I love tennis and know
that anyone can miss a
shot. I try to explain this
to John McEnroe.
AP/WIDE WORLD PHOTO

In the summer, I sit
at my table over the sea
with a glass of mineral
water and catch up on
business matters.
WILLIAM WRIGHT

As a child I loved horses but became too busy for them as I was building my career. I renewed my passion in Ireland in 1979.
AP/WIDE WORLD PHOTO

After lunch in Pesaro, the incredible Nicola holds the attention of my daughter Lorenza, my wife, Adua, and me.
WILLIAM WRIGHT

The main reason for the first three tenors concert was the great affection Placido Domingo and I have for José Carreras, who had recovered from a terrible illness.
HENRY GROSSMAN

People can say what they want, but Placido and I are friends and enjoy working together.
HENRY GROSSMAN

There was a spontaneous, upbeat mood to our first three tenors concert in Rome in 1990. I was afraid we would not be able to equal it a second time. F. ORIGLIA

For all the high spirits in performance, we all three take our work very seriously, and if we didn't, Zubin Mehta would insist on it.
THE RUDAS ORGANIZATION

While I was working hard rehearsing *Ballo* in Naples, Bill and Nicoletta relaxed over espressos.
WILLIAM WRIGHT

July in Peking can be very hot, especially inside the theaters. I was incredibly grateful to the person who thought to bring battery-operated fans.
AP/WIDE WORLD PHOTO

I loved the brief period our schedule allowed for us to stroll around Tiananmen Square.
HANS BOON

When I travel, I like very much to hear young talent, as here in Chile.
CYNTHIA LAWRENCE

The people in China were so open and friendly, they reminded me of Italians.
AP/WIDE WORLD PHOTO

My concerts in Moscow in 1990 were during a tense period of transition.
JUDY KOVACS

A bonus of my profession: meeting beautiful women like Whitney Houston.
ANDREA GRIMINELLI

Leone Magiera, Bryan Adams, and I rehearse for the concert that is the finale of my Modena horse show.
CLAIRE FLAMANT

One of the distinguished visitors to my horse show was the Dalai Lama, who saw what I was going through and took my pulse.
JUDY KOVACS

The vocal competition
I started in Philadelphia
requires many long hours
of auditioning young
singers in cities all over
the world.
HENRY GROSSMAN

Winning a competition
doesn't always mean
much, so I make a point
of performing an opera
with the winners.
TRUDY LEE COHEN

My secretary for seven years, Judy Kovacs is now a sculptress in Vienna. In 1994, she stopped by Pesaro on her way to the south of Italy.
WILLIAM WRIGHT

Franco Casarini, whom we call Panoccia, is probably my best friend—and a bigger clown than I am.
ANDREA GRIMINELLI

I have a fantastic relationship with all my daughters. Giuliana, with me in my hammock, gave us a terrible scare in the 1980s when she got very sick.
JUDY KOVACS

My collaborator is proud of this picture he took on my boat in Pesaro.
WILLIAM WRIGHT

My only sibling is my wonderful sister, Gabriella.
WILLIAM WRIGHT

Two of my daughters, Giuliana and Cristina, came to my opening of *Ballo in Maschera* in Naples in December 1994. Lorenza was too busy with her Modena boutique.
WILLIAM WRIGHT

Crowds are part of my life. If they weren't, I would start to worry.
JUDY KOVACS

I admit it, I love the telephone. In the summer in Pesaro I keep in touch with friends around the world. WILLIAM WRIGHT

only do they see it all but they must live it all with me. We grow very close. Because of that, I think it is a good idea that they not stay with me too long. I get too dependent on them, and they sometimes get too dependent on me. In the past twenty years, I have had eight secretaries. I think I am still friends with all of them.

When Adua is interviewed, she also gets questions about our private lives. Like me, she has become good at brushing aside these efforts to raise matters you do not wish to discuss with strangers— or to have printed in newspapers. At the same time, you don't want to be disagreeable. That can turn the interview into an unpleasant experience for everybody.

When the fashion newspaper, *Womens Wear Daily*, asked Adua about the young women in my life, she had a good answer for their nosy question. She said that I travel all the time and when I do, I might look at another bowl of pasta or another pretty face, but, she added, "there is still plenty of linguine at home." Adua is very smart and very strong. It is not easy for a magazine or newspaper to upset her or make her say something she does not want to say.

Adua and I have had an exceptional relationship. We fell in love when we were teenagers. For seven years we were engaged to be married. For most young Italians, being engaged doesn't mean too much. It is just a formality that makes it possible for young people to go out together without a chaperon. Breaking an engagement is no problem. Usually there is very little to break. Everybody knows this. With Adua and me, however, it was different. Both of us always knew we would marry when we had enough money—or when I had hope of earning some.

Unfortunately, that took seven years. When I won the Achille Peri competition in 1961 and got a chance to sing in the

Reggio Emilia production of *Bohème*, my career could have ended right there. I sang well that night, but if you are unknown, no matter how well you sing, people can easily forget about you. But I was extremely lucky because an important Milanese agent, Alessandro Ziliani, was in the audience that evening to hear another singer. When he took me on as a client and began finding me jobs, I finally felt as though my future looked promising enough for Adua and me to get married. So in that one year, 1961, I made my operatic debut, I got married, and, most important of all, I got my first car.

That, of course, is a joke (so was the car). Maybe it was jokes of this sort that made Adua and me fight all the time. Our seven-year engagement was like one long argument. The morning of my wedding, I said to myself, "Luciano, what are you doing? Do you want to fight all the rest of your life?" I believed I was making a big mistake, but it was too late to escape. Of course, as it turned out, marrying Adua was the best thing I could have done. After our wedding, we still fought, but we fought like adults. The battles would be *about* something. Before, it was two young lovers testing each other and getting rid of all their extra energy.

Few women could have put up with the life of an operatic tenor as Adua has done. In our homes, there are always people around, many of them strangers to my wife and daughters. Some of them come to help me prepare a role, others come for interviews, and in recent years there have been constant meetings concerning the horse show or the Philadelphia vocal competition. All of this activity turns our household into a circus, but Adua never complains about it.

From almost the beginning of my career, I have had to be away from home a great deal of the time. At first, Adua traveled with me. But when our daughters were growing up, she did not feel she could leave them, even though our parents and her sister were there to look after them. Adua wanted to be their mother full-time.

So she stayed home to raise the family and to manage our affairs. Over the years the business affairs have become more and more complicated. So have the daughters, but fortunately not in any way to cause us problems. Adua invested our money, and when we bought property in Modena or Pesaro, she would oversee all the negotiations and details. She is terrific with numbers, which I am not. Until recently she would fly to New York once a year to go over the books of my expenses in America. Because I have two apartments there, it gets complicated. A few years ago my daughter Cristina opened a boutique in Modena. Adua also does the books for this business.

With all her energy and ability, it was inevitable that Adua would want to be more than just the tenor's wife. In 1987, when our daughters were grown, she started her own business, an artists' management firm, which she calls Stage Door. She created offices in the stables next to our Modena house. The building had already been partly modernized when we created apartments for my family. At the other end, Adua put in offices that looked like the headquarters for Fiat—all glass, marble, and steel. She knew from the beginning that the business would be big, and she was right.

Even before starting her company, Adua had a good knowledge of the business side of opera. Until Herbert Breslin became my manager in 1968, she handled most of the arrangements for my singing engagements. Also, she knows singing. It would be difficult for anyone to attend as many operas as she has without developing a sharp ear for good singing. With this expertise and her talent for business, there was no way her business would not be a success.

Stage Door now has a staff of nine people and over eighty clients, most of them singers, but also a few stage directors and other production talents. She is incredibly busy most of the time—

busier than I am, I think—but she has fantastic energy and loves the activity. Because of her years with me, she knows how to deal with impossible singers and she is sympathetic to their problems. She has done well and I am impressed with what she has accomplished.

When people compliment her on her success, I hear her telling them that it doesn't hurt to have the last name of Pavarotti. While I am sure that is true, I don't like to hear her say that. If she didn't represent good singers and if she wasn't a good manager, it wouldn't matter what her last name was.

It's the same when I give young artists a chance to appear at one of my concerts. It is always a great opportunity for beginners to perform with an established artist, but if they don't please the audience with what they do on the stage, they will not have any future. When they thank me, I say, "I am not out there on the stage when you perform—only you."

Everybody knows how important the family is to Italians, but there are signs that this is starting to change in Italy. It is sad to say that for some of my countrymen, the family is not as strong as it once was. This is not true with me. My family is still extremely important to my life, and I think my family feels the same way. In spite of a career that keeps me on airplanes much of the year, we have all managed to stay together.

When I bought the large house outside of Modena, in 1978, I had in mind to build living quarters for those members of my family who wished to live there. In existing buildings on the property we built an apartment for my mother and father, another for my sister, Lela, and her son, Lucca, an apartment for Adua's sister, Giovanna Ballerini, and her family. Each part of the family has separate quarters, and we all live independently. We eat meals together only on special occasions. At the same time, we are all together. It is like a small village made up entirely of Pavarottis and Ballerinis.

In our summer house in Pesaro, we enjoy an even greater degree of togetherness, because here we all eat together. My daughters are usually involved with their own activities, so they come only from time to time, and Adua comes for a long visit only when she closes her office for two weeks in August, but the rest of the time there are still many family members—my parents, my sister, my in-laws, my nieces and nephews, their children.

When Bill and I were working on this book last August, he reminded me that our publisher, Betty Prashker, was coming through Pesaro and wanted to have lunch with us. I suggested we take her to a restaurant. Bill asked why. He said he thought she would prefer having lunch at the house with the family.

I was in the hammock, and I looked around the terrace at all the people. I said to Bill, "Why would she want to come here? Look, there are one, two, three, four, *five* families. This is a mess!" Bill assured me Betty would prefer the mess. Of course, I do too.

My father is a worrier who always finds something to get upset about. My mother must constantly work to cheer him up. I can hear her saying to him, "How could things be better? The family is together and we live right next to our son and daughter. When Luciano returns from trips, the first thing he does is come over to our house and call out 'Mama! Papa!' " It is true, that is the first thing I do. Aside from the love I have for my family, they are my contact with reality. They tell me I have not changed in fifteen years, and I hope they are right. The truth is that none of us have. Maybe staying together has kept us the same.

Now that I think about it, my father has changed. He's gotten better. My father, Fernando, is a fantastic, incredible person and I love him very much. I have spoken often about what a beautiful singing voice he has—even now, at eighty-two—and that his love for singing sparked my interest when I was a little boy. Other people discover they have a singing voice, then study the music and become interested. With me, the interest in the music and the singing came first. I didn't discover until many years later that I had a voice. This passion for the music and the vocal tradition is an important part of who I am as an artist.

I owe it to Fernando, and maybe some to my Italian blood. But the sad truth is that many Italians, even of my generation, do not care anything for opera or the bel canto tradition. They could not have been Fernando's children. Naturally, he is very proud of me and my career, although he sometimes tries to hide his interest.

When he flew to New York last year to hear me sing *Tosca*, for instance, he pretended he came for other reasons. It was amazing that he made the trip at all. He is not a young man and he speaks no English, but he flew from Modena to New York by himself. After all this effort, he told friends in New York that he had come to America not to hear his son sing at the Metropolitan Opera but to see his dentist. Because I just happened to be singing a role he loves, he told people, he had stayed a few days longer to hear me.

I have also spoken often about how my father continues to vocalize every day. He is still asked to sing for special events like weddings and funerals—and gets paid for it. He actually makes quite a good business. One thing that many people don't know about my father is that he believes his voice is better than mine. Now, that may be true, but in the interest of family peace, I would prefer that he say his voice is *as good as* mine. That is not what he believes. He is too polite to say it directly, but it has come out in his comments.

He is a real student of tenor singing, a true authority. He knows the voice of every tenor of the past seventy years, the things that each one did better than anyone else, the things each one did not do so well. He knows which tenors were best in which roles and which roles present-day tenors should consider performing.

When listening to tenors, he is extremely critical. A few years ago a colleague of mine, a very fine tenor in the international opera world, was having vocal problems. My father and I and some others were playing cards while we listened to this singer on the radio in a live broadcast from the Metropolitan. The singing was very bad, and I felt truly sorry for this tenor. I knew this was not the way he usually sang. My father started making jokes about the performance and said some very critical things. I couldn't stand it and got up and turned off the radio. With my father, tenor singing is too important to show anyone a little pity and mercy.

With Fernando's deep knowledge of singing, he knows the great importance of proper study and training that must go on for years and years. These of course are the things he did not have. He has often said he envies me my years of vocal study. He believes his lack of training is the only thing that kept him from having an important operatic career.

Another thing that prevented a career was his nerves. He gets incredibly anxious before singing in public, sometimes a week before. Anybody who performs gets nervous, but Fernando more than most of us. Unlike me, he never learned to conquer his nerves or, better, to convert them into positive energy. Because of these two problems—nerves and the lack of vocal study—Fernando missed having a career. Until recently, I never realized *how* important a career he believes he might have had.

One day not too long ago my father went a little bit further than his usual lament about not having studied singing seriously. After I complimented him on the way he had just sung a piece, he said, "Ah, Luciano, if you only had my voice, think of the career you could have had."

I was too surprised to tell him that even with the voice I have,

I still get plenty of work. But I should have been expecting this. Not too long before he made this comment we were all sitting together in our house in Modena and the telephone rang. One of my daughters said it was an organization in the city who wanted to know if Mr. Pavarotti would be available to sing for them. With a big smile my father said to me, "I know that group. It's me they want. Not you."

Almost more than me, I think, my father lives in a world of opera and voice. He has a dreamy side to his nature and he is often off in his own world of music. When he is by himself, I can hear him singing softly, usually in a falsetto, an aria or a classic song. Even if he did not have the career he might have had, I think he is totally happy when he is off in his private world of music and great tenor singing.

My mother is very different from my father, but they are completely devoted to each other. She is always upbeat and cheerful and looks at the positive side of things. She tells me that I am so good to her, that I make her feel like the daughter, not the mother. I recently gave a big party for her birthday and bought her an overcoat and matching hat, which I had found in the mountains in the very north of Italy. It was in the Tyrolean style and was almost like a costume. She was very pleased with the present. She put it on for everyone to see and looked terrific in it. Even after the ordeal of her knee operations, she still has her same old pep and spirit.

My sister Gabriella, whom we call Lela, is a miracle of nature. She is so much fun and so upbeat you would never know she has ten times as much misfortune in her life as any person should ever have. She lost a baby daughter when the little girl was three months old. Her only surviving child, Lucca, is paraplegic and is confined to a wheelchair. Although Lucca cannot talk, he is very intelligent.

If you recite the alphabet and leave out a letter, he will let you know you made a mistake.

That is how we communicate. You signal a letter to him and, if you have the right one, he will let you know with his eyes. He understands everything that is going on. When I returned from the Los Angeles Three Tenors concert, Lucca spelled out, "You sang better and your heart was bigger." It gave us all goose bumps. He understands Italian, some English and he is interested in science. One night in Pesaro, he pointed out the quarter moon to me.

Lela teaches school, but when she is not working, she spends all of her time with Lucca, who needs a lot of attention and must be lifted in and out of his chair. To help her, she hires young boys from Modena. She doesn't want to ever leave her son alone. I recently invited Lucca to visit me in New York. I thought it was time for him to take a trip. I didn't invite Lela because I wanted her to have time by herself. Instead I invited the boys who help look after Lucca in Modena.

Of course Lucca loves his mother deeply, but he was very happy to come on a trip without her. He was eager to see where I lived, to meet my New York friends, and to visit the Metropolitan Opera. He also remembered a lot about a trip he made earlier. One day the boys and I took him out for a walk and were pushing Lucca in his wheelchair along Central Park South. He asked me if this was the same street the Hotel Navarro was on. That was where I lived in New York before moving into my present apartment. He must have remembered hearing us talk about the location on the park.

My three daughters—Cristina, Lorenza, and Giuliana—are young women now, and I look upon them as wonderful gifts from God. They are terrific—very sensitive, kind, well educated, and intelligent. If I can be immodest in an area where most people are immodest, I'll say they are also very well brought up. Best of all they have their feet on the ground—like their mother and father, I hope. But for them, growing up was not so easy because they had to deal with the famous name. Adua and I did not have this problem when we grew up. But my daughters handled it very, very well. I am most impressed by this part of their characters.

As sisters, they are close, but each one has a very different personality. Cristina is interested in fashion and has her own boutique in Modena called Titi Pavarotti—after the cartoon bird. She works extremely hard for this shop and does very well.

Lorenza has a beautiful soul. She likes people and is interested in everybody. Because she is so concerned and compassionate about us all, she is practically the head of the family.

Giuliana, the youngest, has many talents. I think she could have a career as a pop singer, if she wanted. She sings well and has the personality. Right now, though, she is interested in other things. She has been studying physical education and is working to become a gymnastic instructor. She has also studied massage.

My daughters are not married yet, but they have romances and I do not give up hope that soon I will be a grandfather.

Italians have strong family feelings and the Pavarottis in particular have always had strong family feelings. With the pressures of my career, my family has become still more important to me. I am particularly lucky in all of my relatives, as I hope I have shown in this chapter. All of them—my parents, my wife, my sister, my daughters—are wonderful people in themselves, and each one loves and supports me in a special way. I don't think I could have survived without them.

14
"AH MES AMIS"

After my family, those who are most important to me are my friends. I am very proud that I still see many of the people I knew when I was growing up in Modena. When I return to my city after singing around the world, I look them up and we spend time together. So I only see them from time to time, but it is no different for my friends who remain in Modena. We all have our own families, our own lives, but every now and then we get together to talk and play cards.

I also have many friends outside of Italy, people whom I have known since the earliest days of my career. Newer friends have commented to me about this. They say that as you move up in your profession and you are meeting more and more interesting people, it is natural that you see less of the people you knew at the beginning. If that is true for anyone, it is certainly not true for me. Most of my friends were friends before I became well known.

There may be an unconscious reason for this. My daughters sometimes tell me that when people make an effort to be friends with them, they have the suspicion it is because they have a famous father. They believe this has already happened to them. If some people choose friends this way, it is very sad, and I am glad my daughters can see through such people.

In my own case, I do not think about this very much, but with people who were my friends before I became well known, there is nothing to think about. I know they are really my friends. Maybe in the back of my mind I too am suspicious about people I meet today, just as my daughters are, and, because of this, I value so much the friends from many years ago.

Typical of these old friendships are Bob and Joan Cahen in San Francisco. Bob has had different professions, but when I met him in the 1960s, he was becoming a professional photographer specializing in opera. He and his wife are big opera fans, and Bob was one of the first to take advantage of the new high-speed color films to photograph opera productions with the stage light and in full costume. He takes wonderful pictures and took the picture of me on the cover of my first book and on this book as well.

Shortly after I met Bob, I was rehearsing in San Francisco for my debut performance in *Un Ballo in Maschera* with Martina Arroyo. The rehearsal was in the Old North Gym and Bob was there taking pictures. After I sang my first aria, I was walking past where he was sitting. He jumped up and said, "If I could sing like that, I would throw away these cameras tomorrow." I looked at him and said, "That is what I did when I was a photographer."

We became friends, and pretty soon I was having dinner in the Cahens' home, sometimes staying with them when I had a few days off in order to get away from the atmosphere of hotels. In those days I traveled alone and spoke terrible English. I was very pleased to have found such warm and helpful friends. Every time I returned to San Francisco, Bob and Joan would pick me up at the airport, keep me company, and help me get organized as the opening approached and things got frantic. We ate together frequently and had a lot of fun as they showed me the city.

Bob liked driving me around San Francisco, which was very

good for me, because he knew the city and I didn't. As I got to know San Francisco better, I began to realize that his sense of direction was not too good. One time we were driving back to the city from his house in Burlingame. It is a very simple route: you just drive north on a major highway until you reach the city. Somehow he made a major mistake and took a right turn and headed straight east and crossed the San Francisco Bay. He couldn't turn around on the water, so he had to drive up the Oakland side of the Bay. This took us miles out of our way.

I missed seeing the mistake, as I had gone to sleep. He told me later that he hoped I would stay asleep until he could make it across the Oakland Bridge and into the city. He knew if I saw his mistake I would kid him without mercy. As we started to cross back over the bay, I woke up just in time to see a sign: Leaving Oakland.

I said to him, "Since when do you have to go through Oakland to get from Burlingame to San Francisco?"

When I was in San Francisco in 1974 doing Verdi's *Luisa Miller* for the first time, Bob and Joan asked me to come spend Thanksgiving with them. It had been a busy week. In addition to opera performances, I had sung a concert on Monday. On Wednesday I had flown to Los Angeles to make my first appearance on the Johnny Carson show. José Carreras was singing *Ballo in Maschera* in Los Angeles, so I stayed down there to hear his performance. The Cahens had also invited my co-star in *Luisa,* Katia Riccarelli, for Thanksgiving, and I asked José to fly up and join the party.

We had a terrific dinner, all the traditional American dishes, and afterward I got the group to play poker. The game went on until very late—almost all night. As it got later and later, Bob got more and more upset. The next evening's performance of *Luisa Miller* was to be broadcast. He was afraid if his opera singers didn't get to sleep, we would sing badly. The broadcast would be a disaster, and it would be his fault. He kept pestering us to stop the game, but we were having too much fun. Especially me, as I was winning every pot.

When the game finally broke up, we all got a few hours sleep. The next evening as Bob and Joan were driving me into the city for the performance, I told them I felt guilty that I had taken all my friends' money at poker. I asked Bob and Joan if I could bring Katia and José back to their house that night after the performance to give them a chance to win back their money. When Bob and Joan said that would be fine, I suggested to Joan that she serve the leg of lamb she does so well.

I am not saying it doesn't matter how rested you are before singing an opera performance; it is usually very important. But as it turned out, we were lucky. The broadcast performance was the best of all five we did in San Francisco. Katia and I were both in top form. I think, for all the people listening to the radio, we brought credit that night to the San Francisco Opera. Maybe I was inspired by thoughts of the leg of lamb and the good cards that were waiting for me in Burlingame.

Two very old American friends of mine are Iglesia Gestone and her son, Michael, who live in New Jersey. When I met them, Michael was about twelve. Iglesia wanted her little boy to know and appreciate Italian culture, so she brought him to the opera from time to time. Michael learned to love opera and quickly became extremely knowledgeable. He has a fantastic memory. He knows every performance I have sung, the dates, the names of the other singers. Iglesia said to me she just wanted her son to become familiar with opera so he could appreciate the best of our Italian heritage. Instead, she says, she has created "an opera monster."

Right after I met him, Michael came to hear me at the Met. In the weeks before, I had sung a series of *Puritani*s, then had to sing a *Bohème*, then a final *Puritani*. This last one was the opera Michael came to see. I was exhausted from too much singing. On a high D I did something I almost never do: I cracked. When Michael came backstage to see me, I apologized to him for letting him down. He was very touched that I cared what he thought, and we began to be good friends.

Iglesia is a terrific woman, but she is a little shy. For so long she had gone on to me about how much she admired Zubin Mehta. Her feelings actually went beyond admiration and were more like worship. I finally said to her that, if she liked him so much, I would invite him to have dinner with her. She was very pleased and excited. At the party in my New York apartment, I sat Iglesia directly across from Zubin at a long narrow table.

During the meal, I could see that Zubin was talking to her, but she was saying very little in return. When she got up for a minute, I followed her into the hall and asked her if there was a problem. Did she not feel well, or did she not like her hero so much after all? She said she felt fine and he was wonderful and was being very nice to her. She was simply too awed to say anything.

I said, "Well, you better say something when you sit back down. It's like watching a silent movie."

I think the longer I have been friends with people and the more I like them, the more blunt and direct I become. Another time I was talking to Iglesia at a large party when Frank Sinatra came over to talk with me. She got so excited that she dropped her wineglass and it shattered at our feet. Because of my knee problem, I have trouble bending down. Iglesia stood frozen like a statue. With the two of us just standing there in the broken glass, Frank crouched down and began picking up the pieces.

I said to Iglesia, "Next time for you—plastic!"

One trait I require in my friends is a sense of humor and the ability to take a joke. It is necessary because I am an absolutely terrible joke player. I can't help it. It is part of my nature. It may be childish, but I love to fool and confuse people. Because I don't want to irritate all of my friends, I have appointed one of them that I can play most of my jokes on. Because he is so good-natured and serious, I chose Iglesia's son, Michael, for this position. He is now about thirty, but because I have known him since he was a little boy, I claim special rights. In any case, Michael has accepted the job.

One thing I kid him about constantly is his singing. Because he loves opera and knows everything about singers, especially tenors, Michael would love to be able to sing, but he can't. I tried to work on his singing, but there is nothing to do. He has a terrible voice. His voice is loud, but the sound is truly awful. He admits this.

One time my friend Carlo Bergonzi was visiting me in my New York apartment, and we spent most of the afternoon trying to teach Michael to sing better. No matter how hard we worked, making him sing scales and simple songs, we could not get one note to sound right. It was amazing. We kept trying. After going up a scale, Michael held the top note. Carlo suddenly yelled, "Stop!"

He turned to me and said, "After two hours, Luciano, this is the first note he has sung correctly."

Afterward I said to Michael, "You can tell people I am your friend, but you *cannot* tell them I am your vocal coach."

I have become fascinated by Michael's singing. When I present him to my friends, I always introduce Michael as a talented young tenor. I have introduced him to many of my Met colleagues such as Gwyneth Jones and Teresa Stratas. Once when the great Licia Albanese came backstage to greet me, I introduced Michael to her as a promising young tenor just starting his career and she made a big fuss over Michael.

"Ah, such a fine looking young man," she said, "and you say he has a beautiful voice? Marvelous!"

It made her happy to meet young talent and, for some reason I can't explain, the small deception made me happy. I once told Michael I wanted to present him in a concert. We would tell everybody I was singing, then when all the people were inside the auditorium, we would lock the doors and Michael would sing an entire program.

I have found many different uses for this stupendous voice. One night before a performance at the Met, Michael stopped by my dressing room to wish me luck. We were sitting talking when Gildo Di Nunzio came into the room to warm up my voice as he always does. Gildo sat at the small upright piano in my dressing room, which faces the wall, so he had his back to me. As Gildo hit a chord, I motioned to Michael to sing instead of me. Michael opened his mouth and gave out one of those loud sounds that only he can make. It was the sound for warning ships in foggy weather. Gildo thought something terrible had happened to me and almost fell off his chair.

I have even been mean enough to ask Michael to sing at parties. One night when he was crucifying an aria from *Manon Lescaut* for my guests, I suddenly had a fantastic thought. I made Michael stop. What's the matter? he asked. I told him that I had recently rented my apartment to José Carreras. The neighbors would think José had lost his voice.

The wonderful thing is that Michael doesn't mind my kidding about his voice. He throws himself into it. I think he tolerates my fantasy as part of his friend Luciano's craziness. I told you, he accepted the position.

It is not only Michael's voice I kid him about. I kid him about everything. He called me one day to tell me it was his birthday. I laughed so hard I couldn't talk. "What's wrong with you, Luciano?" he asked.

"Michael," I said, "I know a thousand people. You are the only one who calls to tell me it is his birthday."

Sometimes he gets back at me. For many months, Michael was overweight. He set his mind on losing this extra weight and was able to return to his normal size. He knows how much I envy that. As if that wasn't bad enough, he can also beat me at Ping-Pong. This makes me so angry that I once remembered the score wrong by several of his points. And he still beat me.

One of the best jokes I ever played on Michael does not concern his voice. It happened by chance when he telephoned my apartment one day. At the time, Andrea Griminelli and his girlfriend had stopped by for a visit. When the phone rang, Andrea saw I was busy at my desk, so he answered it for me. When Michael heard Andrea's voice, he asked Andrea what he was doing there. On an impulse, Andrea said he was not anywhere, he was at home and that Michael had dialed the wrong number. That was all I needed to get me started.

Michael hung up and called back a second time. This time I answered and, disguising my voice, said, "Andrea Griminelli's apartment." I told Michael that Mr. Griminelli was not at home. He had gone over to Mr. Pavarotti's apartment. Did he want that number? Now Michael was thoroughly confused. When he called back a few minutes later, I forget what we said, but we kept the joke going. Finally we got Andrea's girlfriend into the act.

We had her telephone Michael in New Jersey. She told him she was the AT&T operator, and then she said, "We would like to know why you are trying to telephone Mr. Pavarotti."

Michael thought he was going crazy, but as the girl spoke more he became suspicious. He asked her for her identification number. She had not expected this question, and she fell apart. I think we made the whole comedy last for a half hour. If that kind of trick proves I have a mean streak, as my friend Gildo says I do, then I must accept the accusation. All I can say is that our joke made my day.

A week or so later I had a plan to have dinner with Michael at

a Chinese restaurant near the Met, Shun Lee's. He was coming by
my apartment to pick me up, but I remembered that I had an
appointment at the Met a short time before. It was too late to
telephone him, as he was already on his way in from New Jersey. I
left a note at the desk of my apartment building telling him to go to
the restaurant and I would meet him there. I was a few minutes
late, which I try never to be, and Michael was coming out of the
restaurant. He looked angry.

"What's the matter with you?" I asked. "I am only five minutes late."

He had gotten my note and come straight to the restaurant,
but the restaurant people said that I had not made a reservation and
they were not expecting me. "I was sure, Luciano," Michael said,
"it was another one of your jokes."

I asked how he could think I would do such a thing to him,
but I made a note to myself to remember this idea for a later date.
It would make a terrific joke. I would just have to wait until Michael forgot about it.

I have spent much time over the years in certain cities, and I
have developed long-lasting friendships in each of them. This
makes it a wonderful pleasure for me to go back each time. The
city may not be my home, but it does not feel like a strange
place, either. If I have not visited a city for a while, one way I
keep these friendships alive and healthy is with the telephone. In
each of these groups of friends, there are usually one or two people who know everybody in the group. I will telephone these
people from different parts of the world to find out how everyone else is doing and to learn their news.

One of those I rely on most in New York to fulfill this function is my friend for thirty years, Umberto Boeri. He is an Italian

from San Remo who went to medical school in Modena, but I didn't meet him there. We met later in the opera world through Mirella Freni. Umberto is a pediatrician in New York, but he is very knowledgeable about opera. He has become a close friend. I can telephone Umberto from anywhere at any time and learn how all my New York friends are doing—who has bad health, whose children are taking exams, who got promoted in their work.

When I am in town, I invite Umberto and all of my New York friends over to my apartment and I cook pasta for them. Sometimes I go to their houses, but not as often as I have them to mine. The weather is usually cold when I am in New York, and I like to avoid going outside as much as possible.

At times it bothers me how little I know about the details of my friends' lives. I get their family news over the phone, but I know little about the way they live. They come to see me in the opera, come backstage to greet me afterward, meet my colleagues. Still I know almost nothing about their daily life. When I try to picture them going about their daily routine I do not see anything in my mind. This is not the way it should be with friends.

For instance, I knew that Umberto worked in a clinic on Manhattan's Upper East Side, but I had no idea what the clinic was like, what they did there, how big it was. So one day I told Umberto I wanted to come see his office. He was surprised but said he had a better idea. His office was having a Christmas party soon. Why didn't I come to it? In that way I could see his office and meet the people he worked with.

I liked the idea but had to stop and think. With all that has happened in my life in recent years—the big outdoor concerts, the Three Tenors—if I show up in a group of strangers, they make a big fuss over me, and that can upset a party—not for me, but for everyone else. I enjoy meeting new people, but I don't like making such a disruption. I told Umberto I would come to his office party but only if he told no one I was coming. I figured that if they didn't have time to think about it, they would treat me like any other guest. Umberto agreed that this was a good idea.

On the day of the party Umberto arrived to pick me up, and I had been dressed and ready to go for fifteen minutes. He told me he was sure I would change my mind about going, but I said, "Let's go."

When we got to the clinic, we went upstairs to the room where the party was going on. There was a woman at the door receiving the guests; she was the clinic's administrator, Umberto said. As the lady shook my hand and looked at my face, she was very surprised and said something like "I am happy you could join our party, Mr. Pavarotti."

When I entered the room, I was happy to see that no one paid much attention to my being there. Umberto said he got a kick out of watching the faces of the other guests. They at first didn't notice me, but little by little he could see them look, then look again in amazement. What is *he* doing here? What is an opera singer doing at a hospital Christmas party? Finally some people crowded around me, but they were very nice, so the party soon got back to normal.

After we had been there awhile and talked with a number of people, I told Umberto I wanted to see his office. He led me back downstairs and showed it to me. I sat in his chair behind the desk and asked if this was where he saw his patients. I asked where the patients sat.

He thought I was crazy to be so curious about everything and said that, in case I was thinking of it, he could not show me his patients' files. I explained that now when he telephoned me from the office or said he was working late, I could picture where he was. I don't like my friends' everyday lives to be a mystery to me. I don't like anything that sets me apart from normal people who lead normal lives.

Umberto spoke often about a hotel in the mountains north of New York where he goes on weekends to relax. He said how beautiful and relaxing it was and how unspoiled. It was a large old-fashioned inn on a lake called the Mohonk Mountain House. It had been run by the same family for many years. I was not only curious, I was also envious, so I told him I wanted to spend a weekend there, too.

We studied my appointment book. The only weekend when I didn't have to sing or be out of town was in October. He said October was when the fall color was at its peak, so it would be difficult to get rooms. But he called them and told them that Luciano Pavarotti wanted to come for a visit, that he had never been to their hotel, had heard much about it, and was only in New York at that time. They were very nice and arranged for us to have several of the most beautiful rooms with spectacular views.

I liked everything about this place—the large rooms, the enormous dining room and lobbies. The food was good, too. The service was from another period, except one time when I asked the young man who was our waiter to bring me some lemon juice. He brought a small dish of juice, but when I tasted it, it was terrible. "What is this?" I asked him.

"Lemon juice," he said.

"Not from a lemon, from a can."

He admitted it was from a can, and I gave him a lecture. Every food store in America has fresh lemons every day of the year, I told him. These lemons cost from twenty to thirty cents apiece. They last for weeks in the refrigerator. They are all delicious. How can he serve guests in his beautiful hotel this horrible juice from a can that tastes like aluminum?

The poor boy was embarrassed, but I really thought it was terrible that such a wonderful hotel would serve such bad stuff. From then on, every time he came out of the kitchen he brought another plate of sliced lemon. Soon our table was covered with dishes of lemon. For me, that made it worse. They'd had lemons in their kitchen all the time, and he had still served that aluminum juice.

I like to do favors for my friends when I can, but sometimes I think they wish I hadn't. One example was when Bryan Miller, the food critic of the *New York Times,* was doing an article about me and the food I liked. To help with his research, I arranged to take him to my favorite New York restaurant, San Domenico, so we could eat together and talk about food. The restaurant is close to my apartment on Central Park South and is run by my friend, Tony May, who has worked in New York for many years but who is originally from Naples.

Miller and I made our eating date a month in advance. When we were finally at the restaurant, our meal started out very well. But when the waiter poured a glass of wine, it didn't taste right. I asked what it was; he told me Lambrusco. When I heard that, I was sure the wine was not right. Lambrusco is a light, slightly sparkling wine that comes from my part of Italy. It is a favorite of mine, and I know how it should taste. When I sent it back and asked for something else, I thought Tony was going to kill me.

First, he was furious that I would send anything back in front of the critic from the *New York Times.* My feeling was that everything at San Domenico was always wonderful and he would not want to serve me and the *Times* critic anything that was not of his restaurant's high standard. From what Tony told me later, he would have preferred to have me drink vinegar with a smile rather than say anything negative in front of an important critic.

What made it worse was that Tony had gone to great trouble to get this wine. He knew Lambrusco was one of my favorites, and he knew how difficult it was to find good Lambrusco outside of

Italy. In fact, I had told him that. To please me, and to show his gratitude to me for bringing the *Times* critic to his restaurant, Tony had flown a case of Lambrusco over for this meal. I did not know anything about this extra effort, and I was very sorry for causing a *brutta figura* for him. But was it my fault the wine had jet lag?

Generally I try to be a thoughtful person, but when it comes to music, food, and wine, I always say exactly what I think. Tony tells me he prefers honesty in his customers. Some of them, he says, when they don't like a dish, they pay the bill and never come back. He would much rather people tell him when they are unhappy. He will either fix the dish or get them something else. If they are still unhappy, he will not let them pay. He thinks Americans are afraid to criticize, but he says restaurant owners would much rather have the criticism and keep the customer. Even so, I now know that Tony would prefer that I don't criticize in front of the food critic from the *New York Times*.

Because I am very well paid, I am in a position to help friends when they have money problems. For me this is one of the best things about being financially well off. My own early years, when money was a constant worry, are still too fresh in my mind for me to not care about my friends' difficulties. Often the problems concern medical expenses, which today have grown so huge. Sometimes, however, my friends get into bigger financial difficulties than I am able to solve personally.

This happened to my friend Judy Drucker in Miami Beach. Several of the concerts that she organized did not sell very well, but she still had to pay the artists their full price. Judy receives no help from the National Endowment for the Arts or from any other government money. As a result she found herself with a big deficit.

When I heard about her problem, I told Herbert to tell her I would sing a benefit concert for her Miami Concert Association. I also got my friends Itzhak Perlman and Vladimir Ashkenazy to appear with me. Each of us would perform for free. In that way all of the money the concert brought in could help pay Judy's debts.

The concert was wonderful, and we all had a great deal of fun both in the rehearsals and in the performance itself. The only problem was Judy. She was driving me crazy with her gratitude. She told me I was her best friend, no one had ever done anything so wonderful for her, and on and on. At first I gave her a serious reply. I told her that with life you never know what will happen. One day I might need a favor from her. She was very touched by that. But I wasn't making pretty speeches, I was sincere. I have had very good fortune in my life, but I also know it could end at any time. Judy knew I meant it, but she still continued with her thanks.

Finally I thought of a way to get her to change the subject. Perlman, Ashkenazy, and I were on stage for our final rehearsal. During a break Judy came out to talk with us. She started in once again to tell us her thanks, but I interrupted her. I said to Perlman, "Tell me, Itzhak, have you ever been to bed with Judy?"

He looked very surprised, but he said no.

I asked Vladimir, "Have you?" He said no.

"Well, neither have I," I said. "So what are we all doing here?"

For many years my driver in New York has been a wonderful Jamaican man named Winston Daley. One of the things I look forward to when I return to the city is to see Winston and catch up on his love life. When I was telling him about the big South American tour that we had planned for 1995, he was very unhappy that we had not included Jamaica in the countries we would visit. He kept talking about it, telling me how excited everyone would be to hear me sing, how his family there had heard so much about me from him, and so on.

I asked Tibor if we could include Jamaica in our tour. He

looked into it and said the island was too small to produce the kind
of revenues he needed to justify all the expense of getting there and
setting up a concert in a large outdoor place. I asked him if it would
be possible if I waived my fee. That would be different, he told me,
and we scheduled Jamaica as part of the tour. And Winston ended
up promoting the concert.

One reason I think I have so many good friends is that I have a very
good attitude toward people. I do not judge people, and if they do
something bad, I assume they did it for a good reason. Nicoletta is
very young, still in her twenties, and she is very different in this
regard. I watch her after she has met someone, and she will say
things like, "This person is not intelligent," "That person is not
nice," and so on.

I say to her, "Why do you do that? Everyone has a good side,
and it is up to you to find that side. You waste your time looking at
the negative. If you do that, you will always find plenty that is bad
and never find the good side."

My sister tells me I am too forgiving. She and Nicoletta point
out the bad things that this person and that person have done to me
and ask how I can remain friendly with them. I believe these people did what they felt they had to do at the time. They probably are
no worse than most people and they still have good in them. For
example, one of the organizers of one of my horse shows left with
a lot of the money we had raised, and I was responsible for paying
the bills. But I still list him in the program as one of the founders,
and if I ran into him I would greet him like any friend.

Many of my friends tell me I am crazy. Maybe, but to me life
is very short, some people are luckier than others, and deep down,
we are all the same.

15

LIFE IN
THE SPOTLIGHT

When you enter into a life of performing, as I have, you cannot be shy and reserved. Many artists work hard to get attention. Then, when they get it, they decide they don't want it. They may spend years trying to win the public's attention, but when they win it, they want the public to leave them alone. I try hard not to be one of those people, and I think it is not too difficult for me. Ever since I was little, when I was the only boy in an apartment building filled with women, I have received more than my fair amount of attention. I confess that I enjoy it. I hope not too much.

Since the Three Tenors concerts and other worldwide television shows, concerts in every part of the world, and all of the publicity surrounding these big events, I am now very well known. The records and videos have had very broad circulation. But I have a theory about another reason many people know me. Because of my size, people see me once and they don't forget me.

Whatever the reasons, I am now recognized wherever I go. Generally I am happy when people come up to me on the street or stop at my table in a restaurant. I take it as a sign of their approval, and how can I get upset at that? I have been told that people approach me more readily than they do other well-known people. If this is true, I am glad. I don't think it is because they like me any better. I think it is because they see that I am the same person they liked on television, that I am myself.

I hope they also see that I do not consider myself better than people who are not famous. I know famous people who work hard at creating an air of aloofness and superiority. They do this in order to keep others from bothering them. I work to create the opposite impression, to make people see that I am a normal, friendly person just like them. If that makes more people come up to me in public, I cannot be upset because that is what I want them to see.

Sometimes they are not sure it is me and say something like, "Are you Pavarotti?"

I usually say, "Yes, I think so." It's not a very clever reply, but what can I say? I heard that someone came up to Elizabeth Taylor as she was getting out of a car and asked if it was really her. She must have been in a bad mood because she looked at the person and said, "Who did you think I was? Groucho Marx?"

When I am asked if I am Pavarotti, part of me would like to reply that I am really Elizabeth Taylor, but the other part, the better part, smiles and lets the person know how happy I am to be recognized.

On a beautiful day in New York I look out over Central Park and can't stand it any longer. I must be outside like everyone else. I'll say to Nicoletta, "Come on. We're going outside for a picnic." We go into the park and find the first bench. We might bring some fruit, cheese, and mineral water. If I am doing well with my diet, I might allow myself two hot dogs, which I love. It is very nice to sit in the fresh air and eat lunch. Sometimes people come up to me, but many times they don't. New Yorkers are accustomed to seeing familiar faces.

I usually like it when people crowd around me when I'm out

in public. But not always. Sometimes I wish it would not happen, like when I am trying to have dinner in a restaurant with friends and people continue to come to the table to talk with me. This happens more in restaurants than any place else. I understand that. They look at me and they think of food. "Ah, yes," they say, "here we are in an eating place, and there is Pavarotti—eating." It is almost an introduction. Also, when I am seated at a table, I cannot run away. Whatever the reason, restaurants are difficult places for me to be alone with my companions.

I must admit, when the visits continue all through the meal, it can become annoying. For one thing, I feel it is not fair to the people I am dining with. All conversation must stop, and they must sit and listen to how much the person enjoys my singing. But I never show any impatience. The person coming up probably doesn't know how often this happens to me. If I feel anything negative, I keep it inside.

I even kept it inside one night at a restaurant in New York's Chinatown when a woman came to my table and said she was a big fan of mine. Her speech was a little slurred, and I think she was drunk. I smiled and thanked her and returned to my meal. She continued to stand beside my chair. Suddenly she said, "I want you to sing for me." I said I was sorry, but I was eating dinner with friends. She got angry and said she wasn't going to leave until I sang for her. I didn't know what to do, but finally the manager came over and asked her to return to her table.

Even when people are very aggressive in that way, I try never to show a sign that I am not happy to meet and talk with them. It's not only that I am naturally friendly and like people; these fans also remind me of how lucky I am. I see the greetings from strangers as part of who I am, part of the success I worked so hard to get. If I am not feeling well and am not in a mood to talk to people I do not know, I stay home.

Sometimes the people who are around me when I am working—my secretaries or close friends—get impatient with the people who approach me every time I go outside, the people who wait outside my building. But when my friends show irritation to the strangers, this makes me upset with my friends. I explain to them that fans are important to all performers. I am grateful that these people go to the trouble to show that they like me. I tell my friends they must never be rude to my fans. It is one of the first things I teach a new secretary.

Sometimes the attention from admirers is funny. In Brazil there is a man who is famous for kissing celebrities. He runs up to famous people and before they know what is happening, he kisses them. They tell me he has kissed many movie stars, sports figures, even the pope. They have a name for him, Il Bacciaciero or something like that.

When I was singing a concert in Rio and was walking from my dressing room to the stage, he popped out of nowhere and was trying to kiss me when the security guards grabbed him. Actually, it got less funny for a few minutes because the police came running in, thinking someone was trying to assassinate me. There was an enormous scene. Even when they discovered it was only Il Bacciaciero they were not too happy.

One of my favorite encounters with the public happened recently in New York. I'm not sure why it delighted me so much, maybe because it was so spontaneous and natural. Jane Nemeth and I were coming out of an audition for our Philadelphia competition that was held on Fifty-seventh Street. The event had been announced in the newspapers, so there were paparazzi and reporters waiting outside. I tried to be polite to them, but Jane and I were late for another appointment up the street, so we hurried through the crowd that had come to see me and were in the clear walking quickly up Fifty-seventh Street.

Coming the other way was a very attractive young African-American woman. She was tall and slender and with a striking outfit and appearance. She was very elegant and must have been an actress or a dancer. This lady looked right into my face, and then she *screamed!* I am not joking, she literally screamed and said "Oh, my God!" She fell back against the building.

I thought at first she was in some trouble, so I stopped. The man she was with looked puzzled. She held one hand over her mouth and, pointing at me with the other, she said very loud, "Oh, my God, it's him!" Her companion looked at her and then looked at me. Other people stopped. I totally cracked up. It was so funny.

Not everybody knows me, though, even in my native Italy. When we were shooting an outdoor scene for the *Pavarotti Returns to Naples* special for PBS in 1987, I had to wait in my car until they were ready for me on the location. Word had gotten around the neighborhood of Naples that I was there, and a crowd had formed around my car. A boy about nine years old was tending a soft-drink cart nearby and watching all the people standing near my car. He left his stand and walked right up to the window and motioned for me to open it. When the window was down, he said to me, "Who are you that everybody is looking at you?"

I said to him, "I am Luciano Pavarotti."

The boy shrugged as if to say, "Is that supposed to mean something to me?"

I said I was a tenor, an opera singer.

"I don't know about opera," he said. "Where do you sing?"

"Everywhere," I said, "In London, Paris, Milan, New York."

"New York?"

I had his attention.

"I am also singing here in Naples," I told him. "I am doing a concert here in three days. Would you like to come as my guest?"

He thought about it for a minute, then said, "What time is the concert?"

I told him eight o'clock.

"No," he said, "it is not possible for me. I must tend the drink stand from eight in the morning until nine every night. My mother insists."

I was liking this boy more and more. I asked him for his phone number and said I would speak with his mother. He said his family did not have a telephone. A neighbor, then? He wrote down a neighbor's number. I said, "I will persuade your mother to let you come."

When I spoke with the mother, she was very polite and thanked me for inviting her son, but she said it was not possible for him to attend the concert. There was no one else to look after the stand. I tried to change her mind, but she had decided and that was that.

Sometimes I get a reminder of what life was like before television made me familiar to incredible numbers of people in every part of the world. I was recently in Vienna to perform an opera. In the car with Larisa and Nicoletta, on the way back to the hotel from a rehearsal, I saw a pizzeria, which you do not expect to see in Vienna. We all decided we were very hungry, so we stopped to get something to eat. It was early—about six o'clock, I think—and the place was empty.

When we sat down at a table, the waiter was friendly but did not make any special deal of my being there. We ordered our pizzas. A few people arrived, but they paid no attention to me. The pizzas were very good and we were able to enjoy the entire meal without one stranger coming to our table. It was very nice and, I must admit, quite rare for me these days. Because of this experience in Vienna, I have started going to restaurants early, when few people are there. In this way I have a much better chance of enjoying a quiet meal. Of course, I would always rather eat sooner than later.

I find I must be careful about one thing: because I stay home whenever I am not in the mood to greet strangers, I might find myself staying home too much. One time in New York Nicoletta wanted to go out for a walk and wanted me to go too. She felt I needed some diversion and some exercise. But I wasn't feeling very sociable—at least, not sociable enough to talk with people I didn't know.

She was irritated with me and said, "How can you live this way? You're almost a prisoner! You are sacrificing too much."

I didn't like to hear that and told her, "My job is my life. It is not a sacrifice."

When I was having trouble with my knee, I had a good excuse to stay home. I could have my privacy, and I could avoid the pain of walking too much. But now my knee is better and my weight is down. Nicoletta keeps reminding me of the improvements and is making sure I don't use these excuses from yesterday to stay home today. She is insisting I go out more, and I think she is right.

This is true not only in cities like New York when I am working, but in places where I go to relax. Last year I went to Barbados for a few days' rest at a hotel where I had stayed many times. Nicoletta had never been there, and she asked me what were the interesting things to see on the island.

I gave her the Italian answer, "Buh," which means I have no idea. I explained that when I came to Barbados, it was to rest. I stayed in the hotel the entire time. In fact, I couldn't remember ever going out. She said she thought that was terrible. "Here you are on a beautiful tropical island, and you never even look at it."

She asked the hotel people about interesting places to visit. They told her about a wildlife preserve which we went to and I must admit that I enjoyed seeing it very much. We also took drives along parts of the seacoast, which were very beautiful and which I had never seen before. Nicoletta started a campaign to make me see the difference between real problems that keep you at home and just being lazy. I am glad she did.

When you are well known, you must make an extra effort to be polite and gracious. If you offend people, even unintentionally, you might hurt them more because of who you are. I like to think I have very good instincts in this way and that I am *educato,* which is roughly like the English expression "well brought up." I have always been sensitive to the feelings of other people, and I hope this has not changed with my success.

The danger areas are the things I care most about. First is my health. If I feel I am being asked to do something that might give me a sore throat or make me sick, I will speak right out, even if someone will be hurt. For example, this might happen when I am sent flowers. Certain types of flowers, especially lilies, give me trouble in the throat. I do not know why this happens, but I assure you it does happen. So even if the person who sent the flowers is right there in front of me, I say, "I am sorry, but you must take them away."

Another example is music. When I am working and I feel one of my colleagues is doing something in an incorrect way, I will speak out even if I know there is a chance of giving offense. I always state my difference as an opinion, not as a hard fact, but I still speak out.

The other area is food. I have a broad range of appetite and understand that different people like different things. But if I am given something that is just plain bad, I will not eat it. If I am asked, I might even say why.

This happened in Berlin not too long ago when I was performing in *Bohème* with the winners of the Philadelphia vocal competition. A dinner was arranged for us in an Italian restaurant. I am always skeptical about Italian restaurants in certain foreign countries, and I am sorry to say Germany is one of them. They have such strong food traditions of their own, and they are on a different culinary wavelength than Italians. But the plans were made for us to eat at this place, so I had to go.

In the restaurant, we were a large group at one table. The first dish, a risotto, was brought out. I took one taste, then turned to Kallen Esperian, who was singing Mimi, and whispered, "Don't eat this. It will poison you."

I don't know what was in it, but it tasted awful. It wasn't Italian food. It wasn't food, even. The next course was not much better. I was certain the chef would come out to receive compliments. I thought about what I would say. When he arrived at our table, I was as friendly as possible. I talked about the atmosphere in his restaurant, the good service—everything but the food. But he could see I had not eaten his terrible dishes, so I joked around with him, hoping to take his mind off my full plate in front of me.

Kallen said later that when I was joking with the chef I said something about not feeding this food to a dog, but I am sure she did not hear me correctly. I don't think I would have said such a thing. But then, maybe I did. I can pretend to be polite about almost everything except these three things—music, my health, and bad food. I believed this situation had to do with the last two.

My mother brought me up always to be polite. You don't have to be rich to have good manners. My friend Renata Nash laughed at me one time for having manners she thought were *too* good. I was visiting her at her apartment on Central Park West, and we were sitting in her living room. She and her husband have a pit bull who decided he liked me. All of sudden the dog jumped up into my lap and stayed there. I have heard the reputation of this type of dog, so I felt very uncomfortable. This must have shown in my expression.

"You don't have to keep Schatzi there, Luciano. If you don't want him, just push him away."

I said to her, "Renata, I am a guest in your home. I cannot tell your dog what to do."

She got the idea and took the dog away, but she said I was being too formal. I don't think so. I want to believe that I know how to behave even if her dog doesn't. Aside from good manners, I wasn't eager to upset a pit bull.

Most of the time, however, I believe in being honest with my friends. If something is bothering me, I will tell them. To do otherwise with close friends is being phony and plastic.

Even though I am now well known, I still am in awe of many people. Since I was a boy, I have worshiped my heroes in the sports world, especially race car drivers and football players. I still do. I am also a complete fan of many people in the entertainment world—Frank Sinatra, for instance, who I am happy to say has become a friend.

For years I have liked very much the recordings of Vic Damone, who has such superb phrasing. One time his wife, the wonderful singer and actress Diahann Carroll, came backstage to see me and said that Vic wanted to meet me. He was outside, but he was such a fan of my singing that he was afraid to come in. I told her to bring him in, but I was such a fan of his singing that I probably would not be able to speak.

Years ago when I was just becoming known in America, Bob Cahen spotted Burt Lancaster in the audience of a concert of mine in San Francisco. Bob knew I was a fan of Lancaster's and had seen every one of his films. In fact, I had learned much of my English from watching Burt Lancaster films. Bob went up to Lancaster and asked if he would like to meet me. Lancaster said he would be happy to.

When Bob brought this legendary movie star into my dressing room after the concert, I was so surprised that I did something foolish: I got down on my knees and bowed to the floor. This was my thanks for all of the fantastic films he had given me, and also for teaching me English. I am no longer quite so enthusiastic about my favorite celebrities. It is a good thing because I am not as quick getting to my knees. Lancaster was a terrific man and we remained friends until his death last year.

At one point I became addicted to the films of Mel Brooks. I remember being in Vienna to sing at the Staatsoper and decided I had to see a particular Mel Brooks film that I knew would cheer me up. I sent my poor secretary all over the city looking for the film in which he plays an actor who spies on the Nazis. It is called *To Be or Not to Be*. We watched it, and I loved it as much as ever.

Then after one of my Vienna performances, I was greeting people in my dressing room and I looked up to see Mel Brooks waiting in the door to see me. I was so surprised and overwhelmed, I could not speak. Even after Brooks and I were introduced, I had trouble saying anything sensible. It was like seeing a Puccini opera and then having Puccini walk into your dressing room. I have seen people who get that confused when they meet me. I assure you, I sympathize.

∽

This is one of the good things about being well known: it makes it easier to meet other well-known people whom you admire. And you get invited to interesting places, too. When I was singing in Washington in the late 1980s during the Bush administration, the president invited me to lunch at the White House. For company, I took my secretary, Judy Kovacs.

At the lunch, I was seated next to Mrs. Bush, and Judy was seated next to the president. Now, Judy is a well-educated, intelligent girl who can converse easily in seven languages, so I was not worried about her sitting next to such an important world leader. One thing about the lunch impressed me. In front of every place there was a little dish of salted peanuts. I asked Mrs. Bush if she always had these nuts on her table. She said the president liked them very much and wanted everyone to have them at all times.

We were all having a nice, relaxed time when suddenly, in the middle of lunch, Judy put her fork to her mouth then let out a loud noise, like a "whoop." The president looked very worried, as if she might be sick. The table was silent and Mrs. Bush said, "Is Miss Kovacs all right?"

I said to everybody, "It's nothing. Judy always does that when she eats something she likes."

I don't know if it was Judy's whoop, but the Bushes became friends and I recently visited them in their new home in Texas.

Through my appearances in benefit concerts and with my own concert for the Modena horse show, I have become acquainted with popular singers, even some rock stars. I find myself particularly fascinated by this world, which is so different from the world of opera, and I am particularly fascinated by the way these singers, who are so much younger than I, handle so easily their worldwide fame.

One who has become a particularly good friend is the British rock star Sting. He and I met and became friends. Later, we both sang at a benefit concert at Carnegie Hall, which he helped organize for the Amazon Rain Forest in 1993. When I agreed to sing for his benefit, he agreed to sing at my horse show concert. I was particularly impressed that he was willing to attempt a little operatic singing with me. I knew he believed he would make a fool of himself, but he did it anyway. He is very brave and a very good sport—and of course sang Verdi with his great style.

I have since visited him and his wife at their amazing home outside London. The place is large and old—a castle, really—and he has recording studios there and a very happy family. His wife, Trudy, is a wonderful person, too. They have three children, ages four, eleven, and thirteen. The eleven-year-old is, I think, my biggest fan of all.

Sting and Trudy have created a fantastic life at their castle. The place is full of love and music, and I envy his freedom to be at home so much. Naturally, he sometimes goes on tour, though. When he was touring South Africa recently, Trudy and the three children came and stayed with me in New York.

Another new friend whom I like very much is Bruce Springsteen. I have always admired his singing. It is so honest and so full of vitality. He does something with a phrase that is remarkable, unlike anyone else. Like me, he appears to draw terrific energy from an audience. I was very pleased, then, when word came to me that Bruce Springsteen wanted to meet me.

The way it happened was that Springsteen and his wife were visiting the director Franco Zeffirelli at his villa in Positano. I have worked with Franco a number of times, and we have a good relationship. A publicity man was also there whom I know, and they were talking about me. Springsteen told them he was an admirer of my singing and would like to meet me. Later in New York, I received a phone call from the publicity man telling me about this conversation, so I invited Bruce and his wife to dinner.

I liked them both very much, and we had a wonderful evening. They urged me to visit them at their farm in New Jersey. I went there for lunch and had a fantastic time. The Springsteens live on a farm that is very secluded and beautiful. He drove me around the place in his Jeep and showed me all the exotic animals he keeps, even an ostrich.

It was a very happy day. The Springsteens have three children, and the actress Susan Sarandon was there for lunch and had brought her three children. I think there were more children from somewhere. Little children were everywhere. It was the end of summer and we had drinks outside under the trees, then went into the house for a delicious lunch.

Inside I saw two unusual chairs I liked very much. They were the style of old-fashioned office chairs made of oak, but they were high, like bar stools. When I was having so much trouble with my knee, I became very fond of chairs this high. I could sit on them and rest my legs without sitting so low that it was difficult for me to get up. I asked for the measurements so I could have a carpenter make chairs like that.

A few weeks later it was my birthday. I got a call from the lobby of my building that there was a large delivery. It was the two chairs we had seen, with a note saying, "Happy birthday from the Springsteens." I have placed the chairs near a window where I can sit and look north across Central Park.

I invited Bruce and his wife to see me sing *Tosca,* and after the performance, I gave a little party for them in my apartment. I also invited my friend Isabella Rossellini and the designers Dolce and Gabbana. These are two very talented and imaginative clothing designers who are very up to the minute. They design for many well-known people, including Madonna. Nicoletta persuaded me to have them design some clothes for me. She said I was too conservative. I agree, but I told her, "Nothing metal."

Nicoletta is also enthusiastic about my doing a performance with Bruce Springsteen. We have not thought of anything specific yet, and I do not know if he would be interested. But I think he is a great singer and I would be happy to perform with him.

I think the greatest thing about being a well-known person is that you can take on projects that are close to your heart. You can help good causes like the movement to save the Amazon rain forest. This was behind my thinking when I started the vocal competition in Philadelphia and my Modena horse show. I have been performing for thirty-five years, and I am extremely fortunate to have won broad recognition. When little boys in the slums of Buenos Aires recognize me and students in Peking ask me to sign my CDs, I would be falsely modest not to acknowledge that I am now very well known. My hope is to use my good fortune in this area for constructive purposes.

When I started out as a singer, I never thought much about becoming famous. For me it was enough to be given opportunities to perform and to earn enough money to support my family. Even when I began having success in the opera world, I knew what a narrow world it was. The idea of becoming famous in the way that film stars are famous seemed very unlikely.

In those first years, however, I did have an experience that made me think a little about this business of fame. When I was touring Australia with Joan Sutherland in 1965, the press was interested only in interviewing Joan. She was singing wonderfully, of course, but so was I. Vocally, I had finally won complete control of my voice—in many ways thanks to her. I was able to sing my best in performance after performance. I knew I was doing something special, something that had taken me years to achieve, but the general public remained completely indifferent to what I was doing.

The audiences were very warm in their applause for my singing, but outside the opera house I did not exist. Joan, on the other hand, was in the newspapers and on television all the time. I saw that the difference was simple: she was famous and I was not.

It made me begin thinking that with fame you get a certain kind of respect you don't get by just being good at what you do. I did not think a lot about this, as I knew there was little you could do about becoming famous. The public either likes you or it doesn't like you. Still, when I had an opportunity to do things that might broaden my recognition—things like television interviews, for instance—I tried to do them when my schedule permitted. If I wanted to win the public's interest, and perhaps their affection, I had to do what I could to make sure they knew I existed.

Now I have a large following, and it is wonderful for me. Everybody wants to be loved, perhaps me a little more than most people. But in many ways being famous is a big comedy. The public says to you, "We have made you a celebrity. Now let us see you fall on your face."

If that sounds bitter, I don't mean it to be. I understand this is part of the game. When the public places you at the top of your profession, they see no place for you to go but down. And many of them are extremely alert to signs that the descent has begun. I know this because for twenty years people have been detecting signs that I am on my way out. They may not be anxious for this to happen, but they do seem to be afraid of missing the end when it comes. Some are eager to be the first to predict this important turn in my fortunes, and I am eager to prove them wrong. I suspect this struggle is healthy, though, because it ensures that I will always make my biggest effort.

I have another attitude that helps me. I never predict how

things will go. I look at every performance as a new experience that can go well or badly. I never feel that because I have performed well in the past, the audience owes me something, that they must react in a certain way. That may sound obvious, but I have colleagues who feel that their reputation has earned them a particular response. I never think that. I know I am judged only on the performance I am doing at the moment. Nothing else.

Celebrities must play another game with interviewers from the media, particularly those on live television, who hope to make things more lively by embarrassing you with references to negative things. I love to tease my friends, so I am sure if I were a television interviewer I would do the same thing. They give you little jabs to make sure you are not too content with yourself.

With me, they might mention a bad performance or my excess weight. Perhaps they want to see how I will deal with a sensitive subject. This happens all the time, and I am good at the game. My secret is that I never take myself very seriously. When the interviewer makes a gentle reference to something bad that happened, I grab it and make a stronger reference.

On *Sixty Minutes,* for instance, Mike Wallace referred to people booing me at La Scala. I knew he was talking about the *Don Carlo* disaster. I said, "Yes, I sang badly that night, and they were correct to boo me." As long as the things the interviewers refer to are true, I have no problem with them and can usually laugh about them. Trouble comes only if you take yourself too seriously and pretend that nothing bad ever happens to you. If they want to talk about my weight, I don't mind and will discuss it any way they like. What else am I going to do? Sit on television in full view of everyone and pretend I don't have a weight problem?

I have talked in this chapter about the pluses and minuses of being well known. I hope the final impression is that I am very happy and grateful that my life has turned out as it has. More than anything else, I believe that fame is an enormous responsibility. If people are good enough to like you, you must do nothing to disappoint them. Each time you sing, you must try to sing as well as you did on their favorite Pavarotti recording. Each time you meet people in public, you must be cheerful and friendly, no matter how you might be feeling. In interviews, television appearances, walking down a street, you must never do anything that would make people sorry they liked you.

This can result in a lot of pressure. Bill Wright has spent a lot of time with me this year, and he sees how hard I try not to disappoint people. He said something complimentary to me about this effort and asked how I can handle the pressure. I told him, "I have big shoulders."

When I start thinking seriously about it like that, something always happens to bring me down to earth. A wonderful example happened in New York recently. I dialed the telephone number of a friend of mine, but a woman answered whose voice I did not recognize. I asked for my friend, and she said in a sharp voice, "Who is this speaking?"

By now I was sure I had dialed the wrong number, but I said, "I am Luciano Pavarotti."

"Sure," she said, "and I'm Maria Callas." Then she hung up.

16
THOUGHTS ON SINGING

When I was nineteen, I dedicated myself seriously to being a singer. Many years earlier, when I was six, for example, I would sing on the kitchen table and tell everyone I would be a singer. When I was twelve and heard and met the great tenor, Beniamino Gigli, I told him I would one day be a tenor. But you say a lot of things at six and at twelve. At nineteen, however, I started seriously planning to become an operatic singer, and I have been a student of singing ever since.

No matter how much success I have had, there has never been a time when I was not working on improving my singing. There is always something new to learn, a different way of controlling the breathing, managing the vocal cords, attacking a phrase.

You cannot think hard about a subject for forty years and not have strong ideas about it. I believe I have learned a lot and understand some of the mystery of the human voice. I would like to pass along some of this knowledge. I am sure most people reading this book are not planning to become opera singers, but I hope they are willing to listen to some of what I've learned. If they do, they might get a better idea of the thought and effort that go into serious singing. The next time they hear beautiful singing, they might appreciate it in a different way.

When I started serious study, I spent the first six months vocalizing only with the vowel sounds. Day after day I would be singing *ay, eee, oh, eye, ooo*. It is not a very interesting way to spend six months, but my teacher, Arrigo Pola, believed it was essential. And he convinced me. Over the years I have become even more convinced of the importance of this. Anyone who wants to be an opera singer must learn not only to manage the voice but also to sing *words*.

With my kind of music, the words carry the drama; the music *is* the words. If from the very beginning you learn to sing notes rather than words, you will get into trouble later. This is trouble that is hard to fix. I believe those six months of singing nothing but vowel sounds locked something into the back of my head that was extremely helpful to me throughout my career.

Probably the most difficult thing to learn for the beginning voice student is the importance of the *passaggio*. Everyone has two voices, the lower and upper registers. If you start singing from a low note and go up the scale, you will hear a place where you switch from the lower to the upper register. The sound becomes different, and in order to make the transition, you switch to a different part of your throat.

The professional singer must learn to manage this transition without any sign. It must all appear to be one voice, a voice without seams. You must not let anyone hear you change gears, but rather you must learn to sing like an automatic transmission of a Cadillac. Learning to do this correctly is one of the most difficult things a young singer must do.

If young people study singing, it is probably because others have told them they have a terrific voice. They must agree or they wouldn't be studying. They hear themselves singing beautiful notes in different parts of their range—down here and up there. But composers do not write music just for down here or just for up there; they write for the entire musical scale. The voice must be trained to pass from one register to the other, not as two instruments, but as one. Although the human voice is a unique musical instrument, it must be trained to be as consistent and versatile as any other musical instrument such as a violin or a clarinet.

Young singers often don't understand this. They know they have a good voice and they want to start singing arias and songs. Learning to control the *passaggio* is very difficult and takes much time and work. There are different techniques for doing this, and different teachers have their preferences. The important thing is to pick one technique and stick to it. For the student, it can get very discouraging, because it is one of those things you work and work on without seeing any progress. But one day it happens, and you are the master of your *passaggio*.

I struggled with this problem for six years before I really had it under control. Time and repetition are more important than which technique you use, but if you get frustrated and change techniques, you will never get the *passaggio* completely under your control so that it is automatic. As a result, you will never have any vocal security.

The other most important thing for the beginning singer is to learn to give full support from the diaphragm. People think you sing from the throat, but you actually sing from the throat *and* the diaphragm working together. I was already a few years into my career before I understood how extremely important this was.

I learned this important aspect of singing from Joan Sutherland when we toured Australia together in 1965. Her brilliant use of her powerful diaphragm was what made it possible for her to sing at the highest level of artistry night after night. In my own performances with her, I was going back and forth between good and not so good. I asked her to show me her secret, and she was happy to do so. It was her very strong diaphragm and the way she used it.

The diaphragm is important not only on high notes, not only to produce the bravura bursts of melody that bring audiences to their feet. It is important for the quiet notes as well. For me, the most difficult notes for the tenor in *La Bohème* are in Act One when Rodolfo sings to Mimi, "Che gelida manina . . ." Those quiet low notes must have a big rich sound—a steady, pure sound that floods the opera house. They may be soft notes, but they must have behind them all your power as a singer. They must have the same amount of support from your diaphragm that you give the big notes.

With the many difficult things a young singer must learn, I realize how lucky I was that I received the finest training from the start. That can make all the difference. I sometimes compare my good luck with the bad luck of Mario Lanza. He certainly had a magnificent voice, but many believe he was improperly trained. They explain this by saying he came from a very poor family in South Philadelphia.

My family was very poor also. Because my father was a baker, we always had enough to eat, but there was no money for anything extra like singing lessons. So the difference was not money or being rich or poor. The difference was that my father was passionate about singing. He loved opera, and he was very knowledgeable about everything concerning operatic singing. Most important, he knew that if I was going to pursue a vocal career, I had to prepare for it properly.

When I decided to make the attempt, my father and I went to talk with the best teacher in Modena, Arrigo Pola, and he agreed to accept me as his student for free. I am sure Philadelphia had good teachers who would have been happy to teach Mario Lanza for no money. I also think there must have been a music school that would have given him a scholarship. America is so rich in this kind of assistance to talented people with little money. I suspect the difference was that his family did not realize how important this was, and mine did. For artists, knowledge is often more important than money.

Another important thing for a singer to learn from the very beginning is how to take care of himself. The voice is a fragile instrument that is vulnerable to many physical ailments that will damage the singing. Young singers must get into the habit of treating themselves like babies. When I first began to work with one of our competition winners, Kallen Esperian, I told her that the most important advice I could give her could be said in three words. In Italian I said, *"Tu sei cantante,"* which means "You are a singer."

I explained that this meant she now had to live her life in a different way from other people. She had to conserve her energy, not do all the things other young women do, be careful to always dress warmly, take extra good care of herself. I know too well that no matter how careful you are, you can still get sick. But if you are going to have a career, many, many people will depend on your voice. It is your responsibility to see that you do nothing to increase the dangers to the voice.

I have many beliefs about how to do this. For instance, I think that an abrupt change in temperature is very bad. You should not go from a warm room to the cold air. To be extra safe, this should be done as gradually as possible. Another thing that is extremely bad for me is when I am so warm that I am perspiring and then I go outside. This is a sure invitation to trouble. I also hate to get my feet cold. Whenever I do, I get into difficulties with my throat.

I have another view about cold that almost contradicts my first one. I believe that cold liquids like iced mineral water are very good for the throat. But for some reason, cold air has a very different effect. It is very bad. That is why whenever the temperature is a little bit cold, I wear a scarf right up over my mouth. I may look like an Arabian bandit, but I am only protecting the voice.

You never know when something will happen that might be bad for the voice. I was flying once on a small airplane, and when the plane took off, jets of cold mist suddenly were shot into my face. I asked the stewardess what it was, and she said it was something to do with the cabin pressure and it would soon go away. As it turned out, it didn't hurt me, but if I had been on my way someplace to sing, I would have had a fit. I have never read any books about the effects of cold mist sprayed on the throat, but I am sure it is not good.

All the things that I have spoken about so far have to do with learning to sing well and protecting the throat. In order to have a successful career there is something else that is essential: you must have great confidence that you have what is necessary, and you must have the determination to make others realize this.

One of my oldest and dearest friends in the music world is Leone Magiera, who has been so much a part of my professional and personal life. When I was studying voice and hoping for a chance to sing professionally, Leone was the husband of my friend Mirella Freni who was also beginning her career. When I first entered the Achille Peri Competition in Reggio Emilia, Leone was my accompanist. I made some mistakes and came in second. He tells me now he remembers the look on my face as the silver medal was being given to another.

He said, "I knew from your expression, Luciano, that you were not someone who was content to be second." I won the next competition, though, and my career began.

I am happy he saw that in my face. Even then I knew what I could do, but I knew I was not doing it. If I looked happy at that moment, I would not have had what I needed to be an opera singer. Even from the beginning I was extremely competitive with myself, not so much with others.

Young singers starting their careers must of course be competitive with other singers, or at least not be afraid of competition. You are trying to win the same role in an opera as many other young singers. Only one of you will get it. Although I had to compete with other singers, like everyone else starting out, I knew that if I did my best, everything else would work out all right. So I concentrated on doing better than I had done the day before and stopped worrying about what other singers were doing.

Eventually a singer reaches a certain level of success when there are plenty of offers of work. That happened to me a few years after I won the Peri competition in 1961. Then I could stop worrying about other singers. There was more than enough opera to keep us all busy, so I could concentrate totally on improving myself and expanding my range as an artist.

I feel about other tenors the way I feel about great football players or horsemen. I am excited and happy when they do well, but I do not feel their achievements have anything to do with me personally. They are them and I am me. If there is a link to me personally, it is a positive one. I have a greater feeling of closeness to the other tenors because I know what they go through with each performance. I think I know this better than anyone, even their wives.

Although confidence is important for a young singer, I also believe it is important not to be too confident. In fact, in my opinion it is good to be constantly scared. In my own career, I am always nervous, no matter what I am doing. Fear can be healthy if it does not cripple you. The main reason my father did not have a career with his beautiful voice is that he could never conquer the fear. Days before he is scheduled to sing a solo, he is frantic with nerves. He would have been miserable in an operatic career where he would always have had another performance coming up.

While I think I have mastered my fear and am confident of my abilities, I never predict how a concert or a performance will go, no matter how good I feel or how good my voice sounds to me. The voice is unpredictable, and so is every aspect of performing. You are feeling good and you believe you are singing as well as you can when—*boom*—something happens to throw you off. A concert or opera that is going well suddenly starts going badly. It might be some quirk in your own performance, something a colleague does, or something that comes from nowhere.

The great soprano Elisabeth Schwarzkopf once sang an outdoor concert—at the Salzburg Festival, I think. She hit a high note and held it. When her mouth was open wide, a bug flew into it and she started choking. This upset her so much that she had to stop singing and wait for a few minutes before she could continue the program.

People think that because I can go out and sing in front of huge crowds, I must have terrific confidence. I don't. I have bravery, and that is different from confidence. If you are confident, it means you believe everything will be fantastic. I never assume that. I am always afraid. In fact, I think the only way to be continually successful is to be a little scared all the time. If you are not scared, it means you think something is easy. If you think something is easy, you won't work as hard and you will not be as good as you can be. Talent and ability are very important for an artist, of course, but fear is important, too.

I am always aware that no matter how much success I have, anything can happen at any moment to knock me from whatever perch I have achieved. I take nothing for granted. I agree with

Herbert when he quotes Yogi Berra: it's not over till it's over. I am always waiting for that bug to fly into my mouth.

Studying to become an opera singer is so difficult and the chances of success are so slight, it is amazing that anyone tries for this career. The other day someone asked me if I thought every young tenor starting out believed he could become another Caruso. I said I didn't think so, and I think the question shows that perhaps people don't understand the motivation of all of us who try for a career in singing.

The young singer starting out believes that he has something to give. In his heart he believes he has something to offer that will make people like him, maybe love him. This is not egotism; it is the opposite of egotism, or a very different kind of egotism than we usually see. He believes he has something inside, but he knows it is hidden, buried so deep that people can't see it. Only he knows it is there. He understands that, so he wants to develop that something, bring it out, show others that he has it.

When I was a young man studying voice, I gradually came to believe I had that something. This belief made me very happy, and even now it makes me very happy. I worked extremely hard to make sure it came out in the best way possible and that I took the best possible care of it. I have been studying how to sing for forty years, and I still work on my voice every day. But not with a teacher. I know when I do it right and when I do it wrong. If after forty years I don't know this, if I still need someone else to tell me, then something is very wrong.

For me, what makes singing exciting is the idea that you are communicating not just the composer's intentions, not the emotions of the character you are portraying, but also part of your own nature that cannot come out in other ways. Of all the rewards, making other people happy is the best. After my Central Park concert in 1993 the *New York Times* wrote that all of the 500,000 people who saw the concert had forgotten their problems by the time they left the park. Maybe for only a short time they were happy. No one can imagine how happy this makes me.

Once you are in a vocal career, you must continue to work on your voice, to be sure, but you must also give a great deal of attention to your repertoire. Singers have ruined their careers at the beginning by selecting the wrong roles. To know which roles are right for you, you must have a clear understanding of your voice. This sounds obvious, but you will remember that a beginner once auditioned for me and announced that she was a mezzo, when I could clearly hear that she was a soprano. If singers don't even know what category of voice they have, how can they pick the right roles?

I was lucky to start my career by singing Rodolfo in *La Bohème*. I was so happy to get a part, which was awarded to the winner of the Peri competition, that I would have jumped into Siegfried without any hesitation. Luckily, Rodolfo has proved to be one of the most congenial roles for my voice and my temperament. I probably have sung it more often than any other role, and I hope to be able to sing it for a long time in the future.

My other two favorite roles are in Donizetti's *L'Elisir d'Amore* and Verdi's *Un Ballo in Maschera*. Apart from the fact that they are both, in my opinion, operatic masterpieces, they have wonderful tenor roles, both musically and dramatically. When it was found that I could manage with not too much difficulty the roles Bellini wrote for tenors, I was happy to take on *I Puritani* and *La Sonnambula*. These operas had not been performed for many years, partly because of the difficulty of the tenor music. Especially *Puritani*, which I think may be the most difficult tenor role. I am proud to have done them.

There is always tremendous pressure on a tenor to expand his repertoire, to take on new roles. Often this pressure comes from the people who like your singing the most. They want to hear you in all of their favorite roles. Others try to push you to your limits. If you can sing *Aïda,* they say, let's hear you in *Il Trovatore.* Okay, now you've done *Trovatore,* how about *Otello?* They want to keep pushing you until you are singing Wagner—or until you destroy your voice.

I have done all of these roles now and have sung all together thirty-seven roles. This year I will add another to my repertoire, *Andrea Chénier.* I have recorded it but never performed it on stage. Many singers have sung many more roles than I have. Placido Domingo knows a hundred roles, I believe. But thirty is quite a lot for me, and I feel my brain is stuffed with music. I was driving somewhere last summer with Bill Wright and I started to sing an Italian folk song that is not well known. Bill remarked on the great amount of music I must have stored in my brain—the operas, the church music, the traditional songs, the popular songs of my youth.

I smiled and said, "Bill, what are you trying to tell me?"

I was thinking about what they say about high notes affecting a tenor's brain. Maybe Bill believed that if my brain was full of music, there was no room for anything else.

There is a natural process in which a tenor's voice becomes darker as he grows older. Singing the more dramatic roles that require a darker voice will help push the voice down, help make it darker. But once you have altered the voice in this way, there is a danger the voice might not go back up. If you sing *Otello,* you may be saying good-bye to *I Puritani.* But maybe you have already said good-bye to *Puritani.* It works both ways.

I will soon find out if that has happened to me. I plan to

undertake for a second time Donizetti's *Daughter of the Regiment*. This is the role with the killer aria, "Ah Mes Amis," with its nine high C's, and it was the part that brought me so much attention when I sang it at the Met with Joan Sutherland in 1972. People felt it couldn't be done, so when I did it, they treated me like Lindbergh flying alone to Paris. But it has been a quarter of a century since I sang that role. It will be an enormous challenge to see if I can still do it.

Many of my friends urge me not to sing this role again. Most tenors, they say, are *never* crazy enough to try it. "But you have done it once, Luciano," they say. "Why do it again?" Because I am crazy, I tell them.

Others say that the many high C's might be difficult for a tenor who is no longer in his thirties. My answer to that is that high C's are just a habit. By that I mean they are like pure athletics. If you train and are in shape, you can do it. For me, the high notes have never been the most difficult part of many operas. I do not mean they are not dangerous. You are usually in a lot of danger in the upper limits of your voice. I mean that to sing other parts of the music really well can be more difficult.

I have often thought about the power of the top tenor notes to move and excite an audience. When I am working hard on the stage throughout the evening and feel I have been singing exceptionally well, I see that the audience appreciates this, but they never show anything like the excitement they feel when you hit a high C and hold it. What is behind this response?

Of course, everyone believes it is more difficult to sing these notes than the rest of the music. That is part of it, I am sure. A high jumper gets more applause going over a six-foot bar than going over a three-foot one. But while high notes may be athletics, music is not athletics. I have a theory that when the tenor voice sings very high, the sound is unnatural. It is not a sound that usually comes from humans; it is more like an animal sound. It may call out to something very deep in our nature. Maybe that is why it is so exciting to many people.

But I do not want to say that high notes are the only way to win over an audience. There are many ways. It might be the turn of a phrase or the intensity of your acting at just the right moment. You must always be alert for opportunities to project the right feeling at the right time.

Whatever happens, I know that when I sing, it is always up to me to move the audience. It is my job, my responsibility. That may sound obvious, but I have colleagues who don't always feel that way. One of them said to me after an excellent performance, "What is wrong with those people? The way I sang tonight, they should have been standing on their chairs cheering." He made it sound as if he had done his part, but they had not done theirs.

I never feel that way. If I want an audience to become really moved and excited by what I do, I must figure out how to make it happen. If it doesn't happen, it is my fault, not theirs.

I am extremely critical of myself. For that reason, I do not pay too much attention to the critics. It is not that I don't respect their opinions, it is that I respect my own opinion more, at least as far as my own voice is concerned. If the critics write that I sang badly when I believe I sang well, I will be upset. If I really did sing badly, then I will know it; I don't have to learn this from them.

It is not only the serious music critics who attack. You must be prepared to receive criticism from anywhere. One time I drove from New York down to Pennsylvania to have lunch with my friends Leona and Nelson Shanks. We were in the kitchen of their house, and Nelson's grandson, a little baby who was not yet two years old, was there also eating his lunch. To test my voice and the acoustics—and maybe to impress the baby—I put my hand over my ear to hear myself better, and I sang a few notes very loud. I was in good voice, and I think I rattled the glasses a little.

The baby looked at me hard, then stuck his tongue out and

made an impolite noise. Nelson called it a raspberry. He and Leona were a little embarrassed, but I told them I was always grateful for a naive opinion.

In recent years I have become more interested in popular music, even rock. It started from my interest in expanding the audience for my type of music with big concerts and television appearances. When I did benefits with performers like Elton John and Sting, I became fascinated with the incredible popularity of these people and their music. There is no doubt they reach a far wider audience than opera singers do.

I learned even more about them when I invited some of them to perform at my horse-show concert in Modena. That was when I began attempting to sing this music myself. Two very popular Italian singers, Lucio Dalla and Zucchero, both wrote songs for me, which I sang at the concert. Neither song took me too far from the operatic idiom, but they were still popular and, for me, a challenge. This was all done in the spirit of fun, and it does not mean I will change my vocal style.

By performing with Sting, Bryan Adams, and the other popular singers, I try to show an appreciation and a respect for their music. But more important for me are the young people in the audience who do not know or care about opera. I want them to see these rock idols showing their respect for my type of music. When the young people see their pop heroes up there on the stage with this heavy opera singer, all singing "La Donna è Mobile" together, they might say, "Hey, if Sting can sing it, maybe this music is not so terrible."

I look forward to singing more concerts with popular singers. My hope is that mixing my music with popular music will bring more people to operatic music and to break down the walls that exist between the two types of music. Tibor Rudas says there is no such thing as classical music; there is only good music and bad music. I do not go that far, but I believe very strongly that most people are capable of enjoying both types; they just don't realize it. Many get trapped in one type of music or the other and think they must stay there.

No one loves the traditional operatic music more than I do, but I have also come to like some of the popular music of today. I tell people I like it if it is good, but I am not sure how to define "good" right now. Maybe I will learn in the future. I sincerely feel I was put on this earth to learn. When I am brought together with something new for me, like rock music, I try not to say "I like it" or "I don't like it." I try first to learn about it, maybe even force myself a little. Then after I have made the effort, I believe I am more entitled to say whether I like it or not.

As far as my effort to understand popular music is concerned, I must give Nicoletta credit for this. When we are driving some-where for me to perform, she puts a rock-and-roll tape on the car stereo. I take it out and put in a classical tape. We used to fight about this, but she has persuaded me to try to appreciate this music which she loves and which is so important to so many people. I saw that she is right.

My interest increased a lot when I began meeting important performers in this field. I saw how serious these artists are about their music, how hard they work on it. I decided I must learn what rock is all about. Now I can really enjoy a lot of it. Still, when Nicoletta is not around, I put on an operatic tape. And when I'm in the shower, I will probably sing Verdi instead of Bryan Adams.

As for my operatic career, I know it cannot go on forever and that it must end before too long. I will know when. What will I do then? I don't think that will be a problem. I love to teach and have been told I am good at it. I taught a master class at Juilliard some years back and enjoyed doing it very much. During my Philadelphia vocal competition auditions, I try to work with the singers in the role of teacher as much as time will allow. I think I have a very good ear and can quickly put my finger on a vocal problem. That is the key to making people sing better. For me, it would be very satisfying to find talented young singers and help them realize their potential.

I also would be interested in working as an impresario for a medium-sized opera company, but I would prefer to do this in partnership with someone. I want to spend more time in Italy with my family, and I don't want to spend the rest of my life working as hard as most impresarios do. Judy Drucker and I have talked about running an opera company together. I think we could do something very good. Any takers?

17
AUGUST IN PESARO

When I arrive in Pesaro each August for my yearly vacation, I shift into cruise gear and just stay there. Compared to my life most of the year, my weeks by the sea have many days that are wonderfully lazy and relaxing. I wake up when I wish, and I know that I don't have to leave my house for the entire day. Pesaro is a resort on the Adriatic, and in the summer the beaches are filled with people who are there only to have a good time and relax. This creates a mood that helps me to relax.

A friend in New York asked me what I do in Pesaro. I said, "Nothing. Absolutely nothing. None of us do anything. Every three weeks we change our underwear. That's it."

My house in Pesaro, the Villa Giulia, is named after my grandmother. It sits on a hillside at the edge of town, and from the terrace I can see the crowds of the summer visitors on the beaches. Because of this location, I can have my privacy and still feel I am part of humanity.

The entrance to my house is at the bottom of a dead-end road that runs along the beach. There is an electronic gate, which I can open from my car or which somebody in the house can open after speaking to the visitor on an intercom. Past the gate my drive twists up the hill to the house. It is always a wonderful feeling to arrive here after working like a dog all year long and to drive up that hill.

I also like coming to Pesaro in the fall and the winter when the crowds have left, although I am not often able to do this. The vacation season lasts from June through September, but most of the visitors leave at the end of August. This is particularly true at my end of town, which is dominated by the beach. In the winter the streets near me are deserted. Also, the light in the sky is beautiful and the sea is furious.

Pesaro is, of course, a year-round city. It was the birthplace of Rossini and has a wonderful small opera house, Il Teatro Rossini, where each August they have a Rossini Festival. People come from all over Europe and America to this festival to see excellent productions with first-rate singers. Many of the singers are at the beginning of their careers, which makes it more exciting because you can discover new people. While Bill Wright was here working on this book with me, he had written ahead for tickets and asked me if I was going to the festival.

I looked at him. "Are you joking," I said. "I work with opera all year long. I am so full of music, I have indigestion. I need two or three months a year to clear my system. I am not going to go sit in an opera house in the summer when I am on my vacation."

I especially like the people of Pesaro, and I think they are among the nicest in Italy. But so are the people in Modena—no, in all of Emilia. They are very nice people generally. Like all Italians, I love my part of Italy the best. Another good thing about the people of Emilia is that they are crazy for tenors.

Our house in Pesaro is not very large, and the family of our housekeeper, Anna Antonelli, occupies one end of it. But there is a large terrace that runs all the way around the house, mostly shaded by trees. Part is a covered veranda. A swimming pool and a small lawn lie off to one side. We also have a fountain and some flower beds that Anna's son Ferdinando takes care of.

Anna cooks all the meals and she generally runs the entire operation at the Villa Giulia. Anna and her family lived in this house when Adua and I purchased it in 1974, and we were very lucky that she agreed to remain and cook for us. She is a fantastic cook. I might be singing in Rome or Milan, and Anna will send me some simple tomato sauce she has made. I cook pasta for her sauce and I am reminded that her food is as good as the food in Europe's finest hotels.

Anna is not just a superb cook, she is also a wonderful character, one of those I call a p.p., a positive person. She is a small woman, not young, with a head of white hair. When she walks across the terrace, she walks quickly, leaning slightly forward, as though pushing herself into a strong wind. She always looks energetic and determined, and she is. Yet she loves to laugh and is quick to see the fun in everything.

I call Anna positive because she sees what needs to be done and she does it. And when you are cooking for me, that is not easy. Some days I tell her there will be six for lunch; then later in the morning I tell her it will not be six, it will be twenty-six. Well, maybe I am not quite that bad, but I am pretty bad. I am hospitable and I don't work on a rigid schedule. People are always arriving at my door. If friends, acquaintances, journalists, or students arrive in Pesaro, they have usually traveled some distance to get there. If they have come a long way to see me, I must ask them to eat with us.

Most cooks would go crazy about this. But not Anna. She handles it all with no complaints. At one time earlier in her life she cooked for a convent, so she knows how to prepare for large numbers. Also, others help her prepare the food and get it on the table. Anna's two grandsons set up the tables and bring out the food. We all help in preparing the meals, even me.

There is never a problem about having enough food. We always have plenty in the house. Of course we try to raise much of it right here. Anna's son Ferdinando is in charge of that. The olive oil is from our own olives. We raise chickens and grow practically all our fruits and vegetables—peaches, pears, lemons, oranges, lettuce, tomatoes. We even grow artichokes, which ripen in the spring before I can get here, but Anna freezes them so I can eat artichokes all through August. She stuffs them with different things and they are fantastic. Anna freezes everything. I think Anna has turned the entire house into a freezer.

In the summer I like to sleep late—in the winter, too, but more in the summer when it's hot but there is a breeze off the Adriatic. I built a bedroom off the terrace into the side of the hill. I did this to avoid climbing the steps to my bedroom when I had problems with my knees. The room has a door to the outside and a window, and a very high ceiling and a minimum of furniture. There is no air conditioning in the room, even though Pesaro can get hot, as it was this past summer. Being built mostly underground, however, the room is usually cool. But if it gets hot, I use a large electric fan.

I once thought of getting air conditioning installed, and I mentioned it to Anna. I always talk to Anna about anything to do with the house; she has lived in it longer than we have, and it is really her house. The idea of air conditioning made Anna very upset. "Why air conditioning, Luciano?" she says. "There is always a breeze up here on this hill over the sea." For the next few days every time I saw her she would jump on me about the air conditioning, telling me again what a terrible idea it was and how it was completely unnecessary. She continued doing this until I promised her I would not do it.

Anna is convinced that air conditioning is not healthy; she may be right. I try not to sleep with it on. But sometimes I believe it is essential. A few days ago, Bill and I drove to Rimini, where we took a private jet to the Rotterdam airport. I had to hold a press conference at the International Jumpers Show about my Modena horse show the following month. Every important horse person from Europe would be there, and it was an excellent opportunity to tell them about my show.

In Rotterdam a car was waiting to take us to the Hague. It was a Mercedes, but it was older than I am, I think—and not air conditioned. It was extremely hot all over Europe that summer, one of the hottest summers in history, and the Hague was as hot as Pesaro. We stepped off the nice cool jet plane and into that heat and then into a very hot automobile. The drive was not long, but long enough to make us very uncomfortable. Most of the cars we passed on the road between Rotterdam and the Hague had air conditioning—their windows were rolled up tight—but for us the trip was terrible. Just waves of hot air and exhaust hitting us in the face.

By the time we got to the Hague I was wet and dirty, but I immediately had to face officials, the VIPs, and preside over a press conference. I don't think I am that demanding, but it does make you wonder what people are thinking of. They go to so much trouble and fuss for you. They furnish private jets to get you there. At the horse show they give you a golf cart so you don't have to walk a hundred meters to the VIP boxes from the VIP restaurant where they first take you. In the boxes you are served by beautiful Dutch girls who speak perfect English as they pour iced mineral water or champagne and feed you almonds, cheese sticks, little cakes. The officials introduce you to every important person in Holland who is there and even to a Swedish royal princess in the next box who has come see the horses perform. They do all these very nice but unnecessary things. Yet they overlook such a basic comfort as an air-conditioned car on a day when the temperature is over ninety. I make sure this does not happen at my horse show.

One of the Dutch officials apologized to me for not having

sent a limousine to the airport to pick me up. I told him that I hate limousines—they symbolize the elite, the rich, the people who feel they are better than everyone else. So I was happy it was not a limo, but I would have liked air conditioning. Actually in New York, I am in limos a lot, but that is not my choice. It's what other people think I want.

For the first hours of the mornings at Pesaro, I like to take it very easy—sit in the sun, read the newspapers, maybe do some exercise, like ride my bike around the house a few times; the terrace is mostly on one level, so that is not too difficult. I might go for a swim and get into a conversation with whomever is in the pool— any excuse to stay in the cool water. I might sit on the covered veranda and chat with my family, discuss with Anna what we will eat that day, what the weather will do.

I also enjoy helping with the food preparation, as long as I can do it sitting down. For instance, if we are expecting many people, we often serve a large bowl of Macedonia of fruit. I love this for dessert. It is delicious and very healthy. So for me it is a pleasure to sit at a table on the terrace, maybe with my sister-in-law, Giovanna, or perhaps with one of her sons, paring the skin from the pears and peaches and cutting pieces to put in the bowl.

Often people come in the late morning to discuss business. Silvia Galli, the manager of my horse show, might drive down from Modena to go over some plans she has, or others will come to talk about the big concert we organize for the end of the horse show. For instance, a few days ago, Silvia came to tell me that Ray Charles would be in Europe next September and there was a chance he might want to be part of the concert. She gave me the phone number of Ray Charles's manager and asked me to call him with our request.

Later I called the manager in New York from my hammock on the terrace at Pesaro. I explained what the show was about, but he had trouble understanding that there would be no fee. I told him what a good thing the show was, how important it was to me, and that I would happily sing at any concert Ray Charles was organizing for a cause close to his heart. I had done this for Sting and others who now sang at my concert. Charles's manager told me they would think about it—but it didn't work out.

Sometimes I have several meetings going at once. At one table a group might be discussing the horse show. At another, people are helping me plan and arrange the concert. At another table a group from Decca is talking about possible new recordings. Leone Magiera arrives from Ancona to work with me on *Pagliacci*. And of course Bill is waiting to work with me on this book.

Friends asks me, "How can you get anything done with all these meetings going on at the same time? With all these people around?" She tells me that I have no attention span. Well, maybe, but I often think decisions don't take as long to make as other people imagine they do. So while they sit and argue, I can go to another meeting.

I join one group for a while and explain my ideas for solving our problems. Then I move to the next table and let the first group talk over my suggestions. When I come back they might say they have talked over my idea and think it is bad or good. Then we proceed. While I am moving around, I make sure they all have what they want to drink—coffee, a glass of wine. In this hot weather almost everybody drinks mineral water. Anna told me that in one day we drank a hundred liters.

Most of those who come for meetings are very busy people who lead high-pressure lives. When I leave their table, they do not always have time to enjoy the view and wait for me to come back. If they have nothing to discuss among themselves, they make calls on their cellular phones and conduct their business. In order not to disturb the others at their table, they usually get up and walk around the terrace. One time I counted five people wandering around my terrace talking on cellular phones. They were so focused on their conversations, I thought they would bump into each other, but they didn't.

Generally I like all the activity, and I like thinking I am not totally wasting time when I am in Pesaro, but sometimes I allow myself to get too busy, which undermines the whole idea of a vacation. My secretary Larisa, who is a trained masseuse, tries each day to give me a massage for my legs and knees, which are still recovering from the problems I had with them. She gets very upset with me when I will not stop long enough for a massage. She and Bill conspire about ways to trick me into doing what they want. I must have people around me all the time, but sometimes all the activity drives me a little crazy and I must walk around the terrace or the garden to clear my head.

Despite all the visitors and activity at my house in Pesaro, I do not forget that my main job is to relax totally and rest up for the year ahead. But in the summer of 1994 it was not easy to unwind. I was still tense from all the excitement of the Three Tenors concert in Los Angeles.

I find this difficult to explain. The concert went very well. It was beautifully organized, the last-minute problems were minor, and we were all in a very happy, upbeat mood. I believe that is what the audience saw. To be very frank, the concert went a lot better than I thought it would. But two weeks after the Los Angeles concert I was still nervous about it.

Why couldn't I relax? I think it was habit. When you worry about something for an entire year, you cannot just turn the worry off with a switch. At least I can't. Everybody talks about how fantastic it was to perform before the biggest audience in the history of entertainment. Over a billion people watched the concert live. I think this is fantastic too. In fact I find the whole idea of a billion people difficult to comprehend. With the Los Angeles concert, everyone on the planet could watch us succeed or fail. You spend your life hoping for the biggest audience possible, but when you get it, you wish you were singing in a church in Modena.

For operatic tenors, every performance is like a bullfight. The high notes are the angry bulls that you must face and overcome. Who wants to be gored in front of a billion people? It was a happy relief that we all got through the concert so well. Still, in those first weeks in Pesaro, I continued to see in my mind that enormous crowd and the bulls coming at me. I had won out over the bulls, but I was still in tenor shock.

Most mornings in Pesaro there are not all those people holding meetings. More likely it will be just the members of my family and a few others. One typical day in August, my good friend Cesare Castallani from Pesaro came up on his Vespa motor scooter to pay a visit in the late morning. He is a wonderful man, over seventy now, but warm, humorous, and a complete gentleman, not from learning so much as from his nature. A friend of mine from New York said to me how nice Cesare was, and I said, "He is from a different dimension."

That morning Cesare and I started arguing about the corruption that exists throughout our country, both in business and in the government. It was, of course, a topic everyone was talking about that summer because Italy had many more scandals than usual. New ones arrived with each day's newspapers.

Cesare believed that the government brought about the corruption. They demanded so much from citizens in regulations and taxes, he said, they forced businessmen to find ways around the rules in order to make profits. I told Cesare I didn't believe that was the reason. I believed that the problem was in the Italian nature. We all want to be *furbo,* clever. We don't like doing things the obvious, straightforward way. We want to find our own way, a clever way.

That, I told Cesare, is what gets us into corruption. We are not dishonest so much as we are determined to be cleverer than the next person. Cesare did not agree with me. It was all the government's fault, he insisted. We argued back and forth. If you put six Italians together you will have six different political opinions. Neither Cesare nor I changed the other's mind—but neither of us got angry, either.

He *did* make me angry, however, when he said he could not stay for lunch. I protested, pointing out that he was retired, a widower, had plenty of time, but he insisted he had things to do, and he rode off on his Vespa down the hill.

It was then almost noon and I was starting to think a lot about lunch, so I went over and sat down at the dining table. We used to have the dining table set up under the covered part of the terrace that runs along one side of the house, but we moved it down to the terrace's edge for a party because of the incredible view of the water. We all liked it there so much we never moved it back. It is not much farther to walk from the kitchen, so we now eat all of our meals right over the sea. The table runs along a metal railing. Behind that the ground drops off sharply to the beach far below.

From the table's new position, you have a wonderful view of the open sea and the green hills to the north. Even though it sits under trees, we placed four or five movable umbrellas along the table in case the sun came through. No one wants to eat in the sun in this terrible heat. Even though I knew Anna would not be ready to serve lunch for at least another half hour, I sat down alone and began to make phone calls.

I must explain that I love the telephone. In New York when it is too cold to go out or too much of a production to face people, I can keep in touch with my friends everywhere by phone. In Pesaro I have two lines, my cellular phone and the house line. I love the idea that I can pick up either phone and talk to anybody I know anywhere in the world.

I also love it when the phone rings. In the Pesaro house there are always about fifteen people wandering around—my family, the people helping Anna, my secretaries. But when the phone rings I grab it before anyone else. My former secretary, Judy, used to tell me I did this because I wanted to control everything. This is not true. I don't need to answer every phone call to do that. I just love to know what is happening, what new thing is coming into the house, maybe a friend I haven't heard from for a long time, or someone with good news. I am a junkie for surprises, for the unexpected.

Others finally began to sit down at the table, and bottles of mineral water and Lambrusco were placed along the table, as were baskets of bread. The first to join me were Bill, my brother-in-law, Gaetano, and Dino Stefanelli, my friend from Fano, a town a few miles down the coast. Dino has a boat business and helps me with my boat, but he was really there because he was courting my secretary, Larisa. It looked to me like she was courting him back, so there seemed to be no big obstacles to their happiness. (They got married last April.)

We sat there chatting, pouring ourselves mineral water. To mine I added a little Lambrusco for flavor. After about five minutes, the food had still not come. I yelled in English toward the kitchen, "I am hungry," but nothing happened. A few minutes later I yelled again. "We want food!" Gaetano helped by yelling for his wife. But no one came out of the kitchen.

Dino had brought some crushed ice. So I filled a wineglass with it and filled it to the top with Lambrusco. I do not drink much wine at lunch, but in this heat, it was delicious, *una granità de Lambrusco*. So I had another. Still not a single sign of action from the kitchen. No one came out. No one called. Silence. If this had been a restaurant, I would have thought the kitchen staff had gone on strike.

"Ho fame!" I shouted again, thinking if I said it in Italian it would get better results. Bill suggested we clink forks on our wineglasses, so we all started banging away. Finally my sister-in-law, Giovanna, came out of the house with a big bowl of steaming penne, a favorite of mine, with a sauce of fresh tomatoes and peppers—hot but not seriously hot.

"What's the matter with you babies?" Giovanna said angrily. "You can't wait five minutes?"

Anna put a superb soft cheese, a local specialty called *stracchino*, on the table. I spread some on a piece of bread and handed it to Bill, who only knows a little about what is good. The penne tasted delicious. We talked about food. I gave my opinion that people change their taste in food every five years. I explained that in the past I disliked calves' liver but now I liked it. Everybody in the world loves balsamic vinegar, which is an important product of my city, Modena. I only like balsamic vinegar on strawberries, but I am sure in a year or two, in my next five-year period, I will like balsamic vinegar on everything—as most people do.

Everybody loved the penne, and I told them that for me, the simpler a pasta was, the better. When we finished the pasta, Anna came out with a large bowl of salad and some platters of cold grilled chicken that was left over from dinner the night before. I was good and did not eat the chicken, just the pasta—and not as much as you think—and some salad. And later some fruit. As we were finishing our meal, Bill's wineglass was empty and Gaetano showed him how to read the future in the dregs of the Lambrusco. Bill asked him if he could see a Pavarotti book in the future.

My cellular phone rang. I didn't mention before that I like to joke around on the phone. I recognized this caller's voice—Dino's mother, who is a good friend of mine. I started speaking Chinese—my own version of Chinese. She got confused and thought maybe a satellite had brought her to the wrong continent. I was afraid she would hang up, so I handed the phone over to Dino.

Another call that brings out my childish side is when people call and ask in a very grave voice if they might speak with "Maestro Pavarotti" or simply "Il Maestro." I know the person is trying to be very polite and respectful, but I can't help having fun with them. I tell them in a serious, low voice that Maestro Pavarotti cannot talk right now as he is in his mud bath with three Norwegian girls. Friends tell me that one day I'll do this, and the call will be from the Vatican asking me to sing for His Holiness, but I don't joke like that every time I answer the phone, and I trust in my good luck.

The conversation at our lunch table is usually not serious or heavy. We talk about food, whether the artichokes are as good this year as last, and how much vinegar to put in the salad dressing. We talk about what everybody did that morning, what we will do that afternoon. Different suggestions are discussed. This summer we also talked a lot about the heat.

Some at the table started talking about the O. J. Simpson case, which had been in the newspapers for the past six weeks. They asked what I thought. I said I had been traveling and knew very little about the details of what happened but that my instinct told me he was innocent. Everybody was amazed at my opinion and told me the evidence against him was very strong. They discussed the loyalty of his fans, how they refused to believe he did it. Bill said he didn't think some of the fans cared whether he did it or not. Others argued about that. Then Bill said a strange thing.

"It's as if you did something like that, Luciano," he said. "There are people who love you so much, they would forgive you anything—even murder."

People at the table got upset and jumped on Bill. How could he think such a thing? Luciano? Murder? Now, Bill knows I am the last person who would ever hurt another person, let alone murder somebody. But I understood exactly what he meant, and I said so. He was not talking about me, but about the passion of some fans. Sometimes that passion can be a little irrational, even frightening.

Maybe Bill was thinking of a conversation we'd had when I was telling him about a movie idea that had been sent to me by Mickey Rooney. The movie would have two main characters played by me and Danny DeVito. The story is about a crime boss who wants to sing like me. He kidnaps me and has my voice transplanted into his body. As I was explaining the story I said, "You see, Danny is a criminal who has the soul of a romantic tenor." Then I had a better thought that made me smile. I said, "The truth is we tenors are romantics who have the souls of criminals."

I meant, of course, that we are naughty, devilish, *cattivo,*—not murderous, thank God.

At the lunch table, I ate some of Adua's penne as Bill was asking her how she liked having so many meetings on her terrace, and if the terrace was not full of meetings, there were journalists, television crews, friends, fans—streams of visitors.

She thought for a moment and then said to him, "For many years I have known no other life. I don't even think about it." She should have added one thing: she is similar to me; she likes excitement and she likes to be busy all the time.

Sometimes the conversation at lunch turns to heavier subjects like politics. We always have many foreigners for meals in Pesaro, and in the summer of 1994 they all asked me about our president,

Silvio Berlusconi, who was receiving so much attention from the international press at that time. I said that when Berlusconi ran for election, I was impressed by him.

He appeared to have the drive for efficiency and getting things done that I think of as an American quality, and not typical of us Italians. You cannot deny his incredible success in business. And you cannot deny that Italy needed some big changes in the way our government is run. Berlusconi and his group got into office on his platform of change. The people around him all said, "Yes, yes, change. That is what we want too." So they were elected.

But these people who came into office because of Berlusconi, they made it clear to him right away that they had no interest in change. None at all. When they saw he was serious about it, that he planned to change things, I think they began to work against him, and he was finished. I would always point out to Americans that at the same time Berlusconi was having so much trouble, many people in the States were against President Clinton. But there is an enormous difference between the Italian system and the American. We can throw our presidents out very easily, while it is almost impossible to throw out yours. You give your presidents a chance to prove themselves, but in Italy we don't. One strike and you're out. Since the end of World War II, we've had fifty-two governments in Italy.

But that day it was too hot to talk politics—and I had already had my political talk for the day with Cesare. Content from my lunch, I looked down on the beach which was crowded with people on this August afternoon. I love watching the people down there enjoying themselves. Some friends once asked me why I wouldn't prefer a vacation house that was more isolated, more cut off from civilization. They thought that with the life I lead all year—a hundred people around me, confusion, noise, pressure—I would want to get as far away from people as possible on my vacation. Why didn't I find a house on a mountain or an island where there was no one for miles around?

But that is not the way I am. I like being up here on the side of my hill, a bit removed and very tranquil and private, but where I can still see life, lots of life, right below me—and I can hear it, too. Up on my terrace, it is quiet and peaceful, but there is always a faint murmur of life coming up from below, maybe yells from a ball game or a squeal as someone gets thrown into the water, all the sounds of people having fun at the beach. When I am relaxing at Pesaro, I almost never listen to music, except when I am working with young singers, of course. But I don't listen to it much for pleasure. That sound of people on the beach, happy, having fun— that is the best music for me, at least for one month each year. I'm like a man who eats rich food and drinks good wine all year long. He loves it, but once a year he must go to Montecatini and drink mineral water to clear his system. That is how I am about music.

The city has made the beach bigger since I bought this house, and they have built breakwaters of large rocks, which stretch maybe eighty meters out into the water. I watched some boys swimming off those rocks and I said out loud, "How much I would like to go down there and go swimming, just like those guys, but I can't."

Dino understood what I meant and said, "Yes, you can, Luciano. I can take you in your boat to a place where no one goes, way out where you will be safe."

"Are you sure?" I said. "No paparazzi? No tourists with telephoto lenses to capture this horrible body? You will guarantee this?"

"I promise," Dino said. "There will be no one."

"A big tuna won't hurt me?"

"Don't worry about it," said Dino. "I know just the spot."

He couldn't take me that afternoon, but we went out in my

boat a few days later to a jetty way off from the others. It was just as Dino promised—completely private. I splashed around in the water for an hour and had a wonderful time. And no photographers or tunas.

After we finish eating, we usually sit around the table for a long time drinking espresso or mineral water, maybe eating some fruit. If I think I have been very good about my diet, I might go into the kitchen and bring out some Häagen-Dazs. The first time I did this, Bill was shocked and asked if I had brought this ice cream with me from New York. "I am sorry to tell you," I replied, "that you can now buy Häagen-Dazs in Italy. I think it is the best ice cream in the world. And I know about ice cream."

People soon began to wander off from the table, and I realized the time has come. I got up and walked the fifteen meters to my hammock, which hangs between two trees farther along the terrace. It wouldn't matter if the president of France was sitting at my table. When it is time for me to take my nap, I'm in that hammock and gone. I could hear the cries of children playing on the beach.

18
SUMMER'S END
❧

One day, for my after-lunch siesta, as usual, I slept in my hammock for an hour or two. It was wonderful to wake up on the terrace with the afternoon sun on the beach below. It was still very hot—I don't remember when it was ever this hot—but there was a breeze, and Larisa saw that I was awake and brought me some cold mineral water.

· Larisa told me that there were three Japanese girls in a taxi down at the gate. They had explained over the intercom that they had come from Tokyo with a present for Maestro Pavarotti. Could they come up and give it to me? They may have come from Tokyo, I told myself, but I am sure they did not come just to see me; they will go to see the sights in Rome and Florence while they are here, too. Still, I told Larisa to let them come up.

They were very charming and sweet, and they gave me a beautiful kimono, which they had made for me in Tokyo. It was made of silk with wonderful colors, and I was very touched. When I put it on, I was very surprised that it was big enough! The Japanese are so clever—maybe they can get a computer to figure out my awful measurements from the television screen.

A phone call came in from a friend of mine who lives down the coast in Fano. They had been out fishing and had caught a 400-pound tuna! I couldn't believe it. I said to Bill that we could work later. Now we had to go see a fish. We got in my Mercedes and made the fifteen-minute drive to Fano. There are a lot of commercial fisheries in the port there, and I could drive right out onto one of the docks.

When we arrived at the spot where my friend told me they would be, there was a small crowd and then I could see the fish hanging by his tail. It was fantastic—about ten feet long and very beautiful. We all had our pictures taken with the fish. (Later someone looked at the photo of me, Bill, and the fish and said, "Ah, The Three Tunas.") That evening my friend brought to my house a big portion of the tuna for me and my family. It was the tail section. Anna sliced the pink meat very thin and served it to us raw, *carpaccio di tonno,* with a pesto sauce. Fantastic!

Before leaving for Fano, I had arranged to meet some of my family at the dock in Pesaro where I keep my speedboat. Bill had said we should go back to my house and continue working on the book. But I told him it was a cloudy day and if we work when the sun is not shining, it will be a sad book. Now the sun was out, but I think Bill had given up on me. Anyhow, he didn't say anything about working.

Bill and I drove up the coast from Fano, passing the long beach where thousands of cars were parked. Many of these cars want to back out of their parking places and hit your car as you are driving by. It is very exciting. We call this stretch of highway La Strada degli Morti, the Street of the Dead, because it has so many accidents. We got through it okay and drove directly to the dock in Pesaro where my boat was waiting. Already seated on board were Larisa, my nephew Vittorio, my niece Carmen, and her stupendous five-year-old, Nicola, who is a beautiful little boy and the master of all he sees. If people think I am the boss at the Villa Giulia in the summer, they are wrong. Nicola is.

When I drove the boat out of the harbor and was in the open sea, I hit the power and headed north away from Pesaro. I love the view of my house from the water. You can see the hillside clearly—even more clearly this year because of the thousand sunflowers we planted in the field that slopes from the beach up to the house. The house itself is almost invisible with the trees covering it.

We discussed getting out the Banana. This is a new toy I had found—a long rubber tube filled with air that you tow behind the boat and people ride on it as if they are riding a horse. It is bright yellow and shaped like a banana. There are handles to hold on to, but your feet hang free in the water, which makes it easy to fall off. Adua loves the Banana and is quite good at staying on—no matter how fast I go or how many turns I make. But Adua was not with us and no one else wanted to ride the Banana. What to do?

I asked Bill if he knew how to water-ski. He said no.

"Do you want me to teach you?" I said.

"Can you do that?" he asked.

"I am an excellent instructor," I told him, so Bill said he'd try it.

He went down into the cabin and didn't come back. I yelled down to him, "What are you doing?" He said he couldn't ski with contact lenses and was looking for something to put them in.

I waited for a minute or two and then yelled, "Look, are you going to do it or not?"

He found two empty coffee cups to put the lenses in, then put on his bathing suit and got into the water. I yelled at him from the boat what to do. He put the skis on and had them pointed up in the air as I told him. He gave me the thumbs-up sign, so I pulled the throttle. I saw a lot of water in the air but no Bill. Then I saw him way behind us in the water. I circled around. He yelled that he got half the Adriatic in his mouth and lost the tow bar. He wanted to try again.

I yelled at him, "Hold on tighter this time, and maybe keep your mouth shut so you won't get so much water in it."

He got ready, his skis in position, and again I gunned the motor. This time Bill held on longer, but as he was starting to come upright, one ski shot out to one side with Bill's leg in it. He was in the water again and looked as if he was in some trouble. I circled back.

"I've done something to my leg, Luciano," he yelled. "It's not supposed to bend in that direction. It hurts like hell."

I ask, "You want to try one more time?"

"One more time?" he said. "I'll be lucky if I walk one more time. I'm done."

When he climbed into the boat he said he was sorry to have disgraced himself. We all said no, no, it happens to everybody the first time. Carmen told him he had the courage of a lion, which I think was an exaggeration, but it made Bill happier. Larisa found a robe for him, one of mine, and we made him sit on the padded seat in the stern of the boat.

Bill asked the others about their first time on water skis, and he was surprised to learn that none of us had ever done it. He had thought he was gaining admission into our little club of water skiers.

"Not even you, Luciano?" he said. "You haven't ever water-skied?"

I said, "Are you crazy?"

Actually, one of our group had tried. Larisa had water-skied a few days ago, and she had pulled a muscle. It turned out this was what Bill had done, too. A coincidence, I think. Larisa showed Bill the back of her leg, which was completely black and blue. He asked us if he would look like that. She told him, "Not right away, but in a few days."

Bill said to me, "Look, Luciano, if you want to get rid of a writer, you don't have to go to so much trouble. Just tell me you don't want to write this book, and I'll go away. It's not necessary to rip my leg off and leave me in the middle of the Adriatic."

I told Bill I did not want to get rid of him. It is necessary to drive the boat fast in order to get the skier standing up.

When Bill came up to the house the next morning, he had a limp. He said his leg only hurt when he walked; he'd had no trouble sleeping. Later when he and I were working, he said to me, "Luciano, I was thinking about yesterday. I've watched movies of people water-skiing and they do not start out so fast. They build up speed gradually." He added to the case against me. "Larisa is young and athletic, and she also pulled a muscle when you taught her to ski. I've come to a conclusion: you go too fast."

My daughters tell me I never admit to being wrong about anything. I don't think that is true. You must be careful how many times you are wrong in front of your daughters. But I must admit that Bill looked very surprised when I said to him, "Maybe I did go too fast."

He told me he was determined to learn how to water-ski. He would find an instructor in Pesaro, learn how to do it, then go out with me again. I asked, "Why find an instructor? I am a very good instructor."

Late that afernoon, three young singers came by to work with me. One was a very good Italian soprano who was young, slim, and pretty, and with a big rich voice. Another was the son of a friend of mine who wanted to become a professional baritone. After I listened to him sing a couple of songs, I knew that he was not very good. Actually, he was pretty bad, and while he was singing I could see my brother-in-law making faces out on the terrace.

But I told the young man to work very hard on vocalizing and nothing else for six months, then to come back to show me his progress. Somebody later asked me why I encouraged somebody who sang so badly. I told them the truth: you never know for sure what might be inside there. And this young man wanted so much to be a singer that I thought he should at least try for a while.

The third was a young tenor sent to me by Jane Nemeth, who runs the Philadelphia vocal competition. His name was Michael Belnap and he was from Indiana. He and his wife had come to Pesaro and were staying at one of the small hotels at the bottom of my driveway. And every afternoon when I could, I would work with Michael for a while. He had a powerful voice with a good sound, but there was a serious problem: he was as heavy as I am. I told him he had to lose some weight. I didn't get too heavy until after I had established myself in the opera world. I wouldn't want to try breaking into that world with the weight I later put on. I don't think they would have given me a chance.

Michael's wife was heavy also. These two young Americans would walk up the hill in the terrible heat, and I would immediately put Michael to work singing. Maybe I could help his singing and make him lose weight at the same time. One day Michael admired my shirt, which was the Hawaiian style, very loose and comfortable with bright colors. He asked where I had bought it. I told him I have a friend who makes them for me, that I have fifty of them and wear them every day. Because he was so hot and sweaty, I asked if he would like one. I had told Michael to plan to stay in Pesaro for a week, but I began to think we were making progress, so he ended up staying three.

I think I am a very good teacher. I can hear right away what the trouble is with the singing, or what I believe is the trouble. The evidence in my favor is that when the singers do what I ask them to do, I can usually hear the difference I am looking for. They tell me the same thing. Also, I have strong ideas about how the music should sound—when a phrase should be emphasized, played down, sung softly, sung loud. It is most often just a matter of following exactly what is in the score. Even working on soprano arias from operas that I have never sung, if I know the music, if I have heard it a number of times, I remember the correct way to sing it. If these young singers make mistakes in the music, I do not have to look at the score to know they are wrong.

Early that evening, Bill and I worked for a while, but I was too tired to concentrate on my past. Also, I get tired of talking about myself. I think Bill would be happier if I were an egomaniac and talked about myself all the time as he tells me some celebrities do.

I suggest that we quit for today and watch a little television before dinner. The television is in my living room where we were sitting. I have a very large screen and a satellite hookup, even though I don't watch television very much when I am at home. I watch it when I am staying in hotels, which I do much of the year. With my television at the Villa Giulia, I think I can get every channel in the world right in this small city on the Adriatic.

When the set warmed up, a movie came on the screen. Right away I said, "Fellini's *Amarcord*." Bill was surprised that I could recognize a film so quickly, but I am a great admirer of Fellini, and I particularly liked that film, which reminded me so much of my childhood. I have watched *Amarcord* several times, so it was not surprising that I recognized it right away. The scene showed a crowd marching through city streets singing. I told Bill they were singing the Fascist song. He also was surprised I would recognize this song after hearing only a note or two, so I told him, "Things like that are important when you are eight or nine. You remember."

A little later a scene showed a man in a metal tub and a lady was pouring hot water over him. This brought back so many memories of growing up. Every Saturday night for the first nineteen years of my life, I took a bath like that. My mother would heat the water, and members of my family would take turns pouring it over each other. I told Bill this and said, "See? I did give you something for our book."

He told me that a fact like that from my childhood should have been in our first book.

There is no pleasing him.

I often work on other projects when I am at Pesaro on my vacation. A few days later my old friend Christopher Raeburn came down from London with a crew from Decca Records, which in America is called London Records. This company has produced all of my recordings, and Christopher has been the producer of most of them. Even though he is now retired, I am very pleased that he will still work on my recordings. Christopher knows as much about singing as anyone alive, and I have great respect for his opinions. He proved this again not too long ago when he discovered Cecilia Bartoli at a group audition and immediately hired her to sing the very important part of Rosina in his recording of *The Barber of Seville*. She was completely unknown then.

Christopher had come to Pesaro to work with me on a recording of *Il Trovatore,* which, I am embarrassed to say, we had recorded four years earlier. Decca gives me the right to approve a recording before it is released, and there were a number of places I did not like. In the last four years we never could get together to go over these places and fix them.

How do we fix them? When we rehearse with the full orchestra, every repetition of an aria or a stretch of the opera is recorded, so when you finish you have four or five different versions of every note of the score—all done with the same orchestra, conductor, and singers. If a section of the final version does not sound right, Christopher and his technicians can take out the bad section and splice in one of the earlier versions that we all like better.

I do not see anything wrong with this. It is your voice in every version, and we are giving the public the best rendition of the opera that is possible. It is not like a live performance when you are being judged on your ability to do it all beautifully in one evening. The idea is to have the best *Trovatore* our voices are capable of providing, the best of every attempt. In any case, we do this editing in just a few places.

The only thing I can see is wrong with this is that now every time I sing before an audience I feel I must sound as good as my records. Because the editing takes out any flaws, I feel I must always try for a flawless performance, and this, of course, is almost impossible. We do this editing work in my bedroom—the room that is built into the side of the hill so it is closed on three sides. It has by far the best and most protected acoustics in the house. Christopher and his crew have been coming to Pesaro often over the years to do this sort of work, and each time they have had to transport heavy speakers and recording equipment. Finally they made a gift to me of an editing setup, which I store here at the house so it is always here when they come. While I had my after-lunch nap, Christopher's crew set up the sound equipment.

When we were ready to work, we all sat in a row at a table across my bedroom from the speakers. Christopher had marked in the score the places I did not like, and he could go to them on the tape very quickly. We listened to the first bad place, which was in a duet between Manrico, my character, and Azucena, his mother. This part was sung by Shirley Verrett. Just hearing her beautiful voice made the session a pleasure for me and not work. I said to Christopher, "That one is so wonderful, I'll sing with her till one of us dies."

Sometimes when I hear the recording again after a long time, I change my mind and decide it is okay. But today a particular high note in the duet sounded strained to me. And I asked to hear the other versions. We played them all several times, and finally I found one I liked better. Christopher agreed with me that the top note was better. But they were both excellent, he said, and in the version I liked, my voice leading up to the top note had not sounded as full and robust. He preferred the version they had. We listened some more. I still preferred the new version. When I could see Christopher was unhappy, I said to him, "You know the top note is better in the version I like, and you can do your tricks to make me sound more robust as I am going to the top note."

Christopher smiled and said, "Ah, yes, the secrets of the kitchen."

We went on to the next place, the trio at the end of Act One. As we listened to the three voices—the soprano, the baritone, and me—I said to Christopher, "I am singing the principal line there, but you can't hear me. The balance is all wrong." He assured me that was an easy problem to correct and he would take care of it back in London. We continued working like that for several hours. When we finished, we had a recording of *Il Trovatore* that we all liked.

When we finished, Bill asked how I liked listening to my own recordings, adding that he always hated reading anything he had written. "There you have your answer about my recordings," I told him. "You always hate what you have done because you know you could have done better."

I thought about it for a minute, and I added, "But wait ten years. After ten years it always sounds fantastic!"

∼

My daughter Cristina's birthday is in August and since that is the month when I am certain to be in Italy, we always plan a big party at the Villa Giulia. It is her party, but it is really a big family party. All three of my daughters are involved with their own projects and cannot spend the entire summer in Pesaro as they did when they were still in school, but at the time of Cristina's birthday, they all arrange to be free. Adua, who goes back and forth to Modena during the summer, closes her office for several weeks and begins her vacation here with the birthday party.

My parents often find summers at the Villa Giulia too busy and chaotic, but they always arrive for Cristina's birthday. Actually they love it here and love especially the view of the sea, so they always stay for a while, but they have developed their own vacation routines. They place two chairs on the terrace, safely out of the way of all the people walking around with cellular phones, and they are happy to sit in the shade looking out at the water and keeping each other company, not paying much attention to all the confusion a few meters away. They have both worked very hard all their lives, and it is a great pleasure for me to see them sitting there, looking out over the sea, enjoying just being together.

As the birthday party drew nearer, we told Anna that there would be about thirty for dinner. That was no problem for her, and we planned a menu we knew Cristina would like. More of a problem occurred when we realized that twenty-two of those people were expecting to sleep in the house that night. Now, we have only six bedrooms, but Anna said no problem, we would manage. She is fantastic.

People began arriving for the party as early as four o'clock. When Cristina got there I was still in the hammock, and she came and sat by me for a private talk. Sometime during the days my daughters were here, I would have at least one private talk with each of them. It didn't matter if there was anything special to talk about or not. I just like to hear what they are doing, who they are seeing, and what interests them most at the moment.

Nicoletta tells me I have a very unusual relationship with my daughters. She knows we are open and honest with each other. I am more like a friend to them, she says, not an Italian father. My daughters tell me about their love life, for instance, sometimes in detail. This surprises Nicoletta. Bill asked Giuliana if this was true. She said, "Yes, he is our friend, but he is also an Italian father. We don't tell him everything."

As everybody began arriving, Adua and her sister, Giovanna, decided to put on funny costumes. They found two of my Hawaiian shirts, which they put on, tying the extra fabric around their waists. They put on shorts with white knee stockings, and they wore porkpie hats. I'm not sure what they were supposed to be. Maybe Hawaiian motorcycle girls, or maybe two crazy Italian sisters. I wanted to take their picture, but I thought they looked stiff. I told them to smile. But the smiles were artificial, plastic, so I said, "Do you remember the time you both made pee-pee in your pants?" I got good smiles.

My daughters have a friend, a composer from Barcelona. He is a big man, very heavy, and has a dark beard. Everyone said he looked just like me. Because we looked so much alike, we decided to get into matching costumes like Adua and Giovanna. When we put on the Hawaiian shirts, the knee socks, and the hats, we did look amazingly alike. I'm not sure what else we looked like. I put this big guy on the motor scooter behind me, and we drove around the terrace a few times while they took pictures. It looked like Pavarotti and his twin brother out for a drive.

The best person in our family for costumes is my sister, Lela. She once fooled everyone by dressing like a Catholic priest, complete with a beard. But for this party, she had just returned from a vacation in Switzerland and was too tired to do her usual production. I was talking to Bill when she came over, gave me a kiss, and said to him, "My brother is an open book and I adore him. You can write that." We are my parents' only two children, and we have experienced a lot of life together.

The dinner was spectacular. Anna and I had planned it for days. We started with prosciutto and fresh figs, then we had tagliatelle with ragout. The main course was a big platter of many kinds of grilled seafood and large bowls of hot spinach with lemon and garlic. Then we had a salad of tomatoes, lettuce, and cold string beans, which was served with a variety of local cheeses.

With our coffee and before the birthday cake Anna had spent all morning baking, people at the table started talking about my friend Gildo Di Nunzio, who is usually present for these parties. Gildo has spent seventeen summers in Pesaro helping me prepare new roles, and he has become a member of our family. This year, however, I did not have that much studying to do. My new role for the season was in *Pagliacci,* which I had already recorded and had sung in a concert version with Riccardo Muti. Everyone was talking about how much they missed Gildo.

Bill, who always has his microcassette recorder in his pocket in case I say anything interesting, got an idea. Gildo was his neighbor in Pennsylvania, he said, and they would be seeing each other in a few weeks. He would pass the tape recorder around the table, and everyone could put greetings to Gildo on the tape.

My family loved the idea, and they were all grabbing the recorder. They first said who they were, then said things like "Caro Gildo, why aren't you here?" Everybody got into the game, even people who didn't know Gildo. The little machine moved from person to person as it was passed around the table. It all went well until the recorder was handed to my father who has trouble getting used to the gadgets we all have these days. He thought it was a cellular phone and expected Gildo to answer.

We got that straightened out as Anna appeared with the large cake she had baked and placed it before Cristina, who blew out the candles. We all sang to her while Anna's grandsons poured champagne for everyone. Since it was now dark, I gave a signal for a surprise. Fireworks shot up in the air from below the terrace and made a spectacular sight high in the air above the beach. From down by the water we could hear people cheering. The show went on for twenty minutes at least.

Later I was still at the table when people began getting up and wandering around the terrace, talking in small groups. I saw Cristina talking to someone, and my youngest daughter, Giuliana, came up behind her and gave her a hug. No reason. It makes me very happy how much love there is in our family.

At the end of the party, Bill said to me, "Luciano, I haven't seen your daughters in thirteen years. They've grown up to be terrific young women. You must be very happy."

I am very proud of all three of them, but all I could say in reply was, "I am. I am."

As the summer came to an end, I started to think of what was waiting for me in the year ahead. After my horse show in September I would go to New York to begin rehearsals for *I Pagliacci*, which would open at the Met at the end of October. Then I come back to Italy later that month for the rehearsals of *Un Ballo in Maschera*, which opens at San Carlo on December 4, with performances going into December.

After Christmas in Modena with my family, I fly to Portland, Oregon, to sing a New Year's Eve concert. On January 4 I sing another concert in Los Angeles, and then begin a tour of South America that Tibor Rudas has arranged, but first I will sing a concert in Mexico City on January 7. I plan to sing concerts in Peru and Chile, then return to Miami for another huge public concert on the beach, which Tibor and Judy Drucker have arranged. Then I fly back to South America for concerts in Rio de Janeiro, Bogotá, and Buenos Aires.

After concerts in Dallas, Barbados, and Jamaica, I finally come to rest for a few weeks in New York where I sing a concert at the Metropolitan Opera house in March, followed by four performances of *Tosca*. In April I fly to London to sing another series of *Ballo* performances at Covent Garden, and after that more concerts in Vienna, Chicago, and Antibes. On July 9 I sing a concert in Wales to mark the fortieth anniversary of the first time I sang in public.

I read over my schedule as I sat alone at the dining table on the terrace. No one was around, which is a sure sign the summer is almost over. The phone had not rung for a while, and the terrace was very quiet. I looked out over the sea, which was still bright with the late-afternoon sun, and I thought about all that would happen before I returned again to this peaceful spot. I raised my arms straight over my head and saluted the sea the way I do an audience. Then I went into the house to pack my bag.

PAVAROTTI DISCOGRAPHY

RECORDINGS OF COMPLETE OPERAS

BELLINI, VINCENZO. *BEATRICE DI TENDA.* Sutherland, Veasey, Opthof, Bonynge, London Symphony (London/Decca), 1966.

————. *NORMA.* Sutherland, Caballé, Ramey, Bonynge, Welsh National Opera (London/Decca), 1984.

————. *I PURITANI.* Sutherland, Cappuccilli, Ghiaurov, Bonynge, London Symphony (London/Decca), 1973.

————. *LA SONNAMBULA.* Sutherland, Ghiaurov, Bonynge, National Philharmonic (London/Decca), 1980.

BOITO, ARRIGO. *MEFISTOFELE.* Caballé, Freni, Ghiaurov, de Fabritiis, National Philharmonic Orchestra (London/Decca), 1980, 1982.

DONIZETTI, GAETANO. *L'ELISIR D'AMORE.* Sutherland, Cossa, Malas, Bonynge, English Chamber Orchestra (London/Decca), 1970.

————. *L'ELISIR D'AMORE.* Battle, Nucci, Dara, Upshaw, Levine, Metropolitan Opera Orchestra (Deutche Grammophon), 1990.

————. *LA FAVORITA.* Cossotto, Bacquier, Ghiaurov, Bonynge, Teatro Communale di Bologna (London/Decca), 1974.

————. *LA FILLE DU RÉGIMENT.* Sutherland, Malas, Sinclair, Bonynge, Covent Garden (London/Decca), 1967.

————. *LUCIA DI LAMMERMOOR.* Sutherland, Milnes, Ghiaurov, Bonynge, Covent Garden (London/Decca), 1971.

———. *MARIA STUARDA*. Sutherland, Tourangeau, Morris, Soyer, Bonynge, Teatro Communale di Bologna (London/Decca), 1974, 1975.

GIORDANO, UMBERTO. *ANDREA CHÉNIER*. Caballé, Nucci, Chailly, National Philharmonic (London/Decca), 1982, 1984.

LEONCAVALLO, RUGGERO. *PAGLIACCI*. Freni, Saccomani, Wixell, Patane, National Philharmonic (London/Decca), 1977.

———. *PAGLIACCI*. Dessi, Pons, Coni, Muti, Philadelphia Orchestra (Philips), 1992.

MASCAGNI, PIETRO. *CAVALLERIA RUSTICANA*. Varady, Cappuccilli, Gavazzeni, National Philharmonic (London/Decca), 1976.

———. *L'AMICO FRITZ*. Freni, Gavazzeni, Covent Garden (E.M.I./Angel), 1969.

MOZART, W. A. *IDOMENEO*. Popp, Baltsa, Gruberova, Nucci, Pritchard, Vienna Philharmonic (London/Decca), 1983.

PONCHIELLI, AMILCARE. *LA GIOCONDA*. Caballé, Baltsa, Milnes, Ghiaurov, Bartoletti, National Philharmonic (London/Decca), 1980.

PUCCINI, GIACOMO. *LA BOHÈME*. Freni, Ghiaurov, von Karajan, Berlin Philharmonic (London/Decca), 1972.

———. *MADAMA BUTTERFLY*. Freni, Ludwig, Kerns, von Karajan, Vienna Philharmonic (London/Decca), 1974.

———. *MANON LESCAUT*. Freni, Croft, Bartoli, Taddei, Vargas, Levine, Metropolitan Opera Orchestra (London/Decca), 1992.

———. *TOSCA*. Freni, Milnes, Rescigno, National Philharmonic (London/Decca), 1978.

———. *TURANDOT*. Sutherland, Caballé, Ghiaurov, Mehta, London Philharmonic (London/Decca), 1972.

ROSSINI, GIOACCHINO. *GUILLAUME TELL*. Freni, Milnes, Chailly, National Philharmonic (London/Decca), 1978, 1979.

VERDI, GIUSEPPE. *AÏDA*. Chiara, Dimitrova, Nucci, Burchuladze, Maazel, La Scala Orchestra (London/Decca), 1985, 1986.

———. *UN BALLO IN MASCHERA*. M. Price, Bruson, Solti, National Philharmonic (London/Decca), 1982, 1983.

———. *LUISA MILLER*. Caballé, Milnes, Maag, National Philharmonic (London/Decca), 1975.

———. *MACBETH*. Souliotis, Fischer-Dieskau, Ghiaurov, Gardelli, London Philharmonic (London/Decca), 1971.

————. *OTELLO.* Kanawa, Nucci, Solti, Chicago Symphony (London/Decca), 1991.

————. *RIGOLETTO.* Sutherland, Milnes, Talvela, Bonynge, London Symphony (London/Decca), 1971.

————. *RIGOLETTO.* Wixell, Gruberova, Weikl, Chailly, Vienna Philharmonic (London/Decca), 1980, 1981.

————. *RIGOLETTO.* Anderson, Nucci, Ghiaurov, Verrett, Chailly, Teatro Communale di Bologna (London/Decca), 1989.

————. *LA TRAVIATA.* Sutherland, Manuguerra, Bonynge, National Philharmonic (London/Decca), 1979.

————. *LA TRAVIATA.* Studer, White, Kelly, Pons, Laciura, Levine, Metropolitan Opera Orchestra (Deutsche Grammophon), 1992.

————. *IL TROVATORE.* Sutherland, Horne, Bonynge, National Philharmonic (London/Decca), 1976.

————. *IL TROVATORE.* Banaudi, Verrett, Mehta, Maggio Musicale Firrentino (London/Decca), 1990.

RELIGIOUS MUSIC

BERLIOZ, HECTOR. *REQUIEM.* Ernst, Senff, Levine, Berlin Philharmonic (Deutsche Grammophon), 1992.

DONIZETTI, GAETANO. *REQUIEM.* Cortez, Bruson, Washington, Fackler, Orchestra of the Arena of Verona (London/Decca), 1979.

ROSSINI, GIOACCHINO. *PETITE MESSE SOLENNELLE.* Freni, Valentini-Terrani, Raimondi, Gandolfi, La Scala Chorus (London/Decca), 1977.

————. *STABAT MATER.* Lorengar, Minton, Sotin, Kertesz, London Symphony (London/Decca), 1971.

VERDI, GIUSEPPE. *REQUIEM.* Studer, Zajic, Ramey, Muti, La Scala (Angel), 1987.

————. *REQUIEM.* Sutherland, Horne, Talvela, Solti, Vienna Philharmonic (London/Decca), 1967.

PAVAROTTI'S FIRST PERFORMANCES IN OPERATIC ROLES

and Significant Subsequent Performances

Rodolfo in *LA BOHÈME*
(Puccini)

Reggio Emilia, April 28, 1961
(Covent Garden, 1963; La Scala, 1965; San Francisco, 1967; Metropolitan, 1968)

The Duke in *RIGOLETTO*
(Verdi)

Carpi, 1961
(Palermo, 1962; Vienna, 1963; La Scala, 1965; Covent Garden, 1971)

Alfredo in *LA TRAVIATA*
(Verdi)

Belgrade, 1961
(La Scala, 1965; Covent Garden, 1965; Metropolitan, 1970)

Edgardo in *LUCIA DI LAMMERMOOR*
(Donizetti)

Amsterdam, 1963
(Miami, 1965; San Francisco, 1968; Metropolitan, 1970; Chicago, 1975; La Scala, 1983)

Pinkerton in *MADAMA BUTTERFLY*
(Puccini)

Reggio Calabria, 1963
(Palermo, 1963; Dublin, 1963)

Idamante in *IDOMENEO*
(Mozart)

Glyndebourne, 1964

Idomeneo

Met, 1983

Elvino in *LA SONNAMBULA* (Bellini)	**Covent Garden, 1965**
Nemorino in *L'Elisir d'Amore* (Donizetti)	**Australia, 1965** (San Francisco, 1969; La Scala, 1971; Metropolitan, 1974)
Tebaldo in *I CAPULETI E I MONTECCHI* (Bellini)	**La Scala, 1966**
Tonio in *LA FILLE DU RÉGIMENT* (Donizetti)	**Covent Garden, 1966** (La Scala, 1968; Metropolitan, 1972)
Arturo in *I PURITANI* (Bellini)	**Catania, 1968** (Philadelphia, 1972; Metropolitan, 1976)
Oronte in *I LOMBARDI* (Verdi)	**Rome, 1969**
Des Grieux in *MANON* (Massenet)	**La Scala, 1969**
Riccardo in *UN BALLO IN MASCHERA* (Verdi)	**San Francisco, 1971** (La Scala, 1978; Metropolitan, 1979)
Fernando in *LA FAVORITA* (Donizetti)	**San Francisco, 1973** (Metropolitan, 1978; La Scala, 1974)
Rodolfo in *LUISA MILLER* (Verdi)	**San Francisco, 1974** (La Scala, 1976; Covent Garden, 1978)
Manrico in *IL TROVATORE* (Verdi)	**San Francisco, 1975** (Metropolitan, 1976; Vienna, 1978)
Italian Singer in *DER ROSENKAVALIER* (Strauss)	**Metropolitan, 1976** (Hamburg, 1977)
Calaf in *TURANDOT* (Puccini)	**San Francisco, 1977**

Cavaradossi in *TOSCA* *(Puccini)*	**Chicago, 1976** (Covent Garden, 1977; Metropolitan, 1978)
Enzo in *LA GIOCONDA* *(Ponchielli)*	**San Francisco, 1979**
Don Carlo in *DON CARLO* *(Verdi)*	**La Scala, 1992**
Canio in *PAGLIACCI* *(Leoncavallo)*	**Philadelphia and New York in concert, 1992** (Metropolitan, 1994)
Chénier in *ANDREA CHÉNIER*	**Projected for the Metropolitan, 1996**

INDEX